WILD
MAGICAL
SOUL

About the Author

Monica Crosson (Concrete, WA) has been a practicing witch and educator for over thirty years and is a member of Evergreen Coven. Monica is the author of *The Magickal Family* and is a regular contributor to Llewellyn's almanacs and datebooks as well as magazines such as *Enchanted Living* and *Witchology*.

MONICA
CROSSON

WILD MAGICAL SOUL

UNTAME YOUR SPIRIT
& CONNECT TO
NATURE'S WISDOM

Llewellyn Publications
Woodbury, Minnesota

FIRST EDITION
First Printing, 2020

Book design by Donna Burch-Brown
Cover design by Shira Atakpu
Interior art on page 166 by Llewellyn Art Department

Llewellyn Publications is a registered trademark of Llewellyn Worldwide Ltd.

Library of Congress Cataloging-in-Publication Data
Names: Crosson, Monica, author.
Title: Wild magical soul : untame your spirit & connect to nature's wisdom
  / [Monica Crosson].
Description: First edition. | Woodbury, Minnesota : Llewellyn Publications,
  2020. | Includes bibliographical references and index. | Summary: "Pagan
  and spiritual self-discovery and self-development through connection
  with the four elements as they are expressed in nature. Includes spells,
  rituals, and hands-on instruction"— Provided by publisher.
Identifiers: LCCN 2019045505 (print) | LCCN 2019045506 (ebook) | ISBN
  9780738760575 (paperback) | ISBN 9780738760834 (ebook)
Subjects: LCSH: Witchcraft. | Four elements (Philosophy)—Miscellanea.
Classification: LCC BF1566 .C68 2020 (print) | LCC BF1566 (ebook) | DDC
  133.4/3—dc23
LC record available at https://lccn.loc.gov/2019045505
LC ebook record available at https://lccn.loc.gov/2019045506

Llewellyn Worldwide Ltd. does not participate in, endorse, or have any authority or responsibility concerning private business transactions between our authors and the public.

All mail addressed to the author is forwarded but the publisher cannot, unless specifically instructed by the author, give out an address or phone number.

Any internet references contained in this work are current at publication time, but the publisher cannot guarantee that a specific location will continue to be maintained. Please refer to the publisher's website for links to authors' websites and other sources.

Llewellyn Publications
A Division of Llewellyn Worldwide Ltd.
2143 Wooddale Drive
Woodbury, MN 55125-2989
www.llewellyn.com

Printed in the United States of America

Also by Monica Crosson

The Magickal Family

Summer Sage

Disclaimer

The publisher and the author assume no liability for any injuries caused to the reader that may result from the reader's use of content contained in this publication and recommend common sense when contemplating the practices described in the work.

Acknowledgments

Thank you to everyone who supported me while I brought *Wild Magical Soul* to life. A special thank-you to my ever-patient family—Steve, Josh, Elijah, and Chloe—who expect nothing more from me than for me to live my dreams. To Michael and Mardi McLaskey, Yolanda Allard, Josh Crosson, and Juliet Hindsley, who listened contently as I read my chapters at our Tuesday night writer's group. You offered solid advice, encouragement, and hugs when needed. Much love and gratitude to Mardi McLaskey, my mentor, friend and fellow Hag Queen, who taught me what real warriors are made of. And to Lauryn Heineman, Eylsia Gallo, and the staff at Llewellyn Worldwide who guided me through the making of this book. This book was truly a team effort.

Dedication

To Chloe and Michelle.

May you both continue to be forever curious, forever growing, forever wild.

Contents

Part 4: Ocean (Water)

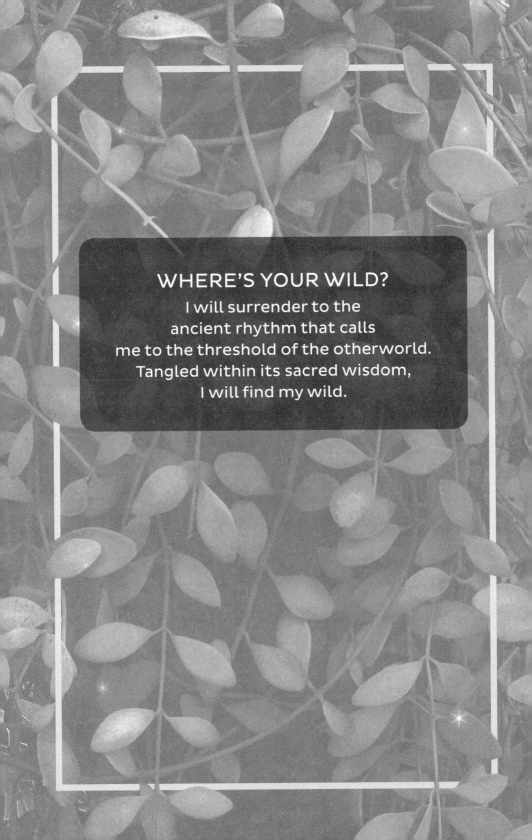

WHERE'S YOUR WILD?

I will surrender to the
ancient rhythm that calls
me to the threshold of the otherworld.
Tangled within its sacred wisdom,
I will find my wild.

It's Not Getting Away— It's Coming Home

We stood together atop the windswept summit of the very mountain that guarded our childhood. A 5,541-foot peak (a mere foothill amongst the North Cascadian giants) that kept our secrets and held tight our dreams—even when, at twelve years of age, we pricked our fingers and made a blood oath that we would always remain friends. And it didn't judge us when these promises were broken or when tears of defeat or disillusionment were shed in its shadow.

From the summit of Sauk Mountain, the entire Upper Skagit Valley lay before us, from the ancient forests that skirted its girth to the massive stretches of agricultural land that lay out like a patchwork quilt westward, all the way to the Salish Sea.

"Right there." My friend pointed to a pocket of land that, from our vantage point, seemed tiny, barely a speck upon our Mother Earth. But to us, as children, it encompassed our entire world; it was our Narnia, our Eden, our home. "Do you remember how we would ride your horse through the forest?" She playfully punched my arm. "I would see that glint in your eye and I knew to hang on."

I chuckled. "We were so carefree back then."

"Yeah." She paused, taking in the breeze that danced around us. "You know, you scared me sometimes."

I was puzzled. "Really? Hmm. I thought we were having fun."

"We were on a horse at full gallop, running through a heavily wooded forest." She snickered. "All I remember is you yelling 'duck!' every two seconds, the whoosh of tree branches, and the sound of your laughter."

"It was pretty nuts." I had to agree.

"Nuts? It was dangerous."

"You don't think about stuff like that when you're a kid." I picked up a small, jagged piece of andesite whose shape reminded me of a small, angular female. I tucked it in my pocket.

"Remember that time you misjudged a tree branch?" She chuckled.

"Oh, yeah! I was clotheslined by a cedar tree—which knocked us both off the horse."

"And you were blind for like two minutes, but wouldn't let me tell anyone." My friend shook her head. "Oh my God, you probably had a concussion."

"Yeah, there's no probably about it." I pointed to a blue-green ribbon that laced its way through the landscape. "Right about there ..." I looked slyly to my old friend. "Isn't that the spot you decided to go swimming in a rushing glacier-fed river?"

She covered her face and shook her head. "Don't remind me!"

"Then I tried to rescue you and, if memory serves me right, we both almost drowned."

"I know. I'm sorry." She smiled. "Do you think our own kids are doing the same kind of dumb antics and not telling us?"

"You bet. And to be honest, I don't think I want to know."

She laughed. "Yeah, me neither."

We wandered lazily down the switchbacks to where alpine meadows offered a crazy quilt of color. Spires of purple lupine released their sweet scent, reminding me of the otherworld; I could almost hear the faerie bells in their midst. There was heady, scented valerian that brought with it a harmonious energy and bright red columbine that punctuated the rocky edges of the trail, spindlier than its hybrid cousin, reminding me to have courage.

But it was the wild phlox that spread in low white clouds across the meadow that stood out. In the language of flowers, it means "our souls united." I looked to my friend, who was busily taking pictures, and I mused: we hadn't seen each other in almost thirty years, but somehow, the spirit of this place had kept us connected.

As we drove back to her hotel, we took the side roads that wound through the forests and fields whose ancient landscapes had once been our teachers. Near a stand of particularly dark trees that we once called Hansel and Gretel's woods, I pulled over.

"You remember this place?" I asked.

"How could I forget?" She smiled.

"Shall we do it?"

"Do what?"

"You know." I pointed to my feet.

"Oh, no. I haven't been barefoot in a forest since I was a kid."

"Well, you're gonna be barefoot today!"

We took off our shoes and socks and immediately started to giggle. "I'll race you to Mama Log," I said, then quickly ran into the forest.

"Wait up, I don't want to get lost!" My friend yelled after me.

I slowed to match her pace and together we were transformed—no longer middle-aged women with busy lives, but two young girls with messy hair and scraped knees who believed that wishes came true, if only you believed in them hard enough.

By the time we reached the massive fallen cedar tree, coated with club moss and nursing sword fern and smaller trees whose roots dug deep into her decaying body, we were both blissfully exhausted.

"Hello, Mama Log." My friend sat on our favorite nurse log, where many faerie stories were created and secrets told. She patted her mossy blanket and closed her eyes.

The forest spoke volumes in the stillness of the afternoon: the wisdom of contentment sifted through the swaying branches; the rhythmic drumming of the pileated woodpecker reminded me that our Earth Mother was alive with a wild beating heart; even the moss that coated the trees and cushioned our seats spoke of protection and the power of the natural world.

"Thank you," my friend whispered.

"You're welcome. It was nice to get away together."

"No, not for getting me away." She looked at me and smiled. "For bringing me home."

I chuckled. "You're the one who paid for the plane ticket. I had nothing to do with it."

She shook her head. "You don't get it. Not for the visit or for the hiking trip, but for reminding me where my wild is." She patted the tree again. "For bringing me…home." She wiped a stray tear and grabbed my hand. "I've spent thirty long years climbing the corporate ladder," she continued. "And too many years trying to find myself. But I forgot to look in the forest. I forgot the wild child who has always been quietly waiting…right here." She patted the log. "And if it weren't for you insisting we go hiking today instead of shopping, I would have never found her. So, thank you."

I pulled the stone I had found on the mountain from my pocket. "Here," I said. "It's called andesite, and metaphysically it's for focusing and letting go of old beliefs. I want you to take this, and every time you feel that big city executive trying to claw her way back out, focus on this stone and remember your wild."

"I promise." She took the stone and slipped it into her shirt pocket. "I will never forget again."

The Wild Soul

"Shall I not have intelligence with the earth? Am I not partly leaves and vegetable mould myself?" Thoreau posed these questions in his 1854 publication, *Walden*, a book based on his two years spent living closely with nature near Walden Pond in Massachusetts.[1] Throughout the book, he encourages the reader to remain "forever on the alert" and "looking always at what is to be seen," because truth can be found in nature, and in nature, we can find ourselves.[2]

I read *Walden* in college and became very attached to Thoreau's ideas of living simply and deliberately. It made me realize that we live in an unprecedented time of disconnection from nature. And that humanity has forgotten how much we depend on the intricacy of living systems that surround us for our own existence. Sadly, I was surrounded by mundane friends and magical practitioners alike who believed that, as humans, we were superior life-forms—mere caretakers of the land, forgetting the Goddess has many children, one no more important than the other. We are brother to the raven and sister to the

1. Henry D. Thoreau, *Walden; or, Life in the Woods* (Boston, MA: Ticknor and Fields, 1854), 150, https://archive.org/details/waldenorlifeinwo1854thor/page/n4.

2. Thoreau, *Walden*, 121.

wind. We are interconnected with all of nature, and we honor the Goddess by honoring her creation.

Our idea of wild has been increasingly tamed, designated to parks and zoos for us to file through and experience what the wild once was. Even the spirits of the wild have long been tamed to stone images in man-made forests of gothic cathedrals or tucked away in museums. I was tired of being a part of a society that had lost its intimacy with nature. With this realization, I knew that my spiritual path would focus on our relatedness with *all* beings, and my magic would reflect the knowledge and wisdom that is present in even the smallest contributor of the web of life.

So, what did I do? I *untamed* myself. I freed that wild child caged within my soul. I took off my shoes, shook free culturized domestication, and danced unabashedly within the bower of my beloved forest. I introduced myself to the spirits of the land, weaved my magic through the use of nature's gifts, and have been living simply and deliberately in harmony with nature ever since.

The untamed practitioner is the practitioner who weaves shamanic teachings into their spiritual practices; they walk in balance with the natural world, trust their animal and plant allies, and work harmoniously with the spirits who dwell in our natural surroundings. The untamed magical practitioner dances between the worlds and has discovered that what have been deemed "supernatural" in the mundane world are only natural gifts that have been forgotten. They have tapped into the ancient wisdom of our Earth Mother and, in turn, have learned to be enlivened by nature's power.

I know what you're thinking, and no, I am not suggesting you trudge off into the wilderness to live like Radagast the Brown. If you want to tuck a bird's nest under your hat, that's cool. But seriously, it is time to reclaim the wild in our soul and to truly live in balance with the land once again. Don't know where to start? Here are a few simple guidelines:

- *Remember to Be Fully Present*: Too many of us spend too much time rooted in a forest of memories, trying desperately to relive past moments and grasping desperately at lost experiences. Others are ever reaching into the future, constantly worried about what *might* be. It's time to bring ourselves fully present. Time to explore the sensations of being alive. I am sure you are familiar with the old saying "stop and smell the roses." Well, it's time to do just that.

- *Be Ready and Willing to Accept Nature's Gifts*: This begins with communication with the natural world and the spirits who dwell within the landscape. Remember that by working with nature's energies, we are opening up to the wisdom of the spirits of the land. We must be willing to accept their knowledge of unseen realities and unheard concepts and their acknowledgment of our own inner truths. If you are ready and willing, nature will open up deep-seated memories of bonds once held between humans and the natural world. And with practice, don't be surprised if your intuitive or psychic abilities become heightened.

- *Change Your Perspective*: Being willing to explore the world through nature's eyes can help us understand and support creation as a whole. What does the world look like through the eyes of the coyote who stands at the edge of the wilderness, one foot between the wild and the tame? Or what about the oak tree in your backyard, reaching endlessly for the sky? Encouraging our children to put themselves in the place of the swallow searching for a suitable place to build their nest or the earthworm who needs the soil to survive is a great way to teach them about symbiosis and practicing empathy for all of nature's creations.

  Another great way to change your perspective is by reaching back to your inner child. Do you remember that curious individual, hungry to explore and thirsty for information? Now go into a natural setting and take a walk from a child's viewpoint. Take off your shoes and put your feet in the mud. Follow a butterfly as it flits through the park. Discover what's on the other side of the hill. As you do this, pay attention to how you feel, the connections made, and the lessons learned.

- *Spend Time Outdoors*: Go outdoors often and spend time in quiet contemplation. Listen to what the universe has to say to you. Spending time outdoors can also improve mental health. According to *Proceedings of the National Academy of Sciences*, a study was conducted that shows people who have access to activity in nonurban settings are found to ruminate over problems less and have a better sense of well-being, less anxiety, and increased memory.[3]

---

3. Gregory N. Bratman, J. Paul Hamilton, Kevin S. Hahn, et al., "Nature Experience Reduces Rumination and Subgenual Prefrontal Cortex Activation," *Proceedings of the National Academy of Sciences* 112, no. 28 (July 2015): 8567–72, doi:10.1073/pnas.1510459112.

When at all possible, practice ritual and spellwork outdoors. If you can get into the wilderness, great, but the backyard, park, or patio will work just as well. Being removed from man-made things can help deepen our awareness of what is sacred to us. For me, there is something very intimate about outdoor ritual—the feeling of contentment from earth under my feet, the breath of inspiration as air moves around me, the strength garnered by the heat of fire, and the healing rhythm of water as it splashes gently against the soil.

• *Learn of Some of the Many Gods and Goddesses Venerated around the World*: Throughout this book I will be introducing you to many gods and goddesses, as well as the spirits of nature who dwell within the otherworld. Before working with their energy, take the time to get know more about them, and don't forget to respectfully introduce yourself to them before working with them ritually.

So what are you waiting for! Take off your shoes as we follow the rhythmic beat of our wild magical souls down twisted paths to a world between worlds. Here, we will run with messy hair and a warrior's spirit to face the mundane world with wild abandon. We will explore the wild magic of earth, air, fire, and water; delight in the gifts of nature; and learn to see the world with a newfound spirit. Here, we are *untamed*, *wild*, and *free*.

Part 1
FOREST

e a r t h

Chapter 1
Into the Forest

As a child, I could be found in woodland that bordered our property, tucked quietly against the protruding roots of a bigleaf maple with club moss caught up in my hair. It was a beautiful soul of a tree, whose green bower was tangled with my song, charms, and childish prayers, and whose roots knew the telling not only of my own soul, but of my grandfather's and the ancient people who walked the virgin forests of the Pacific Northwest before him.

The forest is where I could be found most days after school, especially if the day had been emotionally challenging. Days when my hair was tugged or childish insults were thrown, when a bug was smashed between the pages of my textbook, or when I was once again chosen last for a dodgeball team in PE—these small humiliations peppered my growing years, so it was within the dark, protective covering of the greenwood where I felt as if I belonged. I was transformed every afternoon from the shy, strange girl who sat in the back of the classroom to a free-spirited individual who communed with nature spirits and (whether I realized it at the time) was gleaning magical practices from the elements that I continue to hone even now.

"It's time to come home, sweet girl." My mom always knew where to find me. "It's almost dinner."

"Can't I stay just a half hour more? I promise I'll be home before dark. *Pleazzze?*" I would plead.

"Thirty more minutes." She would smile, then turn and leave me to my magical play.

As an adult, I am still drawn to the towering guardians of our dwindling woodlands. I go there for solitude and respite, for grounding and wisdom, for ritual and magical working. The forest is truly where I find myself over and over again.

The First Tree

What bewilderment must have been felt by our ancient ancestors when they looked upon the largest of plants! The world of trees has always been an integral and essential part of the world of humans. Those glorious beings, the trees, provided ancient people with shelter, fiber, food, protection, medicine, fuel, sacred space, magic, and mystery since the beginning of humankind. My mind wanders to the incredible old-growth temperate rain forests of the Pacific Northwest, where trees like western red cedar, Douglas fir, and California redwoods once rose to staggering heights of up to 350 feet tall with impressive girths up to 20 feet in diameter.[4] These beautiful giants of another time now only dot our Pacific coastal forests—most are tucked within the protective confines of state and national parklands, where, for a fee, we can file through and experience their grandeur.

As I walk the second- and third-growth forested trails where I live, the stories of the ancient forest unfold through the many massive remaining stumps that punctuate the forest's landscape. I know their stories—tales of lightning or fire are scorched upon the bark. Chinks in the wood tell me of the pioneers who came to the West to make a living in a land that must have seemed filled with a resource that knew no end. And the sorrow of the indigenous people whose sacred land was taken and stripped is still palpable; it can be heard in the rustle of leaves and tasted in the mist that clings to chapped lips on foggy mornings.

Trees have held a sacred position in the hearts of humans since the beginning of time. Maybe it was because trees, like humans, stood straight with their feet planted deep within the earth and their mighty heads in the air, much closer to the realm of the gods than we. Or because we follow similar cycles

---

4. Roy F. Douglass, "Silvical Characteristics of Redwood (Sequoia sempervirens [D. Don] Endl.)," US Forest Service Research Paper PSW-RP-28 (Berkeley, CA: Pacific Southwest Forest & Range Experiment Station Forest Service, 1966), 10, https://www.fs.usda.gov/treesearch/pubs/28694.

throughout our lifespans. Or is it that a tree holds a memory bank within its mighty trunk that, much like our own memories, recalls events in the past that had effected its growth and well-being? No matter the reason, one has to look no further than the myths of any culture to find proof of their reverence.

You may be familiar with some, like the Tree of Knowledge in the Garden of Eden, whose fruit would give anyone who partook of it knowledge of good and evil, or the tale of Daphne, who was changed to a laurel tree by her father, the river god Peneios, to avoid the importunities of Apollo.

There was Odin, who hung from Yggdrasil, the world tree, for nine days, staring into the dark water to gain the knowledge of the runes for the good of humankind. Buddha gained enlightenment under the Bodhi tree, and in India, *asvattha*, or the cosmic tree, was thought to have its roots in the sky and its branches growing downward to cover the earth. Wherever you look in mythology, trees served as links between this world and the supernatural: gods and messengers could access worlds by traveling along its trunk or branches.

But if a single tree represented the axis mundi, what did the ancients believe about a forest of trees?

Crossing the Threshold

Primeval forest once covered almost all of central and western Europe. In some forested areas, like the Black Forest of Germany, the wood was so dense the sun couldn't penetrate it. Dangers were real: one did not venture too far into the forest without the possibility of becoming lost, being attacked by bandits, or falling prey to one of the wild creatures that called the woodland home. It was also a place of mystery and rich with symbolism to the people whose settlements bordered the forest's edge.

It is into the forest that we cross a threshold that, according to JC Cooper in *An Illustrated Encyclopedia of Traditional Symbols*, represents the soul entering the perils of the unknown—the realm of death, the secrets of nature, or the spiritual world, which man must penetrate to find meaning.[5] The stories of Brothers Grimm and other folktales illustrate this clearly. Think for a moment of the fairy tales that you remember as a child: "Little Red Riding Hood,"

---

5. JC Cooper, *An Illustrated Encyclopedia of Traditional Symbols* (London: Thames and Hudson, 1978), 71.

"Hansel and Gretel," "Snow White," "Goldilocks and the Three Bears," or even "Rumpelstiltskin." What do they have in common? The deep, dark forest.

It is through the endless forest with its sweeping branches, shadowed corners, and tangled understory that our heroes and heroines must navigate. Along the way, they must face what may lie in wait in those shadowy places—and if they reemerge, they are transformed.

In many cultures, the oldest sanctuaries were groves or woodland areas where great shady trees, such as the oak, yew, or pine, would be dedicated to a specific deity they worshipped with ecstatic dancing, feasting, and communion with the spirits of the land. As Christianity took hold, these first temples that served as a way of uniting man with nature became home to great cathedrals dedicated to the Christian God. But the old gods and goddesses didn't completely disappear from their woodland homes; they are still evident in the many esoteric carvings and in the roots and vines that consume decaying structures … What is that old saying? Oh, yeah—Mama's home!

Trees guarded over rites of passage for our ancestors for generations. In some European countries, trees were planted near the front entrances of the homes of newly married couples to secure their happiness, while in parts of Asia, couples circled a tree during the wedding ceremony to secure the power of fertility, which was communicated to them by the tree.

Trees were sometimes planted for good luck at the birth of a child, particularly an heir. And instead of interning their dead, many cultures placed their dead in trees as a way of ensuring their rebirth. In parts of Europe, when a young man came of age and departed from his home village, he placed his welfare in the keeping of a tree. As long as this "guardian tree" flourished, his loved ones knew he was well, but if the tree withered, it meant the health of the young man too had failed.

Though the world of trees was very much an integral part of our ancestors' daily lives, we seem to take them for granted in our modern world. We forget that trees supply an incredible ecosystem upon which we are dependent. Without these lovely giants, carbon dioxide could not be processed into the oxygen that we breathe. Without rain forests, rainfall would decrease, possibly altering wind and current patterns and creating unstable weather patterns on a global scale.

When you enter the forest, do so with an open heart. Allow the stirring of ancient memories to awaken that intimate knowledge of nature that has laid dormant for far too long.

I have always believed that to walk through the forest is to hold the hand of the Green Lord. His messages can be heard in the whisperings of ancient trees, the scuttling of forest creatures, and the water seeping through the forest floor. They carry with them the lessons of peace, stability, and connection to our Mother Earth. But to fully understand these lessons, we must move closer to the trees themselves. So, if you're ready, step with me across the green threshold into the forest, where the moss clings to the branches of trees that know the telling of a thousand years.

Whispers from the Trees—Run!

The rain in Washington state varies greatly from season to season, from the soft summer mists that plump your cheeks and curl your hair to the pelting winter deluges that sting as they hit, like a million pebbles being thrown by angry gods. It was mid-November when the rain poured in heavy sheets, the kind that soaks quickly through wool and fills shoes. It was the kind of weather that would keep most *sane* people tucked within their warm, dry homes, content in front of a fire, cup of tea in hand, with a cat curled up beside them.

But not me: I felt compelled to cross the threshold between my mundane and magical life. There is a place in the forest I often go to when the whispers from the otherworld tickle my ear and tug at my soul. My entrance is two tangled vine maples that create a natural arbor that borders a small county access road on forested land near the Sauk River just a mile and a half from my home.

On that day, when the rain felt never-ending, I entered as I usually do, grounded and my heart open to the messages nature had to offer. The hemlock and cedar trees, which make up most of the woodland, sheltered me some from the downpour, so I peeled off my heavy sweater and placed it on a moss-shrouded stump.

I followed the same trail I always do, one that leads down a mossy embankment laced with lichen and dotted with fern to a western red cedar that bends over the Sauk River and whose shallow roots have been twisted and deformed by the river's fickle movement. Near the base of the tree, where a few boulders (to which huckleberry bushes desperately cling) keep the tree from being completely swallowed by the river, there is a hollowed section, and it is within this hollow that I tuck myself, neatly and safely surrounded by cedar's purifying and protective energy.

Western red cedar was the most sacred of trees to Pacific coastal tribes. It was used as medicine to treat respiratory illness and worn as an amulet for protection and prosperity. The inner fiber was used to make clothing, blankets, and sleeping mats. Homes were built from the wood, canoes dug from the trunks, and baskets formed by its roots. It was also carved to create totems, masks, and other ritual tools. Its bark was ground into incense, and its lovely scaled leaves were bundled into smudge sticks. None of the tree was wasted. Cedar is a tree of protection, purification, and prosperity, and many tribes believed that the spirits of their ancestors resided within the trees.

As a child of the wood, I was very familiar with cedar's protective energy. And though I work with the energy of many trees, it is the cedar that I am drawn to when I feel at my most vulnerable. So, while the rain continued to pour into the river and saturate the landscape surrounding me, I pulled a simple white candle and bergamot incense from a small bag I had brought with me, lit them, centered myself, and began my meditative work. I felt the tendrils of the otherworld as they reached from beyond the veil (as I always do) and cedar's guardian entity envelope me with its calming spirit. But then something strange happened, something that I have to say frightened me. A sudden, anxious sensation shot through me, followed by one word that rang desperately in my head: *run!* It was so sudden and so severe that I didn't question the demand, but I fumbled as I quickly snubbed out the candle and incense and scrambled back up the embankment, leaving in my wake a breadcrumb trail from my magical bag of tricks and one wool sweater.

Back on the road, I stopped to catch my breath. *What the hell just happened?* I questioned myself. Branches snapped from within the forest's edge, startling me. I swung my head around and saw from the corner of my eye what looked to be a shadowy human form. Was I seeing things? Once again, I heard the snapping of branches and this time I didn't stick around to see what it was. I ran as fast as I could the mile and a half home, and it was when I had finally reached my front porch that I heard sirens and breathlessly watched as two speeding sheriff's cars roared by.

It wasn't until a couple of days later that I found out that the sheriff's office had been in pursuit of a man under the influence of methamphetamines and who was wanted not only for a string of home burglaries but also for assault. Would he have harmed me? I don't know. What I do believe is that the spirit of that tree was protecting me.

Even in this modern world, where urban sprawl and the growing demand for agricultural and forest products have wiped out a huge percentage of our woodlands, the spirits of trees are still very much alive—in the old oak that stands stately in your backyard, in the alder whose branches gracefully sway along the river's edge, or in the stand of pine that shades your favorite park. By taking the time to attune ourselves with their powerful energies, we are tapping into an ancient wisdom that is freely available to all, if only we take the time to listen.

Connecting with Tree Spirits

Second-century Roman author Tacitus is said to have written, "It is wise to listen to the voices of trees for they tell us much that we might otherwise forget." Almost two thousand years later, this still holds true. Sadly, we are living in a world where our alienation to nature continues to increase, and, according to Richard Louv, author of *Last Child in the Woods*, a growing body of research links our mental, physical, and spiritual health directly with our association with nature.[6] I don't know about you, but if I'm not spending time in nature—whether I'm working in my garden, rediscovering forgotten hiking trails, or communing with my favorite tree—I feel the drain, both spiritually and emotionally.

Our ancestors had a direct link with nature: they worked with the land and saw the intelligence in all things. For them, nature provided a window through which to see their connectedness, and they celebrated this connection through dance, song, story, and ritual. They knew the truths whispered through the leaves that quivered on the breeze and paid heed to water's rushing song. Animism (the belief that every object has a soul or spirit) can be traced all the way back to Paleolithic times. Evidence can be found woven into myths, folktales, and fairy tales worldwide.

6. Richard Louv, *Last Child in the Woods: Saving Our Children from Nature-Deficit Disorder* (Chapel Hill, NC: Algonquin Books, 2005).

When you feel ready to connect with tree spirits (or any nature spirit), take it slow. Running to the nearest tree and expecting it to communicate isn't going to work, but going outside is a good start. Here are a few more things to try:

- *Crack Open the Books*: By knowing the stories told by our ancestors, we can begin to understand our connectedness to nature spirits. For it was our ancestors who worked with the spirits of the land, whispered their knowledge around communal fires, and passed their mysteries from one generation to the next. Remember to keep close to the folklore that weaves tales of wood wives and moss maidens who called the ancient groves their home, and seek the stories that speak of the wisdom of the Elder Mother and of the mysteries of the dryads, for there is always a bit of truth in the fantastical.

  Don't forget your study of the trees themselves. Use a guidebook or list of magical correspondences when you go out on your next walk. This will help you familiarize yourself with your local flora and give you an insight to the shape and character of the nature spirit you are dealing with.

  For example, are you looking for new beginnings in your life? Search out the emotional healing powers of the birch tree. This radiant tree is all about light and life. And with its ruling planet as Venus, the spirit within invokes beauty and love in all of its workings. Maybe you're feeling emotionally drained and need a tree spirit who can handle a good release of negative energy—try the mighty oak. With its close association to the thunder gods, this is the tree to go to for strength, courage, and clarity of thought.

- *Get to Know Your Local Woodland*: It is impossible to enter the forest and not be aware of the magic that emanates from softly swaying branches and the flickering of the sun off shady pools. Take your hands and gently hold them around and over the forest's flora and take in its green energy. Let it gift you with healing and comfort. Spend some time with a tree or shrub that calls to you. Read or meditate under its branches. How do you feel when you're with this tree?

- *Approach the Tree as a Child Would*: Did you have a favorite tree as a child? I know I did. Most of us have memories of summer days spent in the shade of a grand tree, one that listened to whispered secrets or watched lovingly as you fell asleep in its shade. Reach back to that child tucked tightly inside you and approach the tree with that same sense of wonder that allowed you to believe that everything had a soul and that trees will whisper your name.

- *Be Patient*: You can't expect to be able to run to the first tree that you see and communicate. In fact, don't be disappointed if you never *literally* talk with a nature spirit. For most practitioners, communication is done through meditation and journeying—and like anything, it takes practice.

Spirits of the Greenwood

There are those times in one's life when an unexpected uneasiness can slip into the fabric of the everyday. What once may have felt comfortable in either our magical or mundane life can become heavy and begin to drag us down. I recall a time, over a decade ago, when I felt I had lost my sense of identity, and it took the wisdom of the hazel to help me discover the solution.

"Mama," my daughter, Chloe, said, handing me a small hazelnut. "The faeries said that this is for you, and they gave me these." She was six years old, and her eyes shined with all the wonder her world offered as she held up three tiny forget-me-nots.

"What beautiful treasures." I turned the hazelnut in my hand. It was perfect and smooth. I knew it would make a nice addition to my magical trove and tucked it away. It was later in the week, as I worked in my garden under a lemony September sun that eased the melancholy I had been feeling, when I thought about the hazelnut again.

Of course, I knew of hazel's associations with wisdom, inspiration, and the otherworld. But was it really meant as a sign for *me*? I went to my daughter, whose natural abilities to connect with nature spirits I never questioned. As a child, I too was gifted with the ability to see through the thin veil to the otherworld. "How do you know, sweetie, that this was meant for Mama?" I held out the hazelnut.

She barely raised an eye as she played with her favorite doll, ragged and tattooed with ink-penned makeup. "I just knew," she said. She was quiet a moment, then said, "It's kinda like the wind tells me, Mama."

I smiled. I knew exactly what she meant. When I was nine years old, I had expressed to my parents how faeries talked to me when I was in the forest and that I could hear their voices carry in the wind. I also learned quickly, after a trip to the doctor, not to talk about my magical play. On an up note, my parents were relieved when the doctor told them I was not schizophrenic and that I probably had an overactive imagination.

As for the hazelnut, I decided it was a sign and set out one evening to discover its symbolism for me. It was twilight, a time that is neither day nor night, when I found a hazel tree growing amongst the bramble rose, alder, and cottonwood near the river's edge. I began by grounding and calling the elements to bless my journey. I tucked myself against the hazel's slender trunk and tapped into its calming energy as I drifted into a meditative state.

My journey took me down a trail that was shrouded with a fog so thick I could hardly make out the path. As I stumbled along, the fog began to slowly dissipate, revealing the beauty of a forest very much like the one I was in but more vibrant. At the end of the trail, there was a being who stood beneath the branches of a hazel tree whose leaves shimmered as they swayed and moved without the presence of a breeze. The being didn't speak, and I honestly couldn't tell you if the spirit was male or female.

It was ethereal in its manner and movements, and I was immediately smitten and at ease in its presence. The spirit motioned for me to sit and held out its hands, its fingers gently enclosing treasures. I instinctively knew I was to pick a hand and I did. As the fingers of this gentle being unfolded, I felt a tinge of disappointment when I looked to see a hazelnut siting squarely on the palm, this time with my name burnt into it. I was confused, as this spirit was showing me the same hazelnut I needed to find the meaning of; this told me nothing. But then the being unfolded its other hand, revealing a chrysalis that quivered as something fought to release itself from its grip. I looked to the spirit, who smiled at me and nodded, and that's when it all came together. I was the creature fighting to set itself free, and the hazelnut was also me, a symbol to trust my intuition and wisdom, to stop allowing others (and myself) to second-guess my abilities. To not hold back the changes needed within me that would allow transformation to take place.

Once the realization was made, a small blue butterfly released itself from the chrysalis and fluttered quickly away. The being smiled and nodded again. I thanked the nature spirit, turned, and walked back into the fog. I have found (through journey work) that nature spirits can help us perceive the world in new and fresh ways. We learn to recognize ourselves in nature, and by doing this we can learn to cooperate with change.

But who are these denizens of nature who appear to us in our dreams and journey work or are felt or even seen in natural settings? The answers to this question are as varied as the forms that nature spirits take on. I can't give you a definitive answer, but I believe they are spiritual beings who exist on a realm that interlaces with our own. These beings have been known by many names and by many cultures. Some possess benevolent qualities, while others were known to be … let's say a bit mischievous. Here is a list of a few of my favorites from around the world:

- *Canoti:* In Sioux folklore, the Canoti are tree spirits who appear as sprites or dwarves. The forest spirits appear in dreams and are considered messengers from the otherworld. Call upon the Canoti for dream magic, divination, liminal magic, and communication with the otherworld.

- *Huldra:* This Scandinavian forest spirit could be called the siren of the forest. An enchanting temptress, she lures men who are wandering the forest landscape to their demise. Possibly connected to Frau Holle, she is protector of the forest and wild animals. Magically, work with Huldra for women's mysteries, protection, and female empowerment.

- *Kodama:* Japanese tree spirits who, according to some legends, could move throughout the forest. Other legends told the kodama were linked to a single tree and that a woodsman who cut a tree and drew blood would be cursed for cutting into the spirit of the tree. Kodama could be heard in the echoes that reverberated through mountains and valleys. Magically, call on the kodama for protection, communication, and hearth and home magic.

- *Lesidhe:* An Irish forest spirit and shape-shifter who can transform into any plant or animal in the forest. Lesidhe can be mischievous and have been known to lead forest travelers astray. Though no one has been harmed by this forest spirit, they are known to dislike humans for their irresponsible treatment of the environment. If you decide to work with the lesidhe, make sure you are treating their domain with respect. Magically, call upon the lesidhe for personal transformation, environmental issues, and shape-shifting.

- *Moss Maidens:* Covered in moss and lichen with limbs resembling maple bark, these wizened guardian spirits of the forest can be helpful to any human who is respectful of their forest domain. These mossy folks come to us from Germany, where they were known as *wilde Leute.* Magically, work with moss maidens when working magic for the environment, healing, and wisdom.

- *Nymphs:* These spirits of the natural world inhabit trees and plant life the world over. They can be sensed if only we try. Their voices mingle with the shushing breeze and seen within the blush of a spring flower. They are the dancing raindrops upon the lake and the vibrancy of summer foliage.

  We are probably most familiar with the Greek dryads, spirits who inhabit the forests. Hamadryads are nymphs that are connected to individual trees, typically oak or poplar; Meliae are nymphs of the ash tree; Oreads are found in pine; and Meliades, in fruit trees. Alseids are nymphs that inhabit groves. Though these romantic, always female nature spirits lend a sense of awe and wonder to any woodland setting, we shouldn't take them lightly. They are very protective of the forest or tree they inhabit. Work with nymphs in magic for the environment, love, healing, creativity, beauty, harmony, and freedom.

- *Skeagh-Shee:* These Irish forest spirits are protectors of the woodlands and can be defensively territorial against humans, but they are willing to share their surroundings with other forest creatures and nature spirits such as dryads. Before calling upon the skeagh-shee, make sure you are treating their domain respectfully. Call upon the them for protection, relationship building, and reconnecting to our natural world.

- *Pukwudgies:* In Algonquian lore, Pukwudgies are forest trickster spirits who can shape-shift into animals and, in some legends, can be identified by their sweet, floral scent. Though these spirits have been known to be helpful to humans, they may also cause forgetfulness or bring harm to people with their malevolent stare. If you think you see or are in contact with a Pukwudgie, it's best to just leave them alone.

- *Lunantishee:* These Irish moon-worshipping spirits of the blackthorn tree (also known as blackthorn sprites) are extremely passionate about the protection of their trees and may even pinch a human who dares to harm their wood. Call upon the lunantishee when working moon magic, for healing, and for strength.

The Elder Mother

If you are walking near the hedgerow on an evening when the air is tinged with the scent of woodbine, the breeze ruffles your magical senses, and you pass an elder tree, don't forget to tip your hat in respect for the wizened woman, Elder Mother, who resides within. She is the Crone of winter whose lessons can be gleaned from the rise of smoke of the communal fire and frost patterns on leaves. She is the aspect of the Goddess that draws us inward so we can gather our energy and eventually blossom. To our ancient relatives, the elder tree was surrounded by taboo and was approached with caution and ritual. According to Charlotte Sophia Burne in her 1914 book *The Handbook of Folklore*, no forester would dare take from the Lady tree before asking, "Owd Gal, give me some of thy wood an Oi will give thee some of moine, when I graws inter a tree."[7]

The Elder Mother was thought to be connected to the White Goddess of Winter, who was known as Hel in Scandinavian lore, Holda or Bertha in Germanic mythology, and Holde on the British Isles. She is the goddess of rejuvenation and transformation; she is the dark mother who holds our hand as we look deep into the cauldron of our soul, knowing that only by manifesting metaphorical death can rebirth begin.

The elder tree is a small tree that grows along country paths and along hedgerows. The European elderberry (*Sambucus nigra*) grows taller (up to twenty feet) than its American cousin (*Sambucus canadensis*), but both bear clumps of sweet-smelling white flowers in the spring and deep blue berries that hang in massive clumps during the late summer and early autumn months. There is also a red variety (*Sambucus racemosa*) that produces berries that are slightly toxic, and of course, there are many other cultivars available at your local nursery or garden center that have been hybridized as ornamental shrubs or for maximum fruit production.

This bent but formidable tree is imbued with the magic of the Crone and leads us through the dark half of the year in more ways than one. The berries of the elder tree, which are harvested in early fall, are rich in vitamin C

---

7. Charlotte Sophia Burne, *The Handbook of Folklore* (London, UK: Sidgwick & Jackson: 1914), 34, https://archive.org/details/cu31924009657283/page/n8.

and chemical compounds called anthocyanidins. Elderberry syrups and tea are powerful medicine for combating wintertime colds and flus. Infusions made of the flowers in late spring can be used to ease head colds and as a gargle for sore throats. The plant may also relieve the symptoms of ailments such as bronchitis, fever, and gout. The bark is a strong diuretic and was used in ancient times as a purgative in cases of food poisoning. Leaves can be used as a poultice for inflammation and the young shoots to clear phlegm from the lungs and head.

Elder guards the gateway to the otherworld. Meditating under her branches brings you closer to the land of Fae—in fact, it is said that if you take in the fragrance of the elder's blossoms on May eve, you will see the faerie king and his entourage. For communication with the otherworld, play a flute or whistle made from the wood of the elder. And for the rest of us who are not adept at making woodwind instruments, sit quietly under the branches and gently ring a bell three times before meditating. This will not only clear away the negativity but will also draw the Fae to you.

Elder guards against negativity. Plant an elderberry in your garden to protect your property and to enjoy its delicious and healthful fruit. Wands made from elder can be used to dispel negativity and in spells for healing, prosperity, exorcism, and protection.

The use of elderflowers at weddings was thought to bring good fortune to the newly married couple, and elder leaves were once carried to help one avoid adulterous temptations.

The planetary correspondence for elder is Venus; element is water; colors are black, green, and deep blue. Deities associated with the elder are Holda, Hel, and Bertha. Use it in magic for transition, funerary practice, protection, faerie magic, regeneration, healing, prosperity, and exorcism.

The Beauty of Transition with the Elder Mother

Transition is a beautiful thing, marking truly magical moments for us. When the universe opens up, absolutely anything is possible, and life becomes an adventure. Yeah … that's what I try to tell myself too. In actuality, transition scares the bejeezus out of me. And if you're anything like me, the uncertainty that can creep up on us during times of transition (whether it's a move to a new city or the first day of a new job) can really cause some major anxiety.

Working with the Elder Mother during times of transition can ease our anxiety and help us see the beauty and magic that can come with change.

It would be nice if this spell could be performed under an elderberry tree. I know that isn't always possible, so just being outside in a comfortable, peaceful area of your yard, patio, or balcony or in a park is great. If you can't get fresh elderflowers, try using a little bit of dried, which can be sourced at your favorite natural grocer or online.

You will need:

Water (enough to fill your cauldron or bowl)

Cauldron or large bowl

Bell

3 fresh elderflower clumps (or ¼ cup dried)

Sit comfortably outside. Remember to ground and center yourself. As you pour the water into the cauldron or bowl, call upon the Elder Mother:

Mother of hedgerows (ring bell)
Mother of gateways (ring bell)
Mother of darkness (ring bell)
I call upon you for wisdom, guidance, and peace

When you feel her presence, slowly begin to stir the water in the cauldron deosil (clockwise) with your index finger. As the water moves, start dropping your elderflowers into the water. Can you feel the arms of the Elder Mother wrapped tightly around you? Good. Now focus on the peace and ease of your transition. Visualize a positive outcome as your transition comes to fruition, all the while continuing to drop elderflowers into the water. As the water slowly stops moving, close your eyes and meditate a while on Elder Mother's green embrace. When you feel you are ready, thank the Elder Mother in your own way for her presence. Give the water back to Mother Earth by using it to water your favorite garden or potted plant.

In the Presence of Trees

For a lifelong resident of the Upper Skagit Valley, every drive into town can turn into a trip down memory lane. There's the old Rockport country store (long since closed), where my mother would buy us creamsicles on hot summer days, or the old dirt road, practically invisible to the average commuter, that led to my grandmother's secret blueberry picking spot. But one of the most significant landmarks for me is an old plum tree that stands elegantly on the edge of an alder stand in a fifty-acre field that is a barrier between the highway and the country road I grew up on.

As a child, I spent many a summer perched in the arms of this tree, feasting on her fruit and dreaming of faeries in her shade. She protected me (on more than one occasion) from a cranky bull my sisters and I would sometimes antagonize, and as I grew, the soil around her roots absorbed the tears of my teenage heartbreak. She was an old tree from which both my mother and my grandmother had gathered plums, which in turn added the sweetness to what could be a meager existence at times for my family. As I travel down the highway, season after season, I am witness to the old plum tree's many battles: the deluges of winter rain and the late summer droughts, the wind storms and heavy snow that snap her branches and threaten her stability. But she always holds strong and is a reminder of my own family's shared roots, our connected struggles, and our growth despite adversity.

We all know that trees are the largest of the plant species, that they absorb carbon dioxide and supply us with oxygen. They also stabilize the soil and provide habitat for animals and birds, but as the longest-living species on the planet, trees can provide us with a link to our ancestors, are a symbol of continual growth and hope for the future, and are a cosmic symbol of our interrelatedness with not only the natural realm but the divine realm as well.

The tree known as the tree of life was used by many ancient cultures to analogize human development both physically and spiritually. In Kabbalist teaching, the tree of life is a sacred map, if you will, used as a transformative guide to reconnect us with the source of all life. In Judeo-Christian teaching, the tree of life symbolizes wisdom and redemption. In Nordic mythology, the tree became a source of inner sight and healing, and in Buddhist teaching, it symbolizes redemption and enlightenment. In North America, Great Plains tribes used a cottonwood as a symbolic tree of life in their sun dance rituals as a means of generating energy to bring life into being.

The tree of life symbolism can be found throughout the ancient world, so which tree sprouted first? The sacred tree of Babylonian mythology was the first in written record, its stylized branches reaching across the regions becoming inspiration for trees of enlightenment throughout the Mediterranean and possibly for myths worldwide. It was said to have grown up in the middle of paradise, whose primordial waters sprang from its roots—a symbol of both regeneration and immortality.

So, reach back and ask yourself, what have I learned from trees? And what can I learn now being in their presence? In the 1980s the Japanese term *shinrin-yoku*, "forest bathing," was coined. If you haven't heard of forest bathing, it's the practice of spending slow, meditative, and connective time in the forest. It's not just taking a walk; it's attuning yourself with the forest's surroundings. It's being mindful of every drop of misty rain, every leaf that falls, and the quiet, distant sound of our Mother's earthbeat. It is gathering magical treasures of smooth stones or stray feathers and listening to the voices of trees.

As an untamed magical practitioner, I know the value of being in the wild. It helps slow me down after a long, strenuous day and reminds me that I am truly a part of the weave of nature. Japanese researchers conducted experiments in which they measured cortisol, heart rate, blood pressure, and pulse of volunteers before and after a walk. Part of the group walked through the forest while the other walked through the city. What researchers found was not surprising. In test after test, they found a walk through the forest lowered blood pressure and heart rate, parasympathetic nerve activity, and cortisol. They also found that the presence of antimicrobial oil emitted by plants and trees (phytoncides) appear to boost the immune system.[8] If just a walk does that, think of all that can be gained by literally bathing yourself in nature!

In the book *The Hidden Life of Trees*, author and forester Peter Wohlleben brings our attention to the social behavior of trees. He explains that trees communicate by sending electrical impulses to one another. They can sense leaf-destroying insects and send signals to predatory insects to feed upon the leaf-eaters. By looking to the canopy, we can find branches growing away from one another, so as to not block another's light.[9]

8. Bum Jin Park, Yuko Tsunetsugu, Tamami Kasetani, et al., "The Physiological Effects of *Shinrin-yoku* (Taking in the Forest Atmosphere or Forest Bathing): Evidence from Field Experiments in 24 Forests across Japan," *Enviromental Health and Preventative Medicine* 15, no. 1 (January 2010): 18–26, doi:10.1007/s12199-009-0086-9.

9. Peter Wohlleben, *The Hidden Life of Trees: What They Feel, How They Communicate* (Vancouver, BC: Greystone Books, 2016), 8–12

So take your time when you are in the woods and get to know these gentle giants, the trees. Listen as the wind rustles their leaves—what is it telling you? Gently run your hand over the bark of their trunk—let their wisdom flow through you. Breathe in, breathe out, feel your pulse slow and your mind clear—take in every earthy note the forest has to offer up, and when you feel ready, give a little bow to the trees and thank them for helping you find your wild.

I have listed some common trees you may find in your backyard, park, or local woodland and the correspondences associated with each:

Tree	Correspondence	Planet	Element	Energy
Alder	Confidence, growth, healing	Venus	Fire, water	Feminine
Ash	Wisdom, curiosity, spiritual love	Earth	Water	Feminine
Aspen	Healing, protection	Sun	Fire	Masculine
Beech	Balance, desire, aspiration	Saturn	Air	Feminine
Birch	Renewal, calm, purification	Venus	Water	Feminine
Cedar	Protection, cleansing, healing	Sun	Fire	Masculine
Cottonwood	Hope, healing, rebirth	Saturn	Water	Masculine
Dogwood	Heart's desire, protection	Jupiter	Earth	Masculine
Elm	Love, creativity, patience	Saturn	Water	Feminine
Fir	Cleansing, protection, change	Jupiter	Earth	Masculine
Hawthorn	Healing, happiness, Faerie realm, fertility	Mars	Fire	Masculine
Hazel	Creativity, abundance, sacred knowledge	Sun	Air	Masculine
Hickory	Abundance, wholeness, strength	Sun	Fire	Masculine

Tree	Correspondence	Planet	Element	Energy
Holly	Protection, dreams, luck	Mars	Fire	Masculine
Locust	Protection, beauty, Faerie realm	Venus	Air	Feminine
Maple	Creativity, abundance, beauty, communication	Jupiter	Air	Masculine
Oak	Strength, prosperity, healing, fertility	Sun	Fire	Masculine
Palm	Protection, fertility	Sun	Air	Masculine
Pine	Healing, protective, prosperity	Mars	ir	Masculine
Walnut	Motivating, health, mental powers	Sun	Fire	Masculine
Willow	Change, renewal, love, emotion	Moon	Water	Feminine
Yew	Rebirth, protection, divination	Saturn	Earth	Masculine

Tree Communion Spell

Finding a tree who is compatible with you can take some time. And more often than not, it will be the tree who guides you to them. So as you search, remember to keep your heart open, and when you think you have found the right tree, spend some time under the tree meditating, reading, or journaling. Place your hands upon the bark of the tree. Can you feel its energy draw you to it? You will know once this has happened.

Once you have made a connection with your chosen tree, pay reverence to them for the lessons that their mighty and wise spirit will be bestowing upon you. Remember this is a privilege not to be taken lightly.

You will need:

A few strands of your hair (or green thread or yarn)

Bowl of water

Large spoon or garden trowel

Just near the trunk of your tree, get down on either one or both knees (if unable to, sit or stand), raise your arms to the tree, and say,

To your roots I am bound
I honor the stability that you give
To your sap I am bound
I will nurture you as you nurture me
To your leaves I am bound
I honor the language of nature and lessons whispered on a breeze
To your wood I am bound
I honor your strength that keeps me upright when I am at my weakest
To you I am bound
Blessed be

Wrap a few strands of your hair (or thread or yarn) around a fallen leaf or twig (of the same tree) three times and say,

Three times three, I am bound to thee

Now, using a large spoon or trowel, bury it near the roots of the tree and pour the water over it to symbolize the sowing of your mutual respect. Remember, dear friend, you are embarking on a kinship that will last your lifetime.

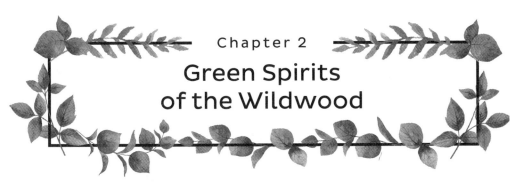

Chapter 2
Green Spirits
of the Wildwood

The next time you walk through the park or along a forest path, listen. For embedded in the crumbling bark and loosened stone are the stories of an ancient spirit whose many guises shift with the changing of the seasons. Linked with the vegetative cycle, he watches from amid the leaves, whispering of the cycle of life, death, and rebirth. In many ways, he is a reminder to us of the strength of the human spirit and our enduring link with nature.

Of all the nature spirits I have been in contact with, it is the spirit of the Green Man whom I gain the most comfort from. It is his green hand that has guided me daily as I work closely with the land. It is his story that unfolds with the changing of the seasons, and it is to him I give thanks for ancient knowledge that I glean each time I walk into the forests that surround my home.

The Green Man has been a presence in humankind's lives for thousands of years. His green spirit has appeared in many forms, be it the wild man Enkidu depicted in the *Epic of Gilgamesh* or in the role of dying and rising gods like Osiris, Attis, or Tammuz. His leafy appearance is woven throughout myth and folklore as Lord of the May, Robin Hood, and the Green Knight, and we sing of him in songs such as "John Barleycorn." He has been painted, sculpted, and carved and has acted as a green guardian to sacred sites all over the world. Even now his message of rebirth is present in the environmental movement: the earth is alive and sacred, and we are just one small part of the whole. So, let's slow down and cast our gaze upon the wildwood as we rediscover that green spirit in some of his many guises and let it shape our untamed soul.

Robin Hood: Reclaiming Your Spirit

It can be said that mythology and magic are deeply intertwined. Weaved within the stories that tell of our quest for identity and unmask the archetypes of every aspect of our human character are the magical elements that speak of mystery and awakening. The tales of Robin Hood, to me, exemplify this. He is an archetypical hero who robs from the rich and gives to the poor. He gets the girl and gains victory over the Sheriff of Nottingham before his own mysterious demise. But interlaced within his story are the leafy green tendrils of something far older and wondrously mysterious that speaks to us of the earth's bounteous energy and our own freedom of spirit.

There is something otherworldly about this cloaked figure who wears the green, something reminiscent of the vegetation myths and kingly sacrifices that harken back thousands of years to a time when the Green Man was the spirit of nature. The mysteries and folk traditions of Maytime festivals are tightly woven into the fabric of his green mantle. Look closely and you will see Robin Hood is champion against the Winter King and becomes consort to the Queen of the May. And his resemblance to trickster spirits such as Robin Goodfellow and Puck seems more than a little coincidental, as much of his exploits were at the expense of the rich monks of the abbeys. As Green Lord over the dominion of the forest, he is also reminiscent of Herne, the huntsman and leader of the Wild Hunt. For both Robin and the riders of the Wild Hunt were said to exact retribution from individuals who had neglected their debts.

We know that the oral traditions of Robin have been around for a very long time (even before his name first appeared in print), and as the ballads evolved, Robin Hood became a champion of the people, which reflected the social injustice acted out by landowners toward their tenants in medieval Europe. But I like to think that the ballads of Robin Hood also held tight to pre-Christian traditions, preserving the myths and traditions of a forest god who holds the secrets of spiritual renewal in his leafy hand and ensures we will never forget.

Reclaim Your Free Spirit with Robin Hood

It is so easy to get lost in the mundane activities of our everyday lives. Mornings spent in a flurry of breakfast dishes or finding your children's lost backpacks and sneakers. Where did your partner put your keys and where did you set your coffee mug? Carpools and express lanes, deadlines, and those coworkers who get under your skin. Afternoons keep you guessing: Can I make it to the gym before my daughter's soccer game? Why did I get that membership to the gym if I never have time to go? Where'd I put my shopping list? What are we having for dinner? Evening catch-up on projects for school or work and—oh, no! You forgot to stop by and help your mother set up her new phone... That will have to wait until tomorrow. Better give her a call.

Life moves fast and before you know it, you've lost that part of you that needs to feel cool soil under your feet and dance under the stars that wink from above swaying branches. More likely than not, to make room for others in our lives, we sacrifice the much-needed time we require to keep that spark in us lit. Let's relight, recharge, and rediscover that free spirit deep within our soul. For this ritual, we will work with the Green Man in the guise of Robin Hood to reclaim our free-spirited nature. This ritual can be done solitary or with a group.

The absolute ideal place to perform this ritual is in a woodland. I know this isn't always easy, but do try to find a place outside. If it is completely impossible, surround your ritual space with potted green plants.

You will need:

Robe that can be easily removed for dancing skyclad... You can do it! But if it might offend the neighbors (I don't want to be responsible for your arrest), wear something flowing and comfortable.

Lit fire (fire pit campfire or even a large candle in a cauldron or firesafe container)

Percussion instrument such as a drum, cymbals, maracas, or even an oatmeal box filled with beans

With your fire central, call your quarters around it. Turn to the east and say,

I cry for a song of unbridled freedom that awakens my tired spirit

Turn to the south and say,

I call to ignite the passion for all that is wild within me

Turn to the west and say,

I ask of you to release all fear that is hidden in the dark waters of my soul

Turn to the north and say,

It is from you I seek the green wisdom that stabilizes my being and keeps me whole

As you stand before the fire, call to the Green Man in the guise of Robin Hood:

Lord of the Wood, I come to you with a trickster's spirit and a twinkle in my eye—join me/us as I/we celebrate the renewal of spirit, of laughter, and of freedom

Drop your robe (if you choose to dance skyclad) and beat your drum. Dance furiously and unabashedly round and round the fire. Yell out! There is no shame for the wild one. For this moment you are a free spirit. There are no other obligations—no work, no home, no family obligations. It is only you and the night and the sound of the wildwood. You deserve this!

When you feel ready, slowly wind down the movement until you are standing still. Take a moment to ground yourself. Thank the Lord of the Wood for this moment of absolute freedom and release the quarters in your own way.

The Green Knight: The Challenger at Your Door

If Robin Hood is the Green Man in the guise of the Summer King that tempts you into the wildwood to dance in celebration of your free spirit, the Green Man in the guise of the Green Knight is his antithesis. The Green Knight challenges us to face the realities of our mundane lives: he leads us down a darker, colder path, calling for courage and sacrifice, so that when we come out of the shadows, we are better for it.

The Green Knight first appeared in a fourteenth-century poem entitled *Sir Gawain and the Green Gome* (better known as *Sir Gawain and the Green Knight*). It is set at Christmastide in Camelot. King Arthur, his knights and guests are just sitting down to dinner when there is a knock at the door and he who enters is described as follows:

Great wonder of the knight
Folk had in hall, I ween.

Full fierce he was to sight,
And all over bright green.[10]

He is an intimidating figure who offers the party to play a "Christmas game." He raises an axe and explains the simple game, in which he will exchange blows with any man on the condition that they accept a blow in return. Sir Gawain accepts the challenge and, with a swing of the Green Knight's axe, quickly takes off his head. But the knight does not fall—instead, he picks up his head, holding it high. Sir Gawain and the other guests watch in horror as the detached head speaks. He tells Sir Gawain that he must journey to the Green Chapel in one year to receive his blow.

The poem continues to tell of Sir Gawain's journey at the turning of the year to find the Green Chapel and courageously face his challenge. Along the journey, he arrives at the castle of Sir and Lady Bertilak, who offer him a place to stay until the day of his trial comes. Sir Gawain is happy to accept their generous offer and settles in at the castle. Because Sir Bertilak was a game hunter, he left every morning proposing to Sir Gawain that he would give him whatever he killed that day in exchange for whatever prize Sir Gawain won at his home. Finding this a strange proposal, Sir Gawain agrees, expecting to win nothing. But every morning, after Sir Bertilak leaves for the hunt, Lady Bertilak enters Sir Gawain's room and offers herself to him. Sir Gawain, being a chivalrous knight, refuses her offers but one innocent kiss. This happens on three occasions, and on every one Sir Gawain faithfully returns the kiss to Sir Bertilak.

As the time draws closer to his challenge with the Green Knight, Sir Gawain finds it harder and harder to refuse Lady Bertilak, finally accepting a gift of a green scarf that she says will protect him from the Green Knight's axe, and this gift he does not offer back to Sir Bertilak but takes with him to the Green Chapel.

Upon meeting the Green Knight, Sir Gawain kneels to accept his fate. Twice the Green Knight feints his swing, finally nicking Sir Gawain's neck on the third blow. To the astonishment of Sir Gawain, he finds that the Green Knight is, in actuality, Sir Bertilak, who had been enchanted by Morgan to test

---

10. *Sir Gawain and the Green Knight,* trans. Ernest J. B. Kirtlan (London: Charles H. Kelly, 1912), 60, https://archive.org/details/sirgawaingreenkn00kirtuoft.

the courage of King Arthur's court. The only reason for the slight wound upon the neck was a punishment for accepting the scarf from Lady Bertilak.

The Green Man in the guise of the Green Knight draws us ever closer to our fears and teaches us to take courage in the challenges of life. He also reminds us that in order for growth to happen, a sacrifice must be made. So what is it, my dear, that is holding you back? Part of realigning to the rhythms of nature is to look at your personal life's journey as part of a challenge that sometimes requires sacrifice. What will you sacrifice in order to regain your wild soul?

Self-Sacrifice and Growth with the Green Knight

There are some things in this life we need to release in order to truly live. I understand how self-doubt and worry can sometimes get in the way of living the creative and magical life you deserve. This spell was created to help you tangibly reject the negativity, self-doubt, and worry that have manifested around you and set you on a path of renewal and self-discovery.

This spell is best performed during the new moon, and, as usual, I encourage you to find a suitable location outdoors to set up.

You will need:

Scrap of paper

Pen

Resurrection plant (These easily obtained and inexpensive plants come dormant and, once placed in a bowl of water, will unfurl themselves and turn a mossy green. Once removed from the water, they curl back up and can be set aside for repeated use.)

Black candle

Sunstone (representing your personal light and strength)

2 bowls of water

Once you have set up your materials, write on your scrap of paper negative vibes, reasons for worry, or self-doubts. Light the black candle and place the resurrection plant in one bowl of water and the sunstone in the other.

Hold the scrap of paper over the flame of the black candle. Look at it, focus on the words you have written, and say,

I release you, (fill in blank)
I reject you, (fill in blank)
I will fear you no more

Light the edge of the paper with the flame of the candle; watch it burn (not too long) and focus on your intention. As you drop it into the bowl with the sunstone, say,

Challenge accepted, Sir Knight
I will plunge into the darkness and regain my life

Now plunge your hand into the bowl of ashes and water and retrieve the sunstone. As you place it on top of the unfurling resurrection plant, say,

In letting go, I reclaim my life

Leave the sunstone atop the unfurled resurrection plant and check it after approximately twenty-four hours at your altar or place of your choosing. You will find it resting perfectly square in the middle of a green living plant. At this time, you can either leave it out as a reminder for you of your reclamation of your life or take the resurrection plant out of the bowl and allow it to go dormant for another use. When you are finished, remember to thank the Green Man in his guise of the Green Knight for his lessons along your life's journey.

Wodewose: Your Wild Soul

We have looked at the Green Man in guises of both the Summer King, who exemplifies our freedom of spirit, and as the Winter King, who challenges us to face our fears and reclaim our lives. Now we will walk deeper into the forest, where the light struggles to break through the thick foliage and the path becomes tangled with vines, and find peeking from behind a tree the steady eyes of the Wodewose, or Wildman. He is the guise of the Green Man who exemplifies the true wildness of nature and is that spark that has been carried deep within each and every one of us since the beginning of time. It is that passion that moves us to create beautiful works, to love deeply, to cry out in anger, and to know fear.

The Wodewose cannot be described as gentle-gazed or beautiful, like the foliate heads seen carved in cathedrals. Neither can he be described as a gallant knight nor cloaked champion of the people. As a personification of nature, he is a combination of human, animal, and vegetative aspects. Feared in medieval Europe, he was thought to live in the far reaches of nature, covered in fur and leaves, except on his face and sometimes the knees and chest area. He was often seen as wielding a heavy club or tree branch and wearing a circlet of green upon his head.

The first accounts of Wildmen can be found in ancient mythology in characters such as Enkidu from the Mesopotamian *Epic of Gilgamesh* or Dionysus, who represented a true wildness of spirit, and as one of many dying and rising gods, such as Osiris or Attis. Merlin, too, could be seen as a Wildman figure. Born from a princess and a faerie (or demon), he arrived into the world hairy and went through a period of madness in the woods. But through this, he was given the gift of prophecy.

There have also been *human* dwellers of the wildwood who could be considered Wildmen. These social outcasts, who existed on the fringe of medieval society, were people who, for whatever reason, left the world of humankind with all of its excess and hypocrisy and formed a kind of subculture. Known for their deep love and knowledge of nature and the animal kingdom, they were sometimes sought out as shamans, seers, or herdsmen. For the most part, the people of our medieval world found them unsavory, and as these "wild folk" made their way into towns or cities, tales of the Wildmen began. Medieval people believed it was their divine right to control the natural world around them, therefore distancing themselves from the wild until its persona became feared and removed from all that was civilized.

To know the Green Man in the guise of the Wodewose is to know a true wildness of spirit, one that can be cruel and aggressive or gentle and kind (much like nature itself). The wisdom we can glean from the Wildman of the Woods is to not deny that part of us that is wild and to always remember our intricate connectedness to nature and the Divine.

Artistic Exploration with the Wodewose

We are going to dig deep into our untamed soul and practice a little artistic expression. By using your body as the canvas, we will tap into that Wodewose spirit of wildness and release the wild one within.

I love this because it not only helps us rediscover that wild child within but also promotes body positivity. We are each a unique and amazing work of art, and what better way to truly understand this than by decorating ourselves as an outward show of love and respect for our own beautiful bodies?

You will need:

> Water-based body paint in the colors of your choosing (There are some really fun ultraviolet paints to use if you have a black light.)
>
> Paint brushes, sponges, etc.
>
> Water and paper towels or rags for cleanup
>
> Drop cloth, plastic sheeting, or old towels to protect surfaces

Begin setting up somewhere where you will be comfortable and that will allow for easy cleanup. Before painting, invoke the Green Man in the guise of the Wodewose for inspiration by saying,

> *I invoke the Wild One of the woods*
> *Who would not deny me my wild*
> *Help me embrace all that is feral, passionate, and free*
> *For I am a wild child*

Now for the fun! Paint as much of your body as you feel comfortable with (or you can reach). Try not to overthink your design—just be impulsive with your strokes. When you're done, take a few selfies, and if you're feeling really brave, post them online (tag me on Instagram—I would love to see them!).

Here's the extra credit: if it's possible, go outside and run around. Dance, laugh, call out to the Green Man, and thank him for this opportunity to express your wild.

The Green Lady

September mornings are one of my favorite times to be in the forests that surround my home. The waning sun of early autumn stretches its fingers through the canopy, and beautiful shafts of lemony light illuminate the moss and tangles with the mist that rises from the understory to create a truly otherworldly feel to an already fairy-tale setting.

It is within the bower of these ancient forests that generations of my family have harvested conifer cones (mostly Douglas fir) for various seed companies as a means to earn extra money. I introduced this environmentally sound practice to my husband almost thirty years ago. Most people are unaware of the practice. You see, there are stands of conifers all over the Pacific Northwest that have specific desirable traits for seedlings that are used to replant areas that have been logged or destroyed by a natural disaster and are sold all over the world.

Once every three to five years, if the conditions are right, the trees produce an overabundance of cones, and just as the mornings begin to cool around the first part of September, we watch the tops of the trees and listen for the chattering of the squirrels. See, it is the squirrels who cut the cones from the trees, and as they do, the tips of the conifer branches spring upward to the sky. We find these areas and pick the cones up from the ground. Don't worry—there are enough cones to go around. We always leave plenty for the squirrels, and our imprint upon the forest is very slight.

On one such year, in the middle of September, my oldest son was almost four, just old enough to carry his own small cone bucket (which, more often than not, he filled with other treasures—discarded snail shells, pretty stones, or pieces of crumbling bark). We were in a beautiful stand of trees clear of underbrush, close to a creek, and most importantly, carpeted with lovely green Douglas fir cones.

As midmorning gave way, I took a break under the lacy branches of a vine maple, which was already reddening by September's chill breath. Steve was still busily picking up cones a hundred feet away, and I could make out the hollow thumps as he filled his bucket with cones. Little Josh was close by me, playing in the cool humus of a decaying cedar stump. He snorted as his stick warriors battled it out for the stump encampment. I closed my eyes and let the speckled sunlight warm my face, enjoying the peace that can only be found in a forest setting.

That's when I noticed it had grown particularly quiet. My mind went suddenly to the creek. Had Josh wandered over there alone? I snapped open my eyes—but Josh was still by the stump, quietly staring into the distance. He giggled and then waved toward a large hemlock tree twenty feet in front of us.

"You having fun, Josh?" I asked.

"Yep," he said, and picked his stick soldiers up again. But then I watched as he looked back toward the hemlock. He cocked his head, then once again smiled and waved. "I'll ask Mama," he said.

"Ask Mama what?" I answered, curious about what or who he was talking with.

"There's a green lady over by the tree." He pointed to the hemlock. "She said I could go over and look at her tree if I wanted."

As a magical practitioner I wanted to scream, "Oh, dear Goddess! Yes! Can I go too?!" But I'm a mom first, so before I got too wound up, I had to make sure there wasn't a human lady over by the tree attempting to abduct my little boy. "Hello!" I called out. "Is anyone there?"

I heard Steve call back, "What!?"

"I'm not talking to you!"

"What?!"

"I said, I'm not talking to you!"

Josh giggled. I tugged at his hair and winked. "Can I go?" he asked.

"Tell you what…" I picked him up. "I'm going to walk you to her tree. Then I'll sit back, and you can look at it with her." He hugged my neck. We walked all the way around the tree (just to make sure). Then I put him down in front of it and plopped myself down in the dirt about ten feet back.

I don't know what I expected—maybe a poof of faerie cloud or the sound of bells. But nothing happened. Josh sat cross-legged right in front of the tree for about five minutes, then he smiled and waved again. That was it.

"Wow. You look like you're working hard." Steve had a seventy-five-pound burlap sack full of cones thrown over his shoulder.

I pointed to my area where there were two seventy-five-pound sacks of cones and gave a satisfied *humph*.

"Oh" was all he managed to come up with.

"Josh has been visiting with a green lady," I said.

Steve, never surprised by anything that happens to us, shook his head and said, "Is it time for lunch?"

The rest of the day was spent in that exceptionally tranquil area of the forest, and as Steve and I worked, I watched Josh as he occasionally smiled shyly toward the distance or gave a little wave. He didn't talk much about it, and when pressed, he would shrug his shoulders and say, "She was nice" or "She was so pretty."

A decade had passed before Josh and I were in that area of the forest picking cones again. I didn't say anything as we worked that clear, crisp September morning. But at the end of the day, we sat in the car tired and covered in pitch. I saw him looking out toward the trees, and I said, "I wasn't sure if you recognized the area, but this is where you saw the green lady."

He turned to me and smiled sweetly, "I know, Mom. I know."

The Obscure Face of the Green Woman

A rare sight among foliate heads, the Green Woman's image is shadowed among the leafier faces of her Green Man counterpart. But if you're paying attention, she can be found. She is typically represented as a gentle creature whose body sprouts from the vegetation. In antiquity, she represented our link with nature and its primitive, innocent beauty. She is there too in the folktales and myths that have grown from the Green Man's origins as a forest deity: she is Marion to Robin Hood and Lady Bertilak to the Green Knight. She can be noted among the Wodewose as well, for there were female and children Wildmen who haunted the edges of the civilized world.

When the ancient gods of Germany and Scandinavia sat enthroned in the trees, it was the Wood Wives (or Wildwomen) who made up their court. These faerie-like spirits can be counted as a link to the Green Woman. Wood Wives were thought to hold the secrets of herbal medicine and were protectors of the trees and thought to possibly be linked to the feminine power of the land.

Also thought to be linked to the Green Woman is the figure of the *sheela na gig*. These female carvings with exaggerated genitalia can be found carved in ancient places of worship all over Europe and closely resemble the yonic statues of Kali, which appear at the doorways of Hindu temples. She is a bit of an enigma for scholars; after all, why would a carving with such strong sexual connotations appear so frequently in medieval religious structures?

One theory is that sheela na gig is a guise of the Cailleach, she who stirs the tempests and shapes the land, an echo of the ancient Earth Mother Creatrix, possibly carved by stonemasons as a way of carrying on the ancient symbolism of their own past. She may also be connected to ancient fertility rites, and like many Pagan symbols, the figure was carved into the churches as a means of showing the absorption (or conquering) of Pagan idolatry. Another theory is that the sheelas were carved to ward off evil or as fertility charms for women eager to bear children. Last, she may have been engraved for the highly illiterate parishioners of the time as a depiction of the sinful nature of sex in order to arouse disgust. No matter the reason for her carvings, she is a reminder of early goddess worship and the reverence our ancient ancestors had for the symbolism of the vulva as a life-giving and regenerative force.

The Green Woman can also be linked with the land itself—she is the *anima mundi* and sovereign goddess. In stories from ancient Greece, Mesopotamia, Ireland, and Wales, the rites of kingship included a ceremonial marriage between the king and the goddess of the land. It was the king's duty to uphold and protect the source of life—the land. In return, the goddess would grant abundance for the king and the kingdom he ruled. But if he somehow broke the terms of the agreement, the land would turn to waste.

I see the image of the Green Woman as representing the world soul and the eternal cycles of growth and rebirth. She reminds us of our interconnectedness with the natural world and our unique and critical role of the well-being of our planet. Look to the Green Woman to reclaim your own sense of empowerment and find balance within yourself. Ground yourself regularly with physical contact to the soil, and as you do, remember the agreements once made between humankind and the sovereign goddess of the land.

Here is a list of just a few goddesses who represent the Green Woman archetype (and their correspondences) whom you may enjoy getting to know:

- *Asase Yaa:* A West African earth and fertility goddess. To the Ashanti she was the upholder of truth and mother to humanity, whom she reclaims upon death. She is invoked for magic involving purity, truth, death and rebirth, bounty, prosperity, fertility, and cultivation.
- *Elen of the Ways:* A Welsh goddess of pathways both astral and corporal and an antlered guardian of the forest. She is invoked in magic for spiritual direction, new beginnings, environmentalism, and renewal.
- *Flidais:* A Celtic woodland and earth goddess. As protector of flora and fauna and mother of cultivation, she is called upon in magic for shape-shifting, balance, empowerment, environmental protection, rebirth, abundance, cultivation, and harvest.

- *Gaia/Terra:* A Greek and Roman earth goddess revered as mother, nurturer, and creator of life. She is a primeval goddess from whom all gods and life itself descended. Invoke Gaia in magic for balance, energy, new beginnings and endings, strength, protection, environmental issues, healing, unconditional love, maternal matters, and abundance.
- *Green Tara:* A Hindu and Buddhist earth goddess. In Tibetan Buddhism she is considered a female Buddha—an enlightened one, attaining the highest wisdom, compassion, and capability. She is called upon in magic for overcoming obstacles, protection, and wisdom.
- *Isis:* An Egyptian Mother Goddess and earth goddess. One of her titles was "Lady of the Green." This goddess was associated with all elements and was considered a life-giver and source of nurturing, devotion, patience, and love. Isis has been called upon in magic for protection, strength, hearth and home, healing, and renewal.
- *Nokomis:* An Ojibwe earth goddess. She was known as Grandmother and the ruler of the earth who nurtured all living things. Nokomis is invoked in magic for protection, abundance, maternal matters, agriculture, fertility, growth, and rebirth.
- *Pachamama:* An Incan earth and fertility goddess. She was thought of as a "dragon goddess" who resided under the Andes Mountains and presided over planting and harvesting. She has been invoked in magic for agriculture, abundance, strength, growth, and protection.

Standing Strong with the Green Woman

We must remember that we are sovereign unto ourselves and that to look at our own reflection is to see the Goddess. The Green Woman teaches us there is beauty in empowerment and balance with acceptance, not only of ourselves, but of others. Our young girls need role models who hold each other up and revere the Goddess within each of us if we want to end mean-girl mentality. So let's unleash the wild Goddess within—let's pledge to be the one who makes the changes, expresses herself in her own fabulous way, stands up for injustice, and does not give in to envy.

This ritual is intended for a group of women but can easily be altered for one. I have set it up pretty loosely because I believe that the words should not come from me but should flow organically from the women who will be sharing this intimate moment.

You will need:

    Green pillar candle

    Floating tea lights

    Table or altar

    Floral wreaths for each member (directions follow this ritual)

    Large tub of water (If you're lucky enough to have access to a garden pool or pond, that would be an excellent place to hold this ritual.)

Let's do this ritual on an evening during the full moon as a celebration of the Goddess within every woman! Invoke the Green Woman in whatever form feels most empowering to you or your group. Set up the green pillar candle with the unlit tea lights on a table or altar near your source of water, and place the floral hair wreaths so they encircle the pillar candle. Circle the altar, and starting with the participant in the eastern quarter and working deosil, have that person take a wreath and place it on the head of the person next to them. As they do so, they will say something positive about the recipient's strength, creativity, and so on.

    Everyone will take a floating candle and light it from the center pillar candle (representing the sovereign energy of the Green Woman). At this point, it is up to you or your group what you want to do or say before placing the floating candles into the water. Just remember to make it beautiful, make it empowering, make it all about you and the beautiful sister goddesses whom you are lucky enough to share your life with.

Floral Hair Wreaths

You will need:

    Floral wire

    Wire cutters

    Floral tape

    Flowers and greenery for each person

    Garden snips or heavy-duty scissors

    Ribbons (optional)

From a length of floral wire, form a circle loosely around your head. Cut the excess and use floral tape to completely wrap your circlet two times.

Lay out the greenery and flowers in a design that is pleasing and will create a look that is beautiful and uniquely you. When you are ready, trim the flowers and greenery, leaving 2 to 3 inches of stem.

Attach each piece to the crown by wrapping with the floral tape.

If you would like to add colorful ribbons, you can either weave them around the flowers or tie lengths of ribbon from the back of your floral crown.

Getting Back to Nature

There was a time in the not-so-distant past when the seasons were not defined by storefronts or Amazon promotions and a look to the heavens revealed so much more than whether or not it was raining outside. People had intimate knowledge of the natural world and of the plants, trees, and animals they shared the land with. Maybe that's why I am so fascinated by the stories of Robin Hood, the Green Knight, and the Wodewose. Unlike our ancestors, we can sit tucked within the confines of our modern world and hear the hum of the refrigerator that guarantees our food will stay fresh and the rhythmic drumming of our dryers and have assurance that we will have clean, dry clothes for the next day. We stare at our smart devices, which keep us in constant contact with the world without us having to move from the couch. And with all these simple conveniences, we are removed from our interconnectedness with nature.

But if we start reacquainting ourselves with the folktales of Robin Hood or poems such as *Sir Gawain and the Green Knight*, they can help us recognize seasonal shifts and the joys and challenges they bring. If we familiarize ourselves with the stories of Wildmen and Wildwomen we can acknowledge the cruelty and gentleness that can be found within the natural world. Study the leafy images carved by artisans, who so beautifully etched their works with a sense of purpose and knowledge of the plants that grew and were sacred to them. If you look closely, you can recognize these depictions of nature as divine.

Making the realization is only the beginning—now go outside and plant your bare feet firmly in the earth, feel the stones under your arches and the soil between your toes, break the separation from our Mother, and relinquish yourself to her sovereignty over the land.

Getting back to nature doesn't mean selling off the condo and living in a tiny house in the middle of nowhere. It means getting to know your local flora and fauna, sharing evening meals on the back deck or balcony, and including technology-free times for your family. Get to know your local state parks and reserves. Observe wildlife and spend some quality time stargazing.

When at all possible, take your magical practice outdoors. Practice meditation to the gentle melody of the birds singing or the rain softly hitting your roof. Be ecologically conscious and remember to feed your body with healthy, nourishing food. Get your hands in the soil—make mud pies and build sandcastles on the beach. Observe the shifting seasons with simple, joyful celebration. Most importantly, sit quietly in nature and listen to her earthbeat and attune yourself at a soul level. The Green Man and the Lady of the Woods still frequent the landscape, but it's up to us to find our way back to them.

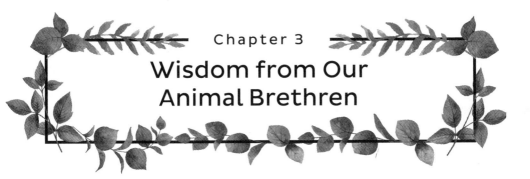

Chapter 3
Wisdom from Our Animal Brethren

As a Witch who can sometimes have a flare for the dramatic, I often visualized myself wandering through the woodland on misty evenings with a stately raven perched upon my shoulder. I would name him Arthur or perhaps Poe, and as I weaved my earthy magic, he would reward me with clicks and caws. The closest I ever came to having a feathered familiar was a crow that found us over twenty years ago when my oldest child was only four. I had come home one morning after running errands to my young son cheering and waving, as he always did, but there was something unusual about his attire. Propped on his shoulder was something quite large and black. I thought it might be a toy, part of some game he was playing—but then it moved. Was that a bird? I rubbed my eyes and looked again. Yes, there was a crow on my son's shoulder.

My husband explained that it had come out of the forest and swooped down, landing on Joshua. Pretty excited about finally having crow as a familiar, I stroked his head and said, "Welcome to the family, Arthur."

"His name is Blackhead, Mom." My son really knew how to blow a mystical moment.

"Like the pimple?" I looked to my husband.

"No, Mom," Josh answered, "because he has a black head."

"Well, don't you think Arthur is a better suited name for him?" I tried to convince my son. "Just like in the stories of King Arthur and Merlin?"

Joshua thought for a moment. "Umm, no. I think his name should be Blackhead because he's so black."

"Great. Welcome to the family ... Blackhead."

We had Blackhead in our midst just over a year before he quietly slipped away. During his stay he was very much my son's bird, watching him from an alder branch as Joshua sifted and played in the sandbox, riding on his shoulder when he rode his bike, and shooing away the dog by flapping madly at her when she jumped on Josh. As for me, I tried to force the poor crow to ride on my shoulder as I wandered into my forest temple, but he would just pick at my hair and suddenly disappear back to our yard to find his small blond human familiar.

Not too long after Blackhead had disappeared, while driving along the winding country road that leads to my home, I would occasionally see a raven hopping around the edge of the forest and scavenging from a carcass or picking at a bit of refuse. I was able to determine quite quickly that this raven had an injured wing, so I started bringing the bird scraps of bread and placing them on the side of the road. The raven soon became aware of my offerings and could be seen pacing back and forth along the side of the road beneath the same cedar tree every day. Was this the bird who was destined be my companion and guide? I determined it was a sign; we were meant to be together.

One morning as the late winter sun reached thin fingers of light through the trees laced with frost, I decided I would rescue the beautiful bird. Because what creature would not want to live with me in my warm home with plenty of food at the ready? The raven was waiting for me to toss the scraps, as I usually did, out of my car window, so when I pulled off the road and got out with the slices of bread held out to him, I think I shocked the poor bird.

"Here you go, beautiful," I said, as I slowly made my way to him. "You can come home with me. It'll be great. You'll love it." I continued to tempt the bird.

But to my surprise, the raven didn't hop over to me and click or croak with affection and appreciation for my effort to save it. In fact, in my opinion, I believe the bird was completely appalled by my attempts. The raven squawked madly, then took off into the forest. And of course, I took off after him. The bird seemed to move and maneuver through the forest, with all of its tangled underbrush and twisted roots and dips and bends, with supernatural speed and grace. I managed to keep up for a short time but suddenly fell victim to my own less than graceful footfall. And as I pulled myself up from one hole or another, I would say, "It's okay—you'll be safe with me!"

After about the tenth time I had to untangle my hair from a salmonberry bush, I gave up. And I felt pretty ashamed. How dare I think that I was somehow superior to this creature or that I could force him to be my familiar or guide or even pet? And who was I to believe that I could save this bird, when it was obvious that he was more adept in the forest on foot than I was?

After consulting with a friend who is a talented shaman (and who had a good laugh at my attempt to "own" an animal guide), I was taught how to connect spiritually with the subtle plant and animal energies that surround me and how to use them in my practice. I soon learned that we have many animal and plant allies throughout our lives who share with us their wisdom, and I was surprised when I discovered it was the deer who was to become my true power animal, gracefully reminding me of my place in nature.

Yes, my personal animal guide came to me in the guise of a shy doe that I found watching me from a stand of cottonwood near the river's edge. Over the course of a summer, I began to see her every day and then every night as she slipped through the tendrils of my dreaming world. And as I thought about it, I discovered it was the wisdom of the deer that I had most often sought out throughout my life without even realizing it. Maybe because they are most commonly seen at the edge of a wilderness setting, representing a bridge between the wild and the tame (much like myself).

In Celtic mythology, deer were able to move between the worlds, and hunting a stag represented the pursuit of wisdom. A stag's antlers were representative of a tree, and because they were shed and regrown every year, they were a perfect symbol of rebirth.

A deer's gentle spirit and swift and delicate movement remind us to have grace under fire, which I have always struggled with. I'm that quiet, gentle soul that turns into a complete whacko when faced with conflict. The deer's innocent nature teaches us to find that lost childlike quality within ourselves and to use that ability to look at things from another perspective. The deer spirit can also be used to help develop your intuition and refine psychic abilities, which I have found very helpful. Magically, the deer spirit can be called upon in spells for renewal, life's mysteries, grace, intuition, and peace. Yes, the deer suits me just fine.

Discover Your Power Animal

To tap into the power of your animal (or plant) spirit guide, I must first ask you to reach back to that time when you still looked to nature with a sense of curiosity and wonder. Find that spirit child within you who knows intimately the music of the wind that rustles the leaves before the rain and can hear the voices of the otherworld that whisper just beyond the silence that insulates the land after a heavy snow. Remember how it felt before you knew that too much sun could cause wrinkles and what the rain did to your hair.

As you enter that temple that is nature's bower, remember that at that moment there is nothing else. Only you and the breeze that tugs at the silvery strands that reach from your soul, the dew that moistens your skin as you brush past softly swaying foliage, and your breath, steady and in rhythm with nature's earthbeat. Recognize that all forms of life have wisdom to share, because it is only when you become in tune with nature that the messages from your spiritual allies can reach you.

Reconstructing our ties to nature is just the first step to discovering the wisdom and magic offered to us by our animal allies. Here are some guidelines:

Your animal guides choose you. It's important to not let your ego get in the way. Allow your own innate powers to be revealed to you through the images that appear through observation, dreams, meditation, ritual, or journey work. And though you will most likely have one power animal who resonates with you, you may also have many animal guides throughout your life. Honor them, for even the smallest shrew has wisdom to share.

Spend time in meditation. Open yourself up to nature and allow your animal guide to stir and reveal itself to you. Take notes after the meditation. Consider what animal or animals appeared, what they looked like, their actions, and most importantly, how the animal's appearance applies to your life.

Be observant of what is going on around you. What kinds of animals are appearing in your everyday landscape? Also, familiarize yourself with the habitats of the animals within your area. Incorporating symbology of the surrounding landscape into your observations may help you understand the animal's significance in your life. That being said, seeing one woodpecker tapping on a tree in the east may just be that—a woodpecker tapping on a tree that happens to be standing toward the east. Which brings me to my next point...

Look for repetition. Are you seeing a lot of woodpeckers throughout the day or maybe dreaming of them, or are they popping up in your journey work? This could be a symbol for a change in part of your daily rhythm. Let's say that the woodpecker in your dream is always pecking on the side of your home, for instance. Incorporating the symbolic representation of the home can help you pinpoint where the changes need to be made. Symbolically, the home typically represents the human spirit. So now you can ask, what is it about my psyche that may need a little change?

Use simple ritual to awaken your animal spirit. Simple drumming or dance can be used to help stir the sleeping animal spirit and guide it to reveal itself to you. Find a quiet place in nature (or a place in your home where you will not be disrupted). Ground yourself and drum out a steady rhythm until you feel relaxed and synchronized with the beat of the music. Allow the images to flow. When finished, journal what you saw. This technique can be used with ritual dance as well. Wear something comfortable and free flowing. Allow the movement of the dance to lead you until you are in a trancelike state. What images did you see?

Use simple journeying techniques to find your animal guide. Applying simple journeying techniques to help guide you through a meditative session may be just the thing to help you make a connection with your animal spirit guide. I suggest writing your own and recording them on a portable listening device. Don't worry; you don't have to be a poet to do this. There are also plenty of prewritten journey scripts that can be found in many of your favorite metaphysical books or online.

The Wisdom of Animals

Below is a list of many common animals and the wisdom they may have to share.

Antelope: Swiftness and adaptability. Antelope wisdom reminds us to grasp on to new opportunities and attune ourselves to life's changes.

Bat: Transition and rebirth. Bat teaches us to face the fear that comes with change and to focus on new beginnings.

Bear: Protection and intelligence. Bear wisdom reminds us to be strong and courageous.

Beaver: Persistence and productivity. Beaver wisdom reminds us to work hard and follow our dreams.

Bee: Sweetness and fertility. Bee wisdom teaches us to grasp on to what makes us happy and to pursue our dreams.

Buffalo: Abundance and manifestation. The buffalo teaches that what we visualize can manifest with time and patience.

Butterfly: Transformation and happiness. The butterfly teaches us to look at the value of change and reminds us of the joy in simplicity.

Cougar: Confidence and power. The cougar helps us understand when we need to be assertive and take charge of our lives.

Coyote: Playfulness and wisdom. The classic trickster teaches us adaptability and how to balance work and play.

Crow: Spiritual strength and watchfulness. Crows remind us to look for the magic that is all around us.

Deer: Peace and quiet. Deer medicine helps us attune to the otherworld and demonstrate grace under fire.

Dolphin: Balance and harmony. The dolphin reminds us to get out and enjoy life.

Dragonfly: Light and change. Dragonfly energy helps us see the light in our lives and understand the power of change.

Eagle: Healing and rebirth. An eagle spirit helps you elicit change and reflect on spiritual and emotional well-being.

Elk: Strength and stamina. The elk helps us understand balance and the importance of pacing oneself.

Fox: Cleverness and shape-shifting. The fox helps us identify growth through change and can act as a guide into the faerie world.

Goat: Agility and new heights. Goats remind us to be flexible when opportunities arise and to reach for new endeavors.

Horse: Freedom and endurance. Horse medicine reminds us to let go of constrictions in life and of power achieved with cooperation.

Mouse: Focus and meticulousness. The mouse teaches us to pay attention to the details.

Opossum: False fronts and sensibility. The opossum helps us see when we need to strengthen our appearance.

Otter: Wonder and playfulness. The otter eminds us to keep that inner child alive and never stop being curious.

Owl: Visions and wisdom. Owl medicine is a link to what is hidden in the shadows of one's soul.

Rabbit: Guile and quick thinking. The rabbit teaches us cyclic attunement and to grasp opportunity quickly.

Racoon: Dexterity and curiosity. The racoon teaches us to question without fear and holds the knowledge of transformation.

Raven: Shape-shifting and magic. Raven wisdom reminds us to set aside ego and seek inner knowledge.

Seal: Creativity and imagination. The seal reminds us of the balance between our inner creative force and our outer realities.

Skunk: Confidence and sexuality. The skunk teaches us to examine our self-image and is associated with increased sensuality.

Spider: Creativity and wisdom. The spider reminds us to maintain balance and that what we weave now in life will affect our future.

Whale: Inspiration and awakening. The whale helps us awaken our inspiration and manifest goals.

Wolf: Intelligence and steadfastness. The wolf helps us discover freedom and teaches us to trust our instincts.

Woodpecker: Rhythm and prophecy. Woodpecker medicine teaches us to follow the beat of our own drum.

Animal Spirit Meditation Beads

An animal spirit guide is much more than just an animal whose qualities we admire. They are the embodiment of our subconscious mind and a guide to help us acknowledge those aspects of our lives that need to be transformed, inspired, or comforted.

There are several ways to cultivate a connection with an animal spirit, including observing nature and keeping track of repetitive sightings of a specific animal, shamanic journeying, dreamwork, and meditation.

By touching each of the beads in repetition, animal spirit meditation beads can work as an aid in focusing your intention on your power animal while in a meditative state.

You will need:

13 beads to represent the lunar months (use turquoise, peridot, hematite, or other stones representing the element of earth)

3 beads representing the Triple Goddess

Spacer beads of your choice (wood is nice)

Charm representing your power animal spirit

Beading string

Lay out your beads in a way that is pleasing to you. String them onto your beading string and knot it securely at both ends.

Shifting Perspective

I think back about the two corvids who came into our lives so long ago. One stood sentinel over my son; he was the watcher who recognized the most vulnerable of us and reminded Steve and I that magic surrounds us every day. Then there was the shape-shifter who not only taught me humility but also stirred my soul and gave me the incentive to hone my magical skills and understand that it's not a game.

It wasn't until another month had passed that I saw that beautiful shapeshifter raven again. The first haze of green was appearing on the trees and the air was sweet with the scent of cottonwood. I was driving in the same area of winding road where I had so often tossed him scraps of bread and feeling horrible (as I had been since the incident when I attempted to catch him). I felt responsible for his disappearance, and as I glanced sheepishly out my window, I felt the familiar pang of guilt catch in my throat. But then a bolt of black swooped past my windshield and landed on a low weeping branch of a vine maple. I slowed and cranked my window. A large raven called out and flapped his wings. Instinctively, I knew who he was—he was the raven who taught me that magic is at play in our lives.

I nodded and smiled. "Thank you," I said, before cranking the window up and driving on into the green mist of spring.

Chapter 4
Amongst the Bramble

There are souls whose hearts beat out an unkept rhythm that can't help but keep them on the margins of our mundane world. I am one of those wild souls—the child in the playground who spied dragons forming from clouds as the other children organized softball teams, the teen who spent more time studying the magical properties of native plants than studying her algebra, and the adult who would rather hold a conversation with a nature spirit than with most people she knows.

We are the ones who teeter between this world and the other, the ones who have honed our intuitive skills and can journey beyond the veil to gain insight from their spirit guides. We are the hedge riders, a term not to be confused with Hedge Witch (one who practices a natural or green witchery). The two practices complement one another, but one does not have to be a Hedge Witch to practice hedge riding or vice versa. So how did the term *hedge rider* become connected with hedgerows?

It was the hedgerows that designated the edges of the settlement. They are considered a "between place" or "liminal space," where the veil between our world and the spirit world are thin. And it was from these borders, a thicket of shrubs, vines, grasses and flowers that separated the wild unknown from the civilized, where the stories of elder women and cunning men who gathered medicinal herbs, bark, roots, nuts and berries took root. Underneath the elder and the hawthorn, it was said, they would sit, teetering between the mundane and the spirit worlds, and amongst the tangled vines and bent branches, many a secret was whispered to them by their spirit allies. Through journey work, they gained the second sight, became spiritual healers, and learned from their spirit allies the healing properties of plants. A modern hedge rider doesn't require a literal hedge to aid them into the spirit world. This can be done through journey work or by the use of entheogens wherever one feels safe and comfortable.

The thought of a hedgerow stirs, for many, images of old superstition, stories of faerie lovers, and folklore about magical cures, and we forget they are also an important and threatened habitat that support a very wide range of plants and animals.

The Importance of Hedgerows

As a child I could be found at the side of my mother and grandmother as we picked the dark, juicy fruit of the blackberry that grew tangled within the hawthorn and elder, nettle and vine maple that partly make up the hedgerows that border the forests near my home.

With blackberry-stained fingertips, my grandmother would point out a nest within the hedge's protective confines: "That, child, is a robin's nest. We need to pick carefully and remember to leave some fruit for the wildlife."

It is from my grandmother that I learned of the importance of hedgerows in nature. Throughout history, hedgerows have been used to mark out agricultural borders and used as formidable defensive boundaries. With the passing of the Enclosure Acts in the eighteenth and nineteenth century in the United Kingdom, hedgerows were planted as fencing borders to separate agricultural fields, and in the 1930s, the United States' Great Plains Shelterbelt program encouraged the planting of hedgerows as windbreaks for farms.

Many hedgerows are now protected, as many small mammals, birds, and insects depend on these tracts of trees, shrubs, and other plants for food and as protective shelter and corridor along which animals can move.

Where I live, I know of many people who think of the hedgerows that border their properties as bothersome bramble and go to great lengths to tear them up, replacing these natural wild boundaries with fencing or replanting them with spiritless shrubs that have forgotten how to bloom. I have purposely left the boundaries of my property untamed: a place for birds such as the thrush and robin to build nests and feast on berries, a green infrastructure for small mammals to ramble and remain protected from predators, a home for many native plant species, and a natural windbreak and noise buffer.

As a magical practitioner, I feel hedgerows tugging deeply at my spirit. They offer a place to gather magical supplies, a "between" place where I feel the threads of the otherworld softly tugging at my soul and a place for meditation and reconnecting with nature. I ask you to take another look at the bramble that may border your property or that you find along fence lines in your neighborhood or along the roadways. These remnants of the wild still beat to an unkept rhythm, teeming with an abundance of life. And tangled within the bramble are the memories of the wise women and cunning men who learned through their interconnectedness with their world and gleaned spiritual knowledge from the spirits of the land.

Here is a list of many important hedgerow favorites, their uses, and their correspondences:

Blackberry (*Rubus* spp.)

Element: Water

Planet: Venus

Energy: Feminine

The natural arches created by the growing habits of blackberry canes were once crawled through ritualistically as a cure for all manner of ills, including whooping cough, blackheads, and rheumatism. Typically ripe in late July or August, blackberry is sacred to Brighid and is an excellent berry for pies and preserves. Try a blackberry pie at Lughnasadh. Use blackberry in magic for health, protection, and money.

Blackthorn (*Prunus spinosa*)

Element: Fire

Planet: Saturn

Energy: Masculine

In folklore, blackthorn was a tree of ill omen and was linked to warfare and death. In Scotland, it was connected to the Cailleach, as it was the striking of the ground with her staff made of blackthorn that began winter. In magic, use blackthorn in spells against evil, shadow magic, creating boundaries, and purification. The fruit of the blackthorn are known as sloes. Too bitter to eat raw, they are excellent preserved in gin or wine and made into jams or jellies.

❧ Crab Apple (*Malus coronaria*)

Element: Water

Planet: Venus

Energy: Feminine

Use apples in spells for love, health, immortality, or garden magic. This favorite tree of Witches (I know it is one of mine!) is popular for making wands. Also known as the "food of the dead," apples are typically seen on altars at Samhain. When cooked down, crab apples make a natural pectin for jams and jellies.

❧ Dog Rose (*Rosa canina*)

Element: Water

Planet: Venus

Energy: Feminine

The dog rose has long been used in love spells, mixtures, potions, charms, and elixirs. Rose hips and petals are also used in healing spells. Use the rose in magic for luck, love, protection, healing, and abundance. Rose hips are high in vitamin C—try making your own rose hip simple syrup to help fight colds and flu.

Rose petals are a wonderful ingredient to add to dream pillows. Here is a great romance blend to stir your sensual nature: 1 cup rose petals, 2 to 3 whole cloves, ¼ cup peppermint, and ¼ cup catnip. Use this blend to fill a small pillow or sachet that can be tucked near you while sleeping.

❧ Dogwood (*Cornus* spp.)

Element: Earth

Planet: Jupiter

Energy: Masculine

The dogwood tree is a tree of wishes and secrets. Collect dew from dogwood flowers and dot it on your Book of Shadows to protect its contents. Dogwood oil can also be used in the same manner. Burn the bark and dried flowers in incense or use leaves in protective amulets. Use it in magic for protection, secrets, and wishes.

❦ Elderberry (*Sambucus canadensis*)

Element: Water

Planet: Venus

Energy: Feminine

Elder guards against negativity. Plant an elderberry in your garden to protect your property and to enjoy its delicious and healthful fruit. Wands made from elder can be used to dispel negativity and in spells for healing, prosperity, exorcism, and protection. The use of elderflowers at weddings was thought to bring good fortune to the newly married couple, and elder leaves were once carried to help one avoid adulterous temptations.

❦ Hawthorn (*Crataegus* spp.)

Element: Fire

Planet: Mars

Energy: Masculine

Sacred to the Fae, the hawthorn is part of the triad oak, ash, and thorn. According to folklore, if all three trees are seen together, one can see faeries. Witches have performed sacred rites underneath the branches of the hawthorn for generations. In British mythology, it was thought that hawthorns were Witches who had transformed to trees. Use hawthorn for healing, happiness, connecting with the Faerie realm, and fertility.

❦ Hazel (*Corylus avellana*)

Element: Air

Planet: Sun

Energy: Masculine

There is a custom of eating hazelnuts before divination, which raises the question, would eating a jar of Nutella be an acceptable substitution? I'll have to try it and find out. Hazel crowns were made to induce invisibility and to grant wishes. Hazel twigs can be used as dowsing rods and make wonderful all-purpose magical wands. Use hazel for creativity, abundance, wishes, sacred knowledge, protection, and fertility. Hazelnuts are high in unsaturated fats, vitamins, and minerals; use them as a heart-healthy addition to your favorite sweet or savory recipes.

❦ Holly (*Ilex* spp.)

Element: Fire, air

Planet: Mars

Energy: Masculine

Holly is a tree of death and rebirth as symbolized in both Christian and Pagan ideology. Plant holly around your property as means of protection. Hang around your home at Yule for luck. It is said that if a man carries holly with him, he will attract a mate. Use in magic for protection, dreams, easing the passage of death, and luck. Holly provides great nesting for many songbirds and is food for animals such as rabbits, squirrels, racoons, deer, and voles.

❦ Honeysuckle (*Lonicera* spp.)

Element: Water

Planet: Jupiter

Energy: Masculine

With beautiful trumpeted flowers, this amazing climber is a favorite of pollinators. Found in the countryside wound around stumps and tangled along fence lines, the honeysuckle teaches us to delight in beauty and appreciate life and laughter. Use it in spells for prosperity and psychic powers.

❦ Laurel (*Laurus nobilis*)

Element: Fire

Planet: Sun

Energy: Masculine

Associated with honor and greatness, laurel was fashioned into crowns and garlands and bestowed upon athletes and other people of honor as a sign of greatness. Laurel was also worn as an amulet to ward off evil and placed beneath the pillow to induce prophetic dreams. Use it in spells for protection, self-awareness, dreams, and love.

❧ Maple (*Acer* spp.)

Element: Air
Planet: Jupiter
Energy: Masculine

Maple is a harmonious tree whose branches have long been used to make magical wands and staffs. The leaves can be used in magic for money, and maple syrup can be used to soothe the psyche. Because of maple's soothing qualities, it's a nice tree to meditate under. Use it in magic for creativity, abundance, beauty, love, and communication.

❧ Red Currant (*Ribes rubrum*)

Element: Fire
Planet: Saturn
Energy: Feminine

Currant can be used to open up the third eye and is said to help those with self-doubt. Use red currant in magic for clairvoyance, healing, abundance, and spirituality. Rich in antioxidants, use these tart berries in your favorite preserves, in pies, or for wine making.

❧ Wild Cherry (*Prunus avium*)

Element: Water
Planet: Venus
Energy: Feminine

Use cherrywood wands for divination. Use wild cherry in magic for unification, love, and intuitive insight. If you use an older spell that requires blood, cherry juice works well as an alternative. There are several varieties of wild cherry throughout Europe and North and South America. The European wild cherry, also known as sweet cherry, is related to the sweet cherries you may find in your local supermarket or roadside stand. The North American black cherry and chokecherry are tarter and appropriate for pies and preserves.

❧ Willow (*Salix* spp.)

> *Element:* Water
>
> *Planet:* Moon
>
> *Energy:* Feminine

Fashion magic wands from willow for practicing moon magic. Folklore dictates that to avert evil, knock on a willow tree three times, hence the saying "knock on wood." This protective tree is great planted around your property or placed in the home to guard against evil. Willow bark can be used medicinally to ease pain and soothe menstrual cramps. Use dried leaves in incense between times of Samhain and Beltane to call up spirits. Use it in magic for protection, healing, love, moon magic, and divination.

❧ Witch Hazel (*Hamamelis* spp.)

> *Element:* Fire
>
> *Planet:* Sun
>
> *Energy:* Masculine

Witch hazel gets its name from its wood because of its resemblance to the hazelnut tree, and it is probably best known for its longtime use as a dousing rod. Witch hazel is a natural astringent and is popular for use on skin conditions such as acne. Use it in magic for protection, chastity, love, and divination.

Lessons from Wildflowers

I went to my local library a while back and was amazed by what I saw. No, it wasn't a new release by my favorite author or a recently added DVD I hadn't checked out. It was the tiny yellow blossoms of a pineapple weed pushing its way through the cracks in the sidewalk. I squatted down close and marveled at the tenacity of this tiny plant.

How many of us go through our lives just surviving? Some of us may feel buried under the responsibilities of our jobs, while others may find their personal lives inhospitable or want to just give up on making a difference in a world that feels, at times, indifferent. I get it because I am guilty of letting circumstances in my life dictate the excuses I use to not grow emotionally or spiritually. But then I look to that tiny pineapple weed, which was not only blooming but thriving. This flower didn't worry about how it was going to bloom … it just did.

Part of the reclamation of our wild soul is to allow ourselves the freedom to bloom where we grow. Yeah, we may not like the situations we find ourselves in due to finances or circumstance. But ask yourself, what can I do despite my situation that will allow for growth and freedom? How can I embrace where I am at this particular moment in my life and facilitate my own change by growing toward the light? Remember the wild Witch that you are—unfurl those petals and bloom.

Grow toward the Light: A Spell to Facilitate Positive Change

This is a very easy spell that is great for spring. I know that daffodils are not a "wild" flower, but I love the way they spread, popping up in fields and on roadsides and delighting us with their cheery burst of yellow that is sunshine for our souls.

In magic, daffodils represent growth, rebirth and renewal, new beginnings, and new love. What I love most about daffodils is their ability to continue to push their way through the soil no matter what nature throws at them. And with unexpected spring snowfalls that can happen for a lot us, it's not unusual to look out and see their happy yellow faces shining on.

In the spring, daffodils can be found still in bud at grocery stores and farmer's markets for very little money. They are an inexpensive way to add a little cheer to what can sometimes be a very dreary late winter and early spring. We are using daffodils for this spell, but any closed flower will do.

You will need:

    1 daffodil in bud stage
    Small vase or jar

This is a very easy way to remind yourself that no matter what your circumstances are, continue to bloom. You can do hard things!

Fill a jar or bud vase with water. Place the closed bloom in the vase and place it in a sunny window. As you do this, visualize yourself as that closed bud. Imagine yourself unfurling toward the light. Now say,

I will unfurl and bloom
I will bloom and grow
Where there is light, I will thrive
Blessed be

Watch as day by day the daffodil unfurls itself and begins to bloom, always reminding you that where there is light, you will thrive. Enjoy the bloom until it withers, and then give it back to the earth by adding it to your compost or burying it in some soil in your yard.

No-Harm Wildflower and Hedgerow Magic

The wildflowers that dot our landscape offer the beautiful messages to embrace our freedom of spirit and that growth and beauty are possible no matter our situation. To work magically with these wild or native plant allies offers an energy that is, for me, far more intense than what I receive from regular hybridized garden plants. I am made completely aware of the underlying pulse that connects us all. It beats in sync with the rhythm of my soul, and I feel at one with the spirits of the land that surround me. And with that comes the realization that we are not only in the universe, but the universe is in each and every one of us.

If you desire to work with the energy of wildflowers, there is one thing you have to remember: it is against the law in many areas to pick wildflowers on public lands, roads, or on private property, and doing so could result in a hefty fine. Picking wildflowers can adversely affect many birds, insects, and small mammals who rely on these plants as a source of food, shelter, and cover. It also reduces the plants' ability to reproduce and will affect their long-term survival in that location. One solution is to buy plants or seeds that are native to your area and plant them in your backyard garden.

Using native plants is a natural form of gardening that can bring into your home joy and contentment that can only be felt in wild places. And what better way to share our oneness with nature than to emulate what the Goddess already knows works right in our own backyards, patios, or balconies? Natural gardening is low maintenance, provides habitat for native birds and animals, and entices the spirits of the wild to your home.

But if planting a wildflower or native plant garden at your home isn't in the cards, there is a way to work with the energies of wild plants without damaging the plants, and you don't need to drag along any magical supplies. So whether you're hiking in the mountains, strolling down a country lane, or exploring a field of wildflowers, you can work magic. Remember, *you* are a part of nature, and as such, you are your most powerful tool. Here are a few ways you can work with plants:

Working with Plant Allies: I have already discussed ways to connect with both tree spirits and animal guides. Connecting with plant allies is similar.

Be Observant: What plants keep popping up in your life or in your dreams?

Be Ready and Willing: Keep yourself open to unseen realities and be ready to accept the wisdom from the spirits of the land.

Get to Know Your Native Plants: Familiarize yourself with your local flora. Use a guidebook or list of magical correspondences when out in nature.

Practice Meditation and Journey Work: Use these techniques to connect with the unique energies offered by each plant. You will know when a plant resonates with you.

Energy Play: Use your hands and move them over the flowers. Play with the sensation. How does it feel to you? Practice energy manipulation. Combine this energy with your own to call the quarters (silently if in a public setting).

Color Magic: Simple color magic can be used when working with flowers. Try meditating in a field of poppies; a combination of the poppy's loving vibes with the strength-giving red color is great for a confident boost of self-love. Or think of the peaceful aspects of the forget-me-not's light blue tones combined with their association with the Fae.

Play in the Dirt: Draw symbols or sigils lightly in the soil to combine the plant's magical energy with your intention. Leave the symbols to be dissolved by the elements.

Take a Walk: Walking is more than a form of exercise. It can be a spiritual act in which we commune with the spirits of the land and manifest our magical intentions. Intensify the energy by matching intention to location. For example, walk through a field of wildflowers to invoke freedom of spirit or down a forest path for transformation.

Shape the Energy with Song: If you're in an area where you don't mind vocalizing, raise energy by singing, chanting, or clapping out a beat with the rhythm of nature.

Magical Wildflowers

Here is a list of common wildflowers whose unique energies may help assist you with your magical needs.

Anemone (*Anemone* spp.)

Element: Fire
Planet: Mars
Energy: Masculine

Also known as wind flowers due to the old belief that they only come out in the windy month of March, these little flowers signify health and hope. Use dried petals in charm bags or healing rituals. Plant anemone around your garden for protection, and use it in spells for health, healing, happiness, and protection.

Aster (*Asteraceae* spp.)

Element: Water
Planet: Venus
Energy: Feminine

A sacred flower to the Greek pantheon of gods, the aster was commonly placed on altars during festivals. Place these flowers in vases in every room, as they bring peace and loving vibrations into your household. Use aster in spells and charms for love, patience, peace, and delicacy.

🌿 Bluebell (*Hyacinthoides* spp.)

Element: Air
Planet: Venus
Energy: Feminine

The beautiful flowers of the common bluebell could be found carpeting forests throughout the English countryside at one time, but sadly, they are now under threat by the introduction of *Hyacinthoides hispanica*, a bluebell native to Spain, Portugal, and North Africa. Bluebells are a favorite of the Fae, and if you have them in a shady nook of your garden, you will be truly blessed. Use dried blossoms in dream pillows to prevent nightmares. Use in magic for truth, luck, and wishes.

🌿 Columbine (*Aquilegia* spp.)

Element: Water
Planet: Venus
Energy: Feminine

Columbine can grow up to three feet tall and is loved by pollinators. The essence of this magical plant is said to help people find their true identity. In magic, use columbine for spells concerning love and courage.

🌿 Cow Parsley (*Anthriscus sylvestris*)

Element: Fire
Planet: Mars
Energy: Masculine

Cow parsley was sometime called devil's parsley because of its close resemblance to the very poisonous water hemlock. Another folk name, mother-die, may have originated from stories told to deter children from picking the plant: because they couldn't tell the difference between the two plants, they were warned that their mother would die if it was brought home. For people who could tell the difference, carrying cow parsley was said to calm emotions and guard against evil. Use it in magic for strength, courage, and protection.

Warning: Cow parsley's sap contains furocoumarin, a compound that may make you very sensitive to ultraviolet light when it comes in contact with your skin. Wear gloves when handling fresh cuttings.

❧ Oxeye Daisy (*Chrysanthemum leucanthemum*)

Element: Water

Planet: Venus

Energy: Feminine

This is the flower of the maiden and the waxing moon. In fact, one of its folk names is moon daisy. Use this lovely flower as part of your Beltane altar, as it is a classic faerie flower and will bring happiness into your home. Use it in magic for happiness, working with the Fae, moon magic, love, and simplicity.

❧ Foxglove (*Digitalis purpurea*)

Element: Water

Planet: Venus

Energy: Feminine

Covered with bell-shaped flowers, this dramatic spiked biennial is a favorite of the Fae. Foxglove grows up to five feet tall and is self-seeding. In magic, use foxglove for protection, faerie magic, and divination.

Warning: This plant is poisonous.

❧ Hyssop: (*Hyssopus officinalis*)

Element: Fire

Planet: Jupiter

Energy: Masculine

Hyssop has been used since ancient times to purify sacred space and as a strewing herb to freshen homes. Hyssop makes a wonderful soothing tea during cold and flu season and can be used as a mouth or eye wash due to its mild antibacterial properties. Use it in magic for purification and protection.

Mallow (*Malva* spp.)

Element: Water

Planet: Moon

Energy: Feminine

Mallow is a protective plant and is excellent to have on hand if conducting spirit work. Plant mallow on the graves of the dearly departed. Use the seeds in sachets to attract love. Mallow is used in spells for banishing, love, and protection

Here is a great protective salve to apply before journeying: gather 1 cup infused olive oil, mallow leaves and flowers, rosemary, 1 cup coconut oil, ½ cup beeswax, and 15 to 20 drops sage or rosemary oil. Infuse mallow flowers and leaves and sprigs of rosemary in olive oil for several weeks in a cool dark place. When ready to make the salve, use a double boiler on low to slowly heat coconut and olive oil. Stir in beeswax. When melted, take off heat and let sit for approximately 10 minutes. Add essential oil. This recipe makes approximately 16 ounces of salve, or enough to fill four 4-ounce containers.

Meadowsweet (*Filipendula ulmaria*)

Element: Air

Planet: Jupiter

Energy: Masculine

Historically used to flavor mead and due to its high content of salicylic acid, this plant of marshes and woodlands was also used as a strewing herb for handfastings and for bridal chambers. Use meadowsweet in spells for divination, love, happiness, and tranquility.

Milkweed (*Asclepias* spp.)

Element: Air

Planet: Moon

Energy: Feminine

So called because of the milky sap that is secreted from the plant, milkweed can be toxic to pets if consumed in large quantities (luckily, because of its bitter taste, animals tend to not eat it). Despite this flower's reputation as a noxious weed, it is beneficial to pollinators, especially monarch butterflies who lay their eggs on milkweed. Just remember to plant varieties that are local to your region. Planted in the garden, milkweed attracts faeries. Add the silky tassels from the seedpods to dream pillows to dream of the Fae, and use milkweed in spells for divination, faerie magic, wishes, and spirit communication.

❥ Self-Heal (*Prunella vulgaris*)

Element: Earth
Planet: Venus
Energy: Feminine

This common field herb is used to dress scrapes and cuts and draw out infection. It was once known as carpenter weed, which gives an indication to its ease of availability and usage for mashed or cut fingers. In magic, self-heal is a great herb to work with in spells for self-love or self-awareness. It can also be used to strengthen healing magic. Use in spells for health, hope, self-love, and banishing.

❥ Wild Ginger (*Asarum* spp.)

Element: Fire
Planet: Mars
Energy: Masculine

Both European and North American wild ginger grow as ground cover in shady or forested areas. One of wild ginger's folk names is wartchase because it was believed that witches used it to rid themselves of warts, thus hiding their true identity. North American varieties of wild ginger have edible rhizomes, though the flavor is subtler and a bit more peppery than regular ginger. Use it in spells for love, success, power, and money.

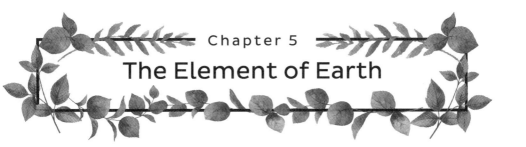

Chapter 5
The Element of Earth

Is it within the cover of the forest that your wild soul longs to be? This mystical place of soul-searching and transformation takes us down twisting paths and shadowy landscapes and invites us to explore dark nooks and listen for its secrets that echo through the trees. For within the ancient wood, magic is more than elaborate ritual or a quick spell found in a book or on the internet. It is working hands-on with the natural world.

In general, it is the element of earth that guides me in my practice. I feel its wild beat resonate deep within my soul and experience its delight through chance encounters of the creatures that we share this world with. Enchantment can be found within the petals of a single blossom found growing in the crack of a sidewalk and heard in the songs of the birds you cannot name. As the oldest magic, earth magic is about revelation—understanding our interconnectedness with the land, digging deep to uncover our personal power, attuning to nature's natural rhythm, and keeping in tune with our own cyclical nature.

Animals associated with the element of earth can remind us to heed life's lessons. The wolf reminds us to listen to that internal voice and take control of our own lives. Protective and intelligent, the bear reminds us of our inner strength and that sometimes courage is needed to navigate us down our path. Coyote's wisdom tells us to stay playful and teaches us adaptability. And then there is the quiet deer standing at the edge of the wood. Pay attention to the message this shy creature extends, for when it shows up, it is to help you attune to the otherworld and, most of all, be gentle with yourself.

Astrological signs associated with earth are Taurus, Virgo, and Capricorn. Well attuned to their natural surroundings, people born under an earth sign are self-disciplined and persistent and can easily reach any goal they set up for themselves.

Magically, you may find these earth signs mixing incense and creating healing salves or stirring up a little magic in the kitchen. They may also enjoy working with plant energies within their own garden sanctuaries or working with crystals, gemstones, bones, or runes.

Earth Deities You May Like to Get to Know

Demeter: Greek goddess of the harvest, the underworld, sacred law, marriage, and the natural cycle of life, death, and rebirth. She is mother of Persephone, who was abducted and taken to the underworld. Demeter's grieving makes the world become cold and desolate for a half year, just to revive in the spring upon her daughter's return. Demeter has been called upon for blessing the harvest and the land, insight, bringing about new ideas and creative opportunities, insight, and legal issues.

Cel: An Etruscan earth goddess of the underworld and of fate, Cel was called upon when interpreting omens. She may be invoked at Mabon to bless a meal of Thanksgiving, as the Etruscan month Celi (our September) was named for her. She has also been called upon for divination, growth, and wisdom.

Danu: An ancient Celtic deity, she was known as the "Flowing One." An earth goddess connected with the faerie hills, she is the mother of the Tuatha Dé Danann and the grand creator who birthed all things. She has been called upon regarding enlightenment, fertility, luck, wisdom, and inspiration.

Correspondences for the Element of Earth

Direction: North

Season: Winter

Hour: Midnight

Days of the Week: Thursday, Saturday

Magical Tools: Drum, pentacle, salt, soil, shield, stone

Qualities: Dry, cold, heavy, passive

Magical Associations: Prosperity, abundance, grounding, stability, growth, protection, nature, cycles, hearth and home, strength, animals, environment, gardening, binding

Gender: Feminine, receptive

Archangel: Uriel

Herbs, Flowers, and Trees: Alfalfa, barely, beet, corn, cypress, fern, honeysuckle, horehound, horsetail, loosestrife, mugwort, oats, patchouli, primrose, rye, sorrel

Stones: Agate, aventurine, granite, jade, jasper, jet, malachite, onyx, petrified wood, rhodonite, ruby, tiger's eye, tourmaline

Colors: Green, brown, black

Elemental Being: Gnomes

Tarot Suit: Pentacles

Metals: Lead, mercury

Runes: Fehu, Wunjo, Jera, Berkano, Mannaz, Othala

Animals: Bear, coyote, deer, wolf

Part 2
MOUNTAIN
a i r

Chapter 6

Mountain Song

Why is it that mountains get under our skin? They inspire writers and are a favorite of artists and photographers. Mountainous areas such as Yellowstone, the Himalayas, the Rockies, and the Alps draw multitudes of hikers, climbers, mystics, and beauty-seekers every year. And whether someone is a weekend warrior who finds joy in the exploration of surrounding hills and midrange peaks or an extreme climber who must answer the mountain's siren call to conquer the challenge of nature's most demanding terrain, the underlying reason we climb is to conquer not the mountain but our own internal challenges, be they physical, mental, or spiritual.

I live in a narrow river valley in the far eastern reaches of Skagit County in Washington state. We are an eclectic lot who have nestled our homes in the shade of giant conifers under threatening skies. Moss coats the roofs of our dwellings and claims abandoned treasures. We have learned to deal with perpetually wet feet and mud that clings to the soles of our shoes. Winter is coffee and woodsmoke and the scent of pelting rain, while summer is green fire and birdsong and the rush of melting glacier water—and surrounding it all are mountains.

We are settled snuggly within the foothills of North Cascades mountain range. The ancient guardians that watch over us hold tight our secrets and keep the dark truths of our more civilized neighbors at bay. We look to these cragged peaks and ponder our immortality; they beckon to us, dare us to reach ever upward. We accept the challenge and climb skyward in order to understand ourselves and to reconnect with our gods.

Mountains have helped shape me into the woman I am today. I grew up comfortably cocooned within my landscape: large trees whose roots tied me to stability, darkened skies and rolling mists that deepened my understanding of my inner self, and cragged peaks that reminded me to continue to challenge myself and not become a victim of my own complacency. They surrounded me and comforted me and I grew strong in their shadow.

But it wasn't until I was in my preteens that I climbed my first peak. The sky opened and I was truly out of my comfort zone. I remember sucking in my breath and feeling how small I was. I wanted to run back down the trail to the comfort of the tree line, but I didn't. I inhaled deeply and slowly blew out the heavy intake of breath, lifted my face into the wind, and let the power of the mountain reveal how vastly amazing my world was. It made me eager to not only explore the world around me, but to step into myself and explore the power I had as an individual.

It was on a mountain with the wind caught up in my hair that I first contemplated a life unlike those of my peers and untangled the constricts of my civilized upbringing. It was in a mountain fire lookout on a night when the moon seemed to wrap itself around the peaks that I first experienced sexuality. From mountaintops I have felt the Divine; I have tasted freedom and I have seen beauty at its most wild. Under the shadow of mountains, I grew to be the woman I am today. Mountains have led me to sing out and dance unabashedly and allowed me to visualize how truly large and vast the world is. And as my daughter said to me at the tender age of four while we were watching the moon rise above the mountains, "I know the Goddess is up there because the mountains wear a crown of moonglow." The divine feminine is definitely alive and her home is on the mountaintop.

Home of the Divine

Mountains are intensely hard places to understand, always remaining elusive, mysterious, mystical, and therefore sacred. Many of our ancient ancestors identified mountains as home of the Mother Goddess. We know the highest point on land as Mount Everest, named in 1856 for George Everest, a British surveyor, but it has been known for centuries in Tibet as *Qomolangma* or *Chomolungma*, meaning "goddess mother of the mountains," and in Nepal as *Sagarmatha*, meaning "head of the sky" or "goddess of the sky."

In the Scottish Highlands, it was the Dark Crone of Winter or Hag Queen, the Cailleach Bhéara, who struck her *slachdan* (staff) atop the mountain, causing the icy waves of winter to ripple across the land. The Cailleach was one with the land, and though she is clothed in the snow of winter, she is the keeper of the seed that holds the very essence of life's continuation. Traces of her name can still be found throughout the British Isles where natural energies are thought to be most abundant: rolling hills and seaside cliffs, glens and tumbling burns, river gorges, and the stillest of forest ponds.

In Hawaii, the mountain Kīlauea is the home of Pele. As both creator and destroyer, she is goddess of lightning, dance, fire, wind, volcanoes, and violence. She governs the great flows of lava that created the Hawaiian island chain and her visibly active power keeps her alive in the hearts of the Hawaiian people. In fact, respect, if not worship, for Pele has lasted longer than that for any of the other old gods of Polynesia. Gifts of gratitude, or *ho'okupu*, of gin, cigars, or fish are offered to this goddess at her mountain quite frequently by residents to this day.

The Hindu goddess Parvati was born of Himavat, the god of the Himalayan Mountains, and a nymph called Mena. This goddess, sometimes also called Lady of the Mountains, was known for her great beauty and as consort to Shiva. She is mother, she is warrior, she is lover, she is demoness, and she is the divine feminine energy that expresses itself as *prakriti*.

Ninhursag, whose name means "Lady of the Mountain," is a Sumerian mountain goddess who, as one of the oldest gods of the Mesopotamian pantheon, is associated with fertility and identified as the mother of the gods and of men.

According to Chinese mythology, Yaoji was the youngest faerie daughter of Wang Mu, the Queen Mother of the West. She and her faerie entourage descended to earth and helped tame and dredge the gorge that formed the Wushan Peaks. By the time her work was finished, she found she loved the area and decided to stay. Eventually she was transformed to *Shennu* Peak, Goddess Peak or Beauty Peak.

In Iran, it was the Persian Mother Goddess Anahita who stood aloft the world mountain, where the source of life-giving water originates. She is goddess of the water, fertility, healing, and wisdom. On the island of Crete, Mount Ida is home to Rhea, mother of the Greek gods.

Not only were mountains home to the feminine aspect of deity, but male deities, too, set their thrones in the lap of the divine mother (or mountain). In Greek mythology, Mount Olympus is home to the whole pantheon of gods and goddesses, with Zeus at the head in his golden palace. The Persian sun god Ahura Mazda lived in a glowing palace atop Mount Hara, and in Canaanite mythology, the god Baal made his home in a heavenly temple, built by himself and without human hands, on holy Mount Zaphon. In England, Gwynn ap Nudd had a palace on the summit of Glastonbury Tor from which he rode out with magic dogs and spectral warriors to collect souls.

Sacred Land

Mountainous peaks were revered by our ancient ancestors, as this place where heaven and earth touch provided an area where one could be close to the Divine, and the mountain itself sometimes provided a means to communicate with their deities or with the earth itself. To secure the presence of the Divine, the erection of shrines, markers (such as standing stones), and statues were established to remind us, even now, that the soul of the earth is alive, and the Divine is present in all of nature.

In China, sacred mountains were believed to be especially powerful sites of telluric power. Sometimes called "dragon veins," this sacred flow of energy runs through the earth at a low frequency and can be a result of both natural causes and human activity. To practitioners of feng shui, mountains are said to embody yang (male) force (earth energy), which is said to give stability.

In Buddhism, there are four holy mountains said to be the dwellings of bodhisattvas (Buddhist disciples) who have reached nirvana but come back to earth to help mortals on their own paths to enlightenment. The four sacred mountains include Mount Wutai, Mount Emei, Mount Jiuhua, and Mount Putuo. The highest of these is Mount Emei at 10,167 feet and, according to tradition, is the site of the first Buddhist temple, which was established in the first century CE.

At 2,507 feet, Ireland's Croagh Patrick is ringed by old sites, monuments, and standing stones that go farther back than its association to St. Patrick. In fact, the mountain was once called *Cruachán Aigle*, of which there is no definitive translation, but the name may have some connection to the fertility god Crom Cruach. Nevertheless, archeological evidence supports the claim of pre-Christian pilgrimages to the summit. In Christian tradition, it was said that St. Patrick fasted, prayed, and wrestled with demons at the summit for forty days in the year 441 CE. In a ritual act of penance, thousands of pilgrims still hike to the peak (some barefoot) on Garland Sunday, which happens the last Sunday in July.

In North America, the boundaries of the Navajo nation are marked by four sacred mountains: in the east is Mount Blanca (*Sisnaajini*, Dawn, or White Shell Mountain), in the south is Mount Taylor (*Tsoodził*, Blue Bead, or Turquoise Mountain), in the west is San Francisco Peak (*D'o'koooslííd*, Abalone Shell Mountain), and in the north is Mount Hesperus (*Dibé Nitsaa*, Big Mountain Sheep, or Obsidian Mountain). According to the Diné Bahane', the Navajo creation myth, the four mountains were formed by the Diyin Dine'é (Holy People) in the fourth world. After the sacred mountains were formed, smoke was prepared and chants were sung to them by the Holy People. Mountain songs are still used by the Navajo to address the mountains with respect and love.

The Inca gave the ultimate gift to their gods. In honor of key calendar events or during times considered to be ominous in nature, the children of high-ranking individuals (typically a chief) were offered as a sacrifice (called *Capacocha*) on the peaks of sacred mountains. This was considered an honor, as the child chosen was thought of as perfect and ensured the link between the chief and the emperor who was considered a descendant of the sun god.

A popular motif in ancient religious practice, especially throughout Asia and Mesopotamia, was the idea that at the center of the world the Cosmic Mountain acted as axis mundi, or a world pillar that connected the three realms of heaven, earth, and the underworld. Depending on the culture, the mountain may have been represented as a real mountain, such as China's Kunlun Mountains, or as a mythological one, as in the case of Buddhist, Hundi, and Jain Mount Meru. Cosmic mountains provided passage from one world to another and acted as a point where creation began and as a point of contact between the physical and the spiritual planes.

As kingship and divinity became interlaced, structures such as ziggurats, pyramids, temples, and earth mounds were built as a way of connecting our physical realm with the Divine. These were places gods were housed and rulers were buried that represented ascending planes and the ascension of the spirit. They may have been built in regions that were remote or absent of hills or mountains as a way becoming *man-made* sacred mountains. These structures occupy a position central to their worlds and represent a place where heaven and earth meet.

Mountain as Mother

Because of their natural curves, peaks, and valleys, sometimes the mountains themselves were identified as feminine in nature. The mountain *is* the Earth Mother, with the rounded boulders as her bones and rushing streams as her blood. She is consort to the sky gods of thunder and lightning. Where I live, we can look across the Sauk River to a series of hills that resemble a woman lying on her back. One of the hills clearly looks like a breast with a protruding nipple and was called "Boob Hill" by my children as they grew up. She watches over me as I spin my magic along the river's edge quietly.

In County Kerry, a pair of rounded hills identified with the Mother Goddess of Ireland, Paps of Anu (Danu) have come to be known as the "stone nipples on the great breasts of the mother goddess" because the peaks are topped with cairns and connected by a line of jagged standing stones.[11] The stones are believed to have once marked a processional route. In Sumer, Mount Mashu's twin peaks were said to nourish the heavens. Mount Sipylus was identified with the goddess Niobe, or the "snowy one," and at the tops of cragged peaks is where her life-giving waters begin. Archaic Mother Goddess images can still be seen carved into the rock near crevices where water seeps out.

Mountain as mother was thought to be life-giving. Glacial water, milky from sediment, was compared to mother's milk or sometimes menstrual blood. *Nilachala*, or "blue mountain," is home to the beehive-shaped temple known as Kamakhya Temple. Kamakhya's *shakti pitha*, a shrine dedicated to the divine feminine, is believed by followers of Tantric Hinduism to be where the yoni of the Goddess fell to the earth. During late July through early August, pilgrims come to celebrate the symbolic menstrual blood of the Goddess, as water that contains iron oxide and red arsenic flows red from a spring that trickles over the cleft of the yoni stone within the temple.[12] Mountain as

---

11. Patricia Monaghan, *The Encyclopedia of Celtic Mythology and Folklore* (New York: Facts On File, 2004), 20.

12. Karen Tate, *Sacred Places of Goddess: 108 Destinations* (San Francisco, CA: Consortium of Collective Consciousness, 2006), 174.

mother is mons veneris; she is the source of origin, she is womb. And when we have taken our last breath, it is to her we return; she is tomb.

There is a purpose hidden in our journey up the mountain. We turn our mind away from the distractions of the outer world and focus it on discovering the profound truths of our soul. The mountain calls for courage and unswerving commitment, but at the same time it is a symbol of constancy and stability.

When I return from extended trips, it is the jagged peaks of the Cascades that are the first to herald me home. The mountain smiles upon me and welcomes me back into the shadow of her protective stance. It is her to whom I go for respite and meditation, it is her to whom I go for perspective, and it is her to whom I go to cry my truth.

Take It to the Mountain: Everything's Going to Be Okay

"Yes, Mama." I wiped the sleep from my eyes. The darkness still hung heavy in the sky, though the first of the morning birdsong had already begun to seep through cracked windows.

"Your cereal is on the stand by Dad's chair, and I've turned on the cartoons. Mommy will be right back." She kissed my head and I stumbled to the recliner where I had spent the early hours of every morning for the better part of the year. "Try not to wake your sisters."

"I know, Mama." I curled up on the recliner where the leather was warm and held the scent of my dad's aftershave lotion. The cartoons blinked in and out, and I stirred my cereal that had already become soggy, just the way I liked it. My three little sisters softly slept in their rooms, and I knew everything was going to be okay because I was eight years old, the big sister who knew she was strong enough to take on the job.

My father had epilepsy. The disease had slowly taken from him a lot of the freedoms most of us take for granted. His ability to drive had been the latest, so my mother got up with him every morning at 4 a.m., fixed his breakfast, and packed his lunch before waking me so I could watch my younger siblings, who ranged in age from one to six years old, while she drove my father the forty-mile round trip to his place of employment. She would always return to find me still vigilant and then send me back to bed to catch a couple more hours of sleep before school. I was okay with my responsibility, and I understood why she didn't want to wake up four little girls and pack them all in the car every morning.

Sometimes, one of my baby sisters would stir. I would hear her muffled cries and would be by her side as quickly as I could. "Hush, now," I would say. "I'm here and everything is okay."

As we grew older, I was the one who led my sisters through darkened woods and dilapidated outbuildings full of spooks and creatures of unknown origin and when they could no longer contain their fear, it was I who yelled, "Stop screaming. I'm with you and everything is going to be okay." They would calm down because they knew they were protected—big sister will keep the boogeyman at bay.

As we became teens and young adults, my role shifted from protector from physical harm to guardian of secrets. Most were childish confidences, crushes whose names were to never be revealed or juvenile antics that needed to be purged. A few were life-changing, the kind of information that once accepted can weigh heavy and burdensome on one's heart, and no matter how many years may pass, their revelation would prove painful. But no matter the secret, my words were the same: "Not to worry. Everything is going to be okay." Because they knew their big sister would never betray nor judge them.

The years went by. We grew up and moved on. My role shifted from big sister to mother and wife. Responsibilities shifted: I was no longer protecting the three wild-haired sisters from monsters under the bed but now protecting my own wild-hearted Witchlings (mostly from themselves) as their youth was filled with hijinks and exploration that on more than one occasion required emergency room visits. But as I held cloths on bleeding wounds and distracted their gaze from broken limbs or carried them away from the contraption they had built and fallen from, I would meet their gaze and know what they wanted to hear: "Hush, baby. Everything is going to be okay." And everything was okay because they knew Mommy was there and Mommy's always made things better.

It was the same with my marriage. Whether it was due to job loss, illness, or injury, during the times we were left struggling emotionally or financially, my husband would walk around in a storm cloud, unable to clearly process the circumstances we were left with. It was up to me to swallow back the anxiety, straighten my shoulders, and look him in the eyes. "Everything's going to be okay," I would say. "I've got this." I took control, and he let me because he knew I was strong and capable of handling the emotional load.

And so it was with friends and extended family: "Monica, I know how good you are with words. Could you please write an essay for me by tomorrow? I completely spaced it and I'm freaking out! It has to be five pages and your choice of essay topics is attached."

"Monica, no one else wants to be a board member and we're desperate. Could you help out?"

"Monica, we need someone to help with our organization's holiday program. By the way, we can't find anyone to dress up as Mrs. Claus this year. Could you help out?"

"Don't worry," I would say. "Everything is going to be okay. I'll help." They knew this to be true because I was dependable, levelheaded, and known to get things done.

But as the years slowly crept by, I found myself feeling muddled and unfulfilled, and by the time I hit my midforties, I felt what I can only describe as a sense of loss. The day before my forty-sixth birthday, just as storm clouds boiled above the bluff that rises above my homestead to the south, I decided to go to the garden to wait for the approaching storm and to ponder my accomplishments.

I had done well. I had helped create a home from scratch and raised an amazing family (and nobody starved). I took on the responsibility of schooling my own children and the children of others when there was a need. I carried many a burden for friends and family so they would not have to feel anxiety or defeat. I helped in the community and gave of my time. Everyone liked me, I thought, and weakly smiled as the first big plops began to fall. But wait a minute—what had *I* accomplished for *me*? I had taken care of others my whole life and put others' needs before my own because that is what I was taught a good person does, but in doing so, I had forgotten to take care of myself. And in that forgetting, I lost a piece of myself.

I gazed to the storm clouds that now boiled and roared above the bluff that guards my home and remembered the exhilaration I had felt standing on its peak looking over the land that I'm so intrinsically connected with. It had been years since I had hiked the bluff; it was time I did it again.

I climbed with purpose, and as I swept back heavy conifer branches and overgrown elder and salmonberry bushes, I asked myself what made me special. I was uncomfortable with my answer, as it was not a practice in my family to brag. But with each exhale of breath, I managed to answer. I am unique. I am creative. I write well. I can draw. Under my hand, gardens bloom.

As I continued up the switchbacks and tripped over roots of giant trees who clung precariously to the steep bluff, I asked myself, what have I done with my gifts? My internal list checked many items:

- I wrote plays and designed sets for various youth organizations.
- I planned engaging lesson plans and lectures for our homeschooling association and for WSU Extension's Master Gardener program.
- I designed and wrote newsletters for my coven's day camp participants and for various ecological organizations.

At this point, I had come to the top of the bluff, thunder crashed, and rain pelted. I stood for a moment and let the wind and rain hit my face. I wanted to feel the sting; I needed the reminder that I was alive and strong and passionate. I stepped as close to the edge as I dared. It's funny how perception can change your reality. I saw my home, which encompassed my whole world and at times had felt a burden, look small and insignificant from my vantage point. The world felt more open than it had in a while and made me wonder who I was, where my place in this world was, and if I was too old to attempt to make my mark.

I am many things to many people: I am the keeper of the home, I am mother, I am daughter, I am sister, I am spouse, I am priestess. I am organizer and doer and maker and mediator. I am protector and caretaker and teacher and friend. So my question was, as I looked out across the majestic Sauk River Valley, who am I to me?

I took a breath and released it. Whisperings of inadequacy stroked my ears —*Selfish, selfish girl. Only thinking about herself.* I shivered and let the thoughts dissolve with the rain that had soaked me thoroughly. With another intake of breath and all the voice I could muster, I released these words into existence:

I am a writer!
My words will inspire!

My words will evoke introspection!
My words will delight!
My words will be read!

When I came off the bluff, I felt good. In fact, I was giddy. I knew after releasing my intention into the universe I had to follow through by putting my power into action. I set up a writing space for myself and hung an inspiration board above my computer. The very first quote I tacked to the board was the popular last line from Mary Oliver's poem "The Summer Day," which asks what you will do with your life. And when I doubted myself, I looked at that quote and replied, "I will be a writer." I researched publishers I thought would be a good fit and put together samples and queries. I took it seriously, and when asked to commit to another obligation that would affect my writing time, I allowed myself to say no guilt-free.

So now, what are you doing with your one life?

Personally, I will spend more time tending the garden of my soul. I will write stories and I will do it for *me,* and everything (and everyone else) ... is going to be okay.

Cry Like a Banshee Spell for Self-Affirmation

Ask yourself, are you living a life that is fulfilling to your soul? Maybe you are giving everything to your job or sacrificing yourself so that others may thrive. It's time to stop for a moment and reflect on you.

What is it that your wild soul longs for? To train for an athletic event or perhaps learn a new skill? Better yet, reacquaint yourself with a passion you gave up on too long ago. For this spell, we will climb the mountain (literally or figuratively) and call upon the banshee as we let go of what no longer serves us and cry out our dreams and positive intentions for ourselves into existence.

The banshee is a female faerie spirit who according to legend is attached to particular families of Irish heritage and whose cries foretell the death of an individual. She is a shape-shifter who may appear as an old woman or a young maid, and she is typically dressed in white but has also been known to wear green or red. A Scottish banshee known as the *bean-nighe* is a washerwoman who washes a death shroud near a stream. Banshees are not to be feared and can be called upon in spellwork for the death of old habits, change in circumstances, or the release of negativity.

You will not need any special tools for this spell, only your voice. Though it would be great if you could do this spell on a hill, bluff, or mountain, it's not necessary. You can stand on your balcony, porch, or deck or on a steady chair—anything that elevates you. Before you begin, ground and center yourself in your own way. If you are hiking up a hill to perform this, use the walk as a form of meditation. Pay attention to the rhythm of your breath and focus on your intention with every step. If you are performing this at your home, meditate for a few moments before you begin and focus on your intention.

Call upon the banshee by saying,

> *I ask for the courage to let go those things*
> *That no longer complete me*
> *Banshee, let your cry be heard as I release*
> *All anxiety and self-neglect completely*

When you feel her presence, join her cry. Let it all out. This is the reclamation of your wild soul—release all the neglect that you have inflicted on yourself. When you have finished, take a moment to collect yourself and thank the banshee for her assistance in your own way. Now you are ready to release your passion into existence.

Position yourself so that you have a good view of the landscape. Take it all in and remind yourself that you are unique and that your talents, skills, and passions matter. Now yell out as loud as you can what *will* exist for you. As you do this, see yourself successful in your hobby, job, passion, or whatever you feel serves you to live a purposeful life.

Now that you have done this, remember that as a practitioner, you are your most powerful tool, and it's up to you to put your power into action. Follow through and live your dreams.

Chapter 7
Taking Flight

On cold January days when the wind howls, pressing the angry clouds against the lowland hills, and the rain falls in hard pellets that sting my face and hands, I can be found down by the river's edge. I go there to watch the bald eagles who come to the Skagit Valley during the winter months to feast on decaying salmon.

Bald eagles, as one of the largest birds, are truly a sight worth viewing in their natural habitat. These amazing birds are powerful, both physically and metaphysically. Watching eagles as they catch the thermals and rise high against the bluff literally takes my breath away.

The eagle was known as the bird of regeneration to the Egyptians and was at one time believed to have the power to procure fire from the heavens and bring it to man. Zeus often shape-shifted to the form of an eagle to help him control thunder and lightning.

As I watch, one of the eagles calls out a piercing cry that gives me goose bumps. *What mysteries do you speak of?* I wonder.

I stand in the stillness of January on the edge of the river until my body shivers with cold, but no matter how cold I am, I feel compelled to watch as the eagles soar ever higher until they are just specks amongst the clouds thousands of feet above me. It's not until they disappear from my view that I wander the trail that leads back to my home, and with me I take a message of freedom and of courage. I am reminded by the eagles' amazing feats to take courage in my own mundane life and that it's okay to let go and soar, free of my comfort zone, and trust in my own abilities.

I am thankful for the spark of divine wisdom I gain with each simple interaction with my natural world. I look at birds as navigators between the worlds, as important messengers of the Divine and as a means to help to keep me in sync with the otherworld.

Navigator between Worlds

Birds have long been linked with the Divine, playing a central role in many creation myths and lending their attributes to both gods and goddesses throughout antiquity. In some versions of her myth, the Egyptian goddess Isis used her wings to fan life into Osiris. The Norse goddess Freya owned a garment of feathers that enabled magicians to fly, and the Celtic goddess Rhiannon was accompanied by birds whose song led the dying sweetly into death. The Egyptian god Ra was born in an egg, and the Celtic god Lugh was associated with the eagle, raven, and crow.

In many shamanic traditions around the world, birds serve as a symbol of magical flight and were a navigator between worlds. Clothing and ritual tools are often made from or ornamented with the feathers, bones, or beaks, aiding the shaman in summoning the bird's power to contact other realms.

Birds were the givers of omens, carrier of souls, and holder of secrets for our ancient ancestors, so there were many forms of divination connected to birds. Oomancy is the art of divining the future through eggs, and augury uses the flight patterns, songs, and entrails of birds to guide in predictions. According to myth, the location of the site for Rome was divined by the flight patterns of birds. Weather predictions using birds were used up until the last one hundred years.

Spirit of Spirit and Other Bird Omens

Have you ever heard anyone say "a little bird told me" when passing on a bit of gossip? Birds have been the purveyor of secrets and have been guiding spirits since ancient times. Watching birds as they flew upward above the surrounding hillsides and faded into heavens before reappearing set firm the connection in the minds of our ancestors that birds were the messengers of the gods.

Birds were sometimes thought of as "Spirit of Spirit," holding the souls of the dead, and it was a long-held belief that if a bird flew into your home or tapped on your window, the bird soul was inviting another to join them. In fact, a common term for death was "flying away." I can attest to the longevity of this superstition, because as a child I remember my own grandmother's distress as we chased many a poor songbird who had mistakenly flown into her home on the first warm days of spring. I can still hear her silly chant as she wielded a broom skyward: "Not this year, bird. Not this year."

Many of the nursery rhymes still read to small children today, like the one below, reflect the superstitions of the past:

One for sorrow
Two for mirth
Three for a wedding
Four for a birth

This rhyme explains the divinatory significance of magpies or, in some regions, crows. Nursery rhymes reinforced folk customs, pre-Christian rituals, and plant, animal, and weather lore in a way that was easy for small children to remember.

Another favorite gives examples of a good omen:

If you see the cuckoo sitting
The swallow a-flitting
And a filly-foal lying still
You all the year shall have your will

As a prognosticator of weather, a bird's behavior was used to divine weather patterns. Gulls that flew inland indicated rain, as did swallows flying low to feed on insects. Crows on a fence indicated sun, and a crow flying alone indicated foul weather was in the forecast.

For many, the owl represented wisdom, but it was also a bird of bad omen. As the screech of an owl was said to bring bad luck, an Old Country tradition was to tie a knot in a handkerchief or an apron string to tie the tongue of the owl so it couldn't screech. It was also said that if an owl cried out during the day, it was a sign of a fire to occur. Another bird that was considered a bad omen was the crow. To see a crow alone meant sorrow would soon follow. To counteract the ill omen, one would tip their hat or bow to the bird.

On the other hand, the presence of a canary in the home brought joy and harmony to its occupants. A young lady graced with the sight of a cuckoo bird in May should kiss her hand and say, "Cuckoo, cuckoo, tell me true when shall I be married."

Birds played an integral role in the spiritual belief systems of almost every culture in the past. But what about today? Watching and connecting with the power of birds is one way to draw us back to nature and deepen our own connection with the Divine. One way to reconnect with the power of bird energy is by creating a backyard bird habitat, which is especially important during the winter months when food can be scarce. Many lessons can be gleaned by watching bird movement and listening to their song and you will feel a much more harmonious energy around your home and yard.

Creating a Bird Habitat

In today's world, most lawns have been primped and trimmed to cookie-cutter perfection, accounting for more than a shocking ninety million pounds of pesticides used yearly to maintain these green carpets.[13] Sadly, our need for the perfect yard is not only poisoning the environment, but partly responsible for increasing habitat loss for our feathered friends. Creating a space with native plants, grasses, shrubs, trees, and a water feature provides much-needed food, shelter and nesting places for local birds. It also creates a space for us to relax, observe, and connect with the bird's powerful energy. Here are a few things to consider when creating a bird habitat:

Multilayered Canopy: Choose trees and shrubs and vines of varying heights. Taller trees provide crucial resting or nesting areas, while shrubs and vines provide a nice shelter from predators. Another thing to consider is fruit-bearing shrubs and vines. They make a great food source for birds such as thrushes, robins, and waxwings.

Grasses and Flowering Perennials: These flowering plants that come back year after year not only provide cover for our feathered friends, but their seeds are also a much-needed food source. Don't forget to plant annual favorites such as sunflowers and bachelor's button.

---

13. "Lawn Pesticide Facts and Figures," Beyond Pesticides, accessed September 19, 2019, https://www.beyondpesticides.org/assets/media/documents/lawn/factsheets/LAWN-FACTS&FIGURES_8_05.pdf.

Water Source: A bird bath, small pond, fountain, or even a large saucer provides a place for drinking and bathing.

Bird Feeders and Nesting Boxes: To maintain a varied diet and to attract specific bird species to your yard, try putting out bird feeders with nuts, seeds, and fruits specific to your local birds' needs. Do some research and hang nesting boxes that will help foster interest from your local bird species. Let the kids get involved by decorating small birdhouses with witchy symbols before hanging to lend a magical feel to your environment.

Remember, even if you don't have a traditional grassy yard, many small trees, shrubs, and flowering plants can be potted and placed on patios or balconies. Hang bird feeders near windows and provide nesting boxes wherever you can.

Especially during the winter months, life can be tough for our feathered friends. Food is scarce or hidden under snow, and water can be hard to find. To help keep your backyard birds warm and energetic, provide high-fat, high-calorie options including suet, black sunflower seeds, peanut butter, millet, meal worms, thistle, fruit, peanuts, and a good-quality mixed seed. If you live in a colder climate, keep an open source for water nearby.

Feather Fetish

Fetishes are natural objects that can be used in your magical practices whose energy you feel closely associated with. As a Witch who closely associates herself with the natural world, a walk in the woods can reveal a treasure trove of magical objects for me, and feathers are one of my favorite fetish finds.

Feathers are not only ruled by the element of air but are *the* ideal representation of the element. Feathers work well in spells for communication and faerie magic and are often used to aid focus and promote change. A good tip when using feathers in magic is to literally breathe your intentions onto the feather itself. Knowing which bird your feather came from can really help refine your spell crafting by giving form and focus on a particular energy.

Something to consider when finding feathers is whether or not the feather was meant as a message to you. As with any communication from the otherworld, it's typically not going to be yelled into your ear but will come to you through symbolism. You must first think about the repetition of the findings.

So if you're finding a lot of robin feathers under one tree, chances are you found a nest. But if you're finding them everywhere you go, that's probably a message intended for you.

The second thing to think about is what has been going on in your head when you find the feathers. Let's say you're experiencing a lot of worry about some upcoming changes. Robins are birds of new growth. Along with the gray color of the feather attributing to peace, this could be a symbol to let you know to stop worrying—everything is going to work out for the best.

Below is a list of common birds whose feathers you may find and their magical correspondences. Note that according to the Migratory Bird Treaty Act, it is illegal to take or possess the feathers of migratory birds. Decorating plain white feathers obtained from a craft store and using them to symbolically represent a given species is always an alternative.

Bluebird: Happiness, confidence, transformation

Blue Jay: Follow-through, personal power

Cardinal: Passion, vitality, self-love

Chickadee: Adaptation, communication

Crow: Wisdom, past-life, mourning, letting go

Finch: New experiences, increased potential

Grosbeak: Family values, healing old wounds

Grouse: Change, manifestation, desire

Hummingbird: Finding joy, faerie magic, continuity

Owl: Wisdom, self-truth, clairvoyance, occult wisdom

Raven: Transformation, spirituality

Robin: New growth and beginnings, fertility, domestic bliss

Rooster: Strength, determination

Sparrow: Ambition, triumph, self-worth

Thrush: Awakenings, inner truth

Woodpecker: Earth's rhythms, prophecy, life's cycles

Wren: Divinity, wisdom, clarity, socialization

You may also consider a bird's feather color. Here's a list of common feather colors and their correspondences:

Black: Protection

Black and White: Change

Blue: Awakening

Brown: Grounding, friendship

Gray: Peace

Red: Passion

White: Hope

Faerie Spirit Wand

There are those places in our landscapes that we somehow connect with. Be it because of spirit of place or familiarity, it becomes sacred to us and therefore creates a link to that which is divine to us. My reason to call a part of nature sacred may be different from yours. Yours might be a piece of property that has been in your family for generations, where the tall grass seems to dance under the touch of the breeze and ancestral voices guide you to the Divine. Or maybe it's on a bluff high above the ocean where the wind whirls and waves crash, the scent of sea brine intoxicating you, and you are drawn by a siren's song to dance unabashedly in the presence of the Divine.

I feel the tendrils of the otherworld grab tight the strings of my soul and lead me to the Divine in a small section of forest where the land meets the water. Faerie activity is strong there. I see it in the dappled sunlight that splashes the forest floor and hear it in the rustling of leaves in the breeze—this song guides me through nature's veil as I journey to the land where messages are tied to what is seen in a ripple of water or the appearance of a stag.

It is there that I am free to quiet my soul, and I bathe in a sea of bleeding heart, absorbing the earth's loving energy or dancing ecstatically in wild abandon to the earth's primordial vibrations. And it is there I pay tribute to the Fae, whose presence can always be felt and sometimes seen as twilight sweeps the land. As part of my practice, I create faerie spirit wands and plant them around my sacred space as means to set intention and send prayers to the nature spirits.

Medicine (or prayer or spirit) sticks are used by shamans and medicine men in rituals that vary among tribes but include the calling of spirits in prayers for hunting rituals and ceremonies, protection of warriors during battle, healing and cleansing rituals, and funerary rites. They could also be used to make offerings or to petition the spirit world. Planting or burying a prayer stick is done where the land has sacred significance.

The wood of the wand is chosen for its strength and spiritual association and decorative symbols are painted on the prayer stick that are reflective of the prayer or message. Feathers are often attached to call to the spirit bird or totem to carry the prayer or message to the spirit world.

Combine the power of the element of air with feather and faerie magic by creating a faerie spirit wand. This wand can be used as you would use your typical wand (or you could choose to make a staff) to direct your magic, or you can plant it in a place that has spiritual significance to carry your intention and prayers to the Divine.

You will need:

Length of branch for your spirit wand or staff that is right for you. Ask the spirits of place to guide you to a tree for the wand or staff. Ask permission from the tree to have this gift and remember to thank the tree spirit when you are done.

Feathers of your choice. You can also use craft feathers that you can paint to symbolically represent the feather of the spirit bird you seek as a guide.

Leather, ribbon, or twine for attaching feathers

Paint (optional)

Once you have chosen your branch, it is up to you whether or not you want to remove the bark or paint it. Use colors that are associated with your intention. You might also consider sigils or symbols. Tie or use a dab of glue to secure lengths of leather, ribbon, or twine to the quills of the feathers and attach them to your wand or staff in a way that is pleasing to you.

When you have completed your wand, focus on your intentions or prayers. Use your breath to breathe your intentions into the feathers, then plant the wand in a significant place, maybe in the east, as that is the direction of the element of air, or perhaps near an altar or sacred tree. That's up to you. Another idea is to make one for each of the elements to mark out your ritual space.

Below I have listed examples of trees and birds that are sacred to the Fae and their correspondences:

TREES

Alder: Element of air, faerie invocation

Birch: Wards negativity, protection, purification

Elder: Wisdom, faerie blessings

Hawthorn: Fertility, creativity, protection

Hazel: Healing, luck, protection, communication

Holly: Balance, winter, dreams

Oak: Strength fertility, health, abundance

Rowan: Protection, inspiration, knowledge

Willow: Love, protection, divination

BIRDS

Hummingbird: Action, wonder

Owl: Truth, wisdom, liminal magic

Raven: Shape-shifting, mysteries

Swan: Loyalty, protection, commitment

Wren: Resourcefulness, courage

Gaining Self-Knowledge with Owl (Feather Chime)

The owl maneuvers through night with purpose and ease and possesses the keen ability to see when others cannot. Metaphorically, this is the definition of true wisdom. Let the owl's magic guide you through the darkness of your soul to help you acknowledge a deeper understanding of your own self-worth so you can grow and blossom. This is a great spell to perform at winter, as winter is a time for self-reflection.

You will need:

9 white craft feathers (to represent the feathers of a snowy owl)

Twine

Driftwood or branch approximately 12 inches long

Marker

Hot glue

Glue gun

On each of the feathers, carefully write a beautiful truth about yourself (examples: peaceful warrior, kind heart, happy spirit, generous nature) or traits that you would like to work on over the coming months.

Cut 9 varying lengths of twine plus another 24-inch piece for 10 total.

Use hot glue to glue the tips of each quill to each of the nine lengths of twine

Tie each length around the branch so when it is held up, the feathers all hang with the vanes down and the writing facing in one direction. Tie the 24-inch length of twine to each end of branch as a hanger.

Hang your feather chime in a place outdoors (porch, balcony, gazebo, patio, etc.) where you can comfortably watch it.

Now go outside on cold nights when the stars are twinkling and the frost shimmers and gaze at your feather chime. As the night air moves the feathers around, imagine the owl whispering each of the power words in your ear. Repeat the words *I am (fill in the blank)* for all 9 power words, then thank the owl spirit for its guidance.

Chapter 8
The Winds of Change

There are nights the north wind asserts it surly howl, blowing wildly in mad swirls around my house. It seeps through cracks in my panes and breathes desperately in my ear as I try to sleep, reminding me of my insecurities, lost dreams never to materialize, projects left unfinished, and plans forgotten. I wake tired and weary in the knowledge that my life is somehow escaping me.

But there are other times, when I am worried or upset and feel the need to be wrapped by the Goddess's soothing embrace, that I will walk the two-mile stretch of road that leads to a single-lane bridge that spans the Sauk River before meeting the highway. There, under the cover of magical bigleaf maples, towering conifers, and the ever-present shushing of the river, a soothing breath from the west envelopes me. It dances around me and plays in my hair, intoxicating me with the scent of fresh earth. Carried on this breeze is reassurance and hope for a better tomorrow, promises of greener days, and a message that with each new dawn, there is joy.

As summer disintegrates, leaving behind only golden memories that touch barren fields, anxious clouds roll above the southern hills. The breeze that accompanies the oncoming storm is scented with rain and reminds me of the days of introspection yet to come.

There, there. The wind seems to understand why I'm uneasy. *There is no light without darkness.*

"There is something in the wind," my grandfather always said, his face drawn toward the sky and gray tufts of hair caught up in the wind's play.

"What do you mean, Grandpa?"

"Well, if you listen, sweetheart, the air speaks. The words can be very gentle and kind, or sometimes it can be shrill and scolding, but it always tells you what you need to hear. You have to listen very close." He paused. "Can you hear it, the words?"

I leaned into the breeze and perked my ears, trying desperately to receive the message I knew rode on the breeze. But all I heard was the scuttle of dry leaves as they tumbled in the wind's wake and the quiet murmuring of branches that trembled in the tall trees above me. "I think I hear it, Grandpa," I said, unsure.

"Don't worry. It doesn't work if you try too hard." He pulled at my braid. "But it will happen."

My grandfather (or rather step-grandfather—my mom's real dad died when she was two) was an old Southern farmer, a stern Baptist whose strict religious upbringing blended smoothly with the old folkways that had been passed down through generations of his family. He gardened by the phases of the moon and told stories of haints that haunted my grandparents' barn. He believed in the power of mojo bags and made poultices from plants he gathered from the surrounding woods. But on the other hand, he never missed church, had a bible quote for every scolding, and when excited, used "Praise the Lord!" like a comma.

Of all the things I gleaned from my grandfather, his message of "something in the wind" fascinated me most. It wasn't until years later that I realized he was talking about the element of air and the four winds associated with the cardinal directions.

Ancient people who relied heavily on maritime trade depended on the wind to fill the sails of the vessels that kept goods moving and defended their cities. The wind blew in the rain that sustained fields and filled the rivers and wells that provided clean water. Among these people were the Greeks, who worshiped wind deities collectively known as the Anemoi. They are the children of Astraeus, the Titan god of the dusk, and Eos, goddess of the dawn, and are depicted as winged beings with loose and blowing mantles or sometimes as mystical horses who grazed upon the shore of the cosmic river that was said to encircle the earth.

When practicing wind magic, one can harness the power of the four winds to intensify the energy associated with the intention of your spellwork.

Boreas, the North Wind

Call upon Boreas, the north wind of winter, whose cold embrace challenges us to dig deep, for change, to banish bad habits, for growth, for prosperity, for funerary practices, and for wisdom. Boreas is associated with the color black and the hour of midnight.

Winds of Change Spell for Moving On

There are times in our lives we need to cut the cords from what is holding us back in life and move on. This winds of change spell is intended to help free you from whatever it is that is holding you back and keeping you from being the best *you* you can be.

You will need:

Black cord

Scissors

For this spell you will need to go outside on a windy day and stand in a northerly direction. Hold up your black cord and say,

North wind, I conjure thee
To free me from (fill in the blank)
Move me, inspire me, set me free
With the power of air, movement, and song
So mote it be

Now hold up your scissors and say,

I cut the cords that bind me

We will be cutting three lengths. With the first cut say,

The winds of change move through me

With the second cut say,

The winds of change inspire me

With the third cut say,

The winds of change set me free

Stand for a moment and let the breeze blow through and around you. Feel it manifest a newfound spirit for freedom. Imagine yourself moving on to bigger and better things.

Euros, the East Wind

Call upon Euros, the wind of the east, whose breath beckons the new dawn, for spellwork concerning growth, new beginnings, transformation, herbal knowledge, and harmony. Euros is associated with the color white and the hour of dawn.

Tangled Breeze Spell for Harmony

This is a great early morning meditation using a little incense that adds a sense of well-being such as lavender, violet or cedarwood. This will help you carry a harmonious vibe throughout the day.

You will need:

Incense blend (recipe below)

Charcoal tablet

Firesafe container

Get up early and find a nice relaxing place to sit outside facing east. Say,

Euros of the east, I welcome this new dawn
Let your gentle touch dissolve all negativity
Stress, strife, and anxiety be gone
In the name of air, wind, and peace
Let the magic take hold—so mote it be

Sprinkle the incense over the lighted charcoal tablet in a firesafe container. Sit in a comfortable position for several minutes, allowing any breeze to clear away the negative residue that has built up from toxic people, stress, or any chaos in your life. Allow the smoke from the incense to draw in harmony and peace.

Incense Blend for Well-Being

1 part cedarwood

½ part lavender

½ part sandalwood

Notus, the South Wind

Call upon Notus, the wind of the south, whose fiery gales can be used for strength, hex breaking, passion, and change. Notus is associated with the color yellow and the hour of noon.

Raise the Wind Spell for Passion

Let the winds of change rekindle your passion for life. Be it an emotional, physical, or spiritual reboot, call upon the south wind to clear the fog of complacent behavior.

You will need:

Feather

Stand on a hilltop facing south and raise your feather into the wind. Invoke the power of the south wind by saying,

Fiery gale, lend me your power
Stir the embers of desire with your wild embrace
By the might of mountain, air, and movement
Let the magic take hold in this sacred place

Whisper your intention to the feather and set it free.

Zephyrus, the West Wind

Call upon Zephyrus, the wind of the west, whose gentle healing breath can be used in spellwork for love, healing, cleansing, dreams, and intuition. Zephyrus is associated with the color blue and the hour of twilight.

Something in the Wind Spell to Enhance Intuition

You know that feeling that creeps up on you, letting you know something is or isn't quite right? Sometimes it's an inner voice that whispers over and over, or (as in my case) you wake up with an anxious gnawing in the pit of your stomach, a signal to be prepared for a bad day.

That is our intuition, and it bridges the gap between our instincts and reality. To enhance and deepen our intuition, we must move beyond the idea of trusting our gut and really tune in to how the universe is trying to guide us.

One way to do this is to use healing stones or crystals to activate your third eye. I like amethyst, as it's a wonderful stone to help increase your spiritual awareness and make those intuitive symbols become clear.

You will need:

Amethyst stone

Something to comfortably lie on (optional)

To do this spell, go outside and find a comfortable position facing west. Hold up both hands with the amethyst in your dominant hand and call to the west wind:

I call upon the west wind to help me see
Let your soft breeze awaken three times three

If you don't want to lie on the grass, lie on your back on a blanket or yoga mat. Place the amethyst on your third-eye chakra and close your eyes. Relax and imagine the amethyst opening your third eye. If there is a breeze, imagine it clearing any obstacles that might hinder your intuition.

Putting on Airs: Auras 101

Have you ever heard the expression that a person has an "air about them"? It's usually used in reference to someone who radiates a certain quality from their being. We see them walking down the street and we turn and stare. Some might think of them as confident, others might call them arrogant, and still others might just describe these people as mysterious. Basically, this term and others such as "air of confidence," "putting on airs," or "air of mystery" all refer to an energy field that they exude. This is also the reason that you can sometimes walk into a room and be immediately drawn toward an individual. This energy field that emits in layers from our physical body is called our aura, and we all have one.

As an extension of your physical self, your auric field is a blending together of layers (or planes) of electromagnetic energy that radiates, leaving its own frequency. Theses layers are as follows:

Ketheric Template Field (Seventh Body): Correlates with the crown chakra and is associated with universal consciousness. Golden-threaded or violet in color.

Celestial Field: (Sixth Body): Correlates with the third-eye chakra and associated with enlightenment and intuition. Pearly white to indigo in color.

Etheric Template Field (Fifth Body): Correlates with the throat chakra and is associated with the physical plane and overall energy. Color can vary but is most often blue.

Astral Field (Fourth Body): Correlates with the heart chakra and is associated with physical, mental and emotional expression. Green or rosy in color.

Mental Field (Third Body): Correlates with the solar plexus and is associated with thought and mental processes. Bright yellow in color.

Emotional Field (Second Body): Correlates with the sacral chakra and is associated with inner feelings. Orange or rainbow in color.

Etheric Field (First Body): Correlates with the root chakra and is associated with your physical well-being. Red in color.

There are people such as energy workers or sensitives who can easily see and interpret our auras and what they reveal about our physical, mental, spiritual, and emotional well-being. And though our auras are made up of many colors, there are typically one or two dominant colors that can gave an instant insight into one's true nature or their emotional state at any given time.

Aura colors and their meanings include the following:

Red: Passionate, thrill-seeking, sexual. More apt to focus on the physical and monetary aspects of life and less on emotional or intimate relations.

Orange: Passionate, creative, intelligent. Strong leaders who are actively involved in meeting their goals.

Blue: Relaxed, nurturing, harmonious. Intuitive souls with a forgiving nature who may best express themselves through art.

Green: Abundant, balanced, harmonious. Natural healers with a peaceful disposition who naturally draw abundance into their lives.

Pink: Loving, balanced, spiritual. With a harmonious spirit, these nurturing souls are natural caregivers.

Yellow: Witty, expressive, playful. Freedom-loving individuals who exude an inner joy and generosity.

Purple: Spiritual, powerful, passionate. Individualistic souls who have no problem dancing to their own tune and seem grounded in both this world and the otherworld.

Turquoise: Influential, authentic, intuitive. Devoted individuals whose creativity and grounded sensibility are a light to others.

The Unbalanced Aura

A balanced aura should emit bright, clearly defined coloration in an egg shape around your body. I'm lucky enough to have a friend who can see the beautiful auric fields that we radiate. Mine, she said, was a bright blue, which I think defines me quite well most of the time.

If you are interested in seeing what your own aura looks like, there are ways you can hone these abilities on your own. The simplest way to start is to hold a plain white piece of paper at arm's length and hold up your index finger in front of it. Look at your finger with resting eyes. As your finger starts to blur, you should begin to see colors radiating from around your finger.

An unbalanced aura will be muddy, dark, or poorly defined. You may feel fatigued, disconnected, or overly frustrated. Just as stress, unhealthy habits, and unprocessed emotions can cause your physical body to become unbalanced, these can also become a factor for an unhealthy aura. One big cause for an aura to become unbalanced is interacting with toxic people. You know the type—you can feel their negative vibrations, heavy and looming as soon as you walk into the room they are occupying. As my mother always says, "Stay away from toxic people. They will suck the life right out of you." And that is exactly what they are doing, drawing your bright energy and leaving you with a residue of their negative gunk.

Cleansing your aura by smudging is a great way to reclaim your radiance. When your energy field is rid of the negative energy, it becomes cleaner, brighter, and more defined, and you will begin to feel vibrant and whole again.

Making Your Own Smudge Bundle

Smoke has been used for fumigation and clearing space, purification and bless-ing, and healing and preservation for thousands of years by cultures all over the world. The use of a smudge stick or bundle is actually a modern take on a collection of very old practices from varying cultures and belief systems.

You can buy a smudge bundle at any metaphysical store, but it makes the ritual that much more meaningful if you make your own. Almost any herb can be used to smudge, but let's begin by looking at some common herbs whose sacred spirits vibrate a bit deeper than their physical constituents and the asso-ciations used for smudging:

❧ Bay (*Laurus nobilis*)
> *Element:* Fire
> *Planet:* Sun
> *Energy:* Masculine

When added to your smudge bundle, these leaves add a big punch. They are known for their protective, purifying, calming, and healing smoke and are also a mood booster.

❧ Cedar (*Thuja plicata*)
> *Element:* Fire
> *Planet:* Sun
> *Energy:* Masculine

Cedar provides a wonderful purifying, protective, and sweet-smelling smoke that burns slowly, which makes it great for ritual use, especially for beginners.

❧ Eucalyptus (*Eucalyptus globulus*)
> *Element:* Water
> *Planet:* Saturn
> *Energy:* Feminine

Eucalyptus provides an energizing boost to your smudge bundle and is great for healing and protection.

❦ Lavender (*Lavandula* spp.)

Element: Air

Planet: Mercury

Energy: Masculine

The purifying, protective smoke of this fragrant herb also lends a sense of peace and harmony to your smudge bundle.

❦ Lemongrass (*Cymbopogon* spp.)

Element: Air

Planet: Mercury

Energy: Masculine

Lemongrass provides an energizing and refreshing smoke that also encourages clarity and focus.

❦ Rosemary (*Rosmarinus officinalis*)

Element: Fire

Planet: Sun

Energy: Masculine

The smoke of this Mediterranean herb encourages a sense of peace, purifies, and is excellent for removing negative vibrations.

❦ Sage (*Salvia officinalis*)

Element: Air

Planet: Jupiter

Energy: Masculine

Cleansing, healing, and protective, the smoke of sage is the ultimate purifying herb.

❦ Sweetgrass (*Hierochloe odorata*)

Element: Air

Planet: Jupiter

Energy: Masculine

Sweetgrass provides a sweet-smelling smoke that is excellent for blessings or for attracting good spirits, but only after smudging with an herb that is meant to repel. Never mix this herb with your smudge bundles meant for purification and cleansing—it defeats the purpose.

Smudge Bundle

Choose any of the herbs from the list to create a basic smudge bundle.

You will need:

4 to 10 sprigs of fresh herbs 4 to 8 inches in length

Twine (a natural fiber such as hemp or cotton)

Scissors

Paper bag (optional)

Lay out your sprigs, making sure they are uniform and keeping stems together. Wrap twine around stems a few times times and knot-off. Wind the twine around the bundle upward, working at an angle. Wrap around the top of your bundle and continue the wrapping back down to the stem. Wrap around twice and knot-off.

Dry your smudge by hanging in a paper bag or in a dark place for approximately 2 weeks.

Cleansing your Aura with the Goddess of Breezes

For this spell, we will invoke Aura, goddess of breezes. She was a nymph and minor Greek goddess whose name means "breeze" or "breath." She was the swift mountain maiden and huntress of Rhyndacos; she was a virgin huntress who could woo the breeze.

You will need:

Smudge bundle (your choice of herbs)

Matches

Abalone shell or safe container to hold and burn your smudge

Feather

Light your smudge bundle and with your feather fan yourself from head to toe and front to back. As you do this repeat this smudging prayer:

Goddess of breezes, I invoke thee
Cleanse my head so that I may remain clear and focused
Cleanse my eyes so that I may recognize true beauty in its many forms
Cleanse my heart so that I may express through the language of love
Cleanse my hands so that they may create for beauty and wonder
Cleanse my feet so that they might lead instead of follow
Cleanse my spirit so I may soar
In the name of all that is flowing, wild, and free
Let the smoke cleanse away all negativity
Blessed be

Here are a couple of other ways to quickly rid yourself of negative vibrations with the power of air:

- Use a feather to quickly fan yourself from head to toe and front and back.
- Stand facing the breeze with your legs apart and arms raised and let the power of the wind blow away negativity.
- Spritz yourself with a little sage smudge spray (recipe follows), then stand for a moment in front of a fan to swiftly cleanse negative vibrations.

Sage Smudge Spray

1 ounce distilled water
1 teaspoon vodka or pure grain alcohol
10 drops sage essential oil
4 drops lavender essential oil
Pinch of sea salt
2-ounce glass bottle with spray head

Put the ingredients in the bottle and charge it to purify and promote healing vibrations.

Chapter 9
Soul Dance

There is something about the mysterious breath from the eastern realm that blissfully moves us to lift the veil just ever so lightly—a glimpse of enlightenment, if you will, that helps a soul find all its pieces...

It was early and April's dawn was just seeping through dark clouds that spat pellets of rain that hit the roof like a million tiny pebbles. I looked out the window and sighed, as it seemed the maiden hands of spring were never going be strong enough to break the crone's icy grip. The wind sung out haunting notes, drawing me closer to the fire along with a cup of coffee, stronger than I'm used to. *But what the hell*, I thought to myself. *You only live once.*

Just beneath the sound of the wind and rain that made a mockery of spring's grand return, there was something else gnawing at me, something I can only describe as a longing or emptiness that all the coffee in the world could never fill.

I sat awhile trying to soothe myself with the warmth that surrounded me: the woodstove's full belly that burned hot and dry, my coffee warm against my palms and easy going down, a robe that embraced me snuggly. I should have felt all the contentment that this idyllic cottage scene had to offer, but I didn't.

I thought about the winter that still desperately clung to swollen buds and quivering blooms. It had seemed especially cruel, and not just atmospherically speaking, but emotionally as well. After several months of recuperation from heart failure, my husband suffered a stroke that almost killed him and had left him partially paralyzed for over a month. And my oldest son, who was diagnosed as bipolar years before, had stopped taking the medication that kept his demons at bay and had slipped back into darkness, resulting in a short stay at a mental health facility. Both incidents had exhausted me physically, emotionally, and spiritually. I was left drained. But spring was on the horizon and we were all healing... Right?

I went to the window and watched as the rain fell in sheets, streams of healing liquid that beckoned me. I opened the front door and stood for a moment on the porch, allowing chilly gusts to whip at my face and remind me that I was whole. There was something in the wind that morning, something pulling at my soul strings, something urging me into the deluge.

I slipped off my slippers and stepped into the storm. Wren, a grumpy black cat who hated everyone but me, jumped from his bed on an antique cookstove that rests by my front door. He knew something was up. He stayed close behind me as I made my way across the lawn, meowing as if to say, "What the hell are you doing now and where's my breakfast?!"

"Not now, dear friend," I spoke softly. "I've got something that needs my attention." I moved swiftly across the grass that numbed my feet, splashed mud onto my calves, and splattered my robe. Wren understood—or maybe he was just tired of the rain—because he turned and ran back to the safety of the porch.

I kept running, across the lawn and past my gardens, through the trees that marked the boundary of our property, and to the field that once belonged to my dear neighbors and friends who had traded their lives on the edge of this wild land for something more civilized. I forgave them, but only after I came to learn that the property they once tried to tame was being donated to a land trust and allowed to return to its natural state.

So strange it felt to be where the grass, once kept trim and tidy, was growing in abandoned tufts, and salmonberry and hazel, whose growth had been restricted to hedgerows, were already escaping their confines for the pleasure of open land. The wind tugged at my rain-soaked robe, which now felt as burdensome as the anxiety that strangled my spirit. I dropped the robe in the tangles of grass and let the rain and wind sting my naked body. The shock was sudden and exhilarating; it took my breath away, and as I began to spin about, hands held upward, my mundane world withered around me. I closed my eyes and welcomed the darkness—spinning, spinning, spinning—a meditative dance led by the beat of my own heart drum.

It was within this meditative state that from the darkness I encountered a young woman who was very much like my maiden self. Her hair was strawberry fire and her eyes churned gray and stormy. Had I once looked like her? I mused. She smiled coyly and motioned for me to follow her into the darkness. As we descended deeper and deeper to the darkest part of myself, she pointed to fading orbs of light, and in an instant, I knew to gather what I recognized as shattered remnants of my own soul that had been fractured by the stresses of my mundane life.

"Yes," she said. "Take back what is yours and know yourself, Witch." She smiled again before disappearing into the dark realm of my inner being. I looked to the bright points of light I had gathered and watched as they absorbed into my solar plexus, my center of power and individuality, that part of me that burns with resistance and stirs the effects of change, leaving me, once again, in complete darkness. I opened my eyes and gasped, shocked by the journey and dizzy and numb with cold. I dropped to the ground and wept.

A good cry does as much for the soul as anything, I find. And I wondered, as I lay in the mud and tufted grass soaked with rain and tangled with the breeze, what my neighbors would have thought seeing me naked and balled up in a fit of tears on their lawn. If they still lived in that small house that was now dark and empty at the back of the field, would they have come out and checked on me or just chalked it up to Monica being Monica? Probably the latter.

When the tears subsided, I gathered up my drenched robe and squeezed out as much of the rain as I could before throwing it loosely around my shivering form and running back to my home. When I got to the front porch, Wren glowered at me from his bed on the old wood cookstove. "I'm sorry," I said. "I'll be right back with food."

The house was warm and glowed with soft candlelight and smelled of cinnamon toast. My teenage daughter wandered from the kitchen with her toast breakfast and blinked.

"Hey," I said.

"Witch stuff?" she offered.

"Yeah."

She took a bite of toast and continued up the stairs to her room.

I smiled at her understatement.

As for me, it took a while for my spirit to feel at ease again in a world so full of uncertainty. I did what I could to heal myself both physically and emotionally. I began a vegan diet, meditated more, spent every second that I could in nature, and tried not to flinch when someone coughed, tripped, or expressed even the slightest change in their mannerism.

The coming of spring has a way of reminding us that we are all part of the embodiment of the Divine and that the power to endure winter's darkness is positioned deep within ourselves. Hold on to your soul-light even as its flicker grows dim and know you are strong enough to take back what is yours (no matter what that means to you). Know yourself, Witch.

Dance Beat

Everything is alive and dances to the rhythms of nature. As Witches and Pagans, we can leave our inhibitions and self-doubt behind within the dance and become absorbed into nature's rhythm. We are the dance. Through dance we can enact a form of self-hypnosis that can aid in our journeying practices. As we weave and shift and move about, the dance acts as a catalyst in guiding us to achieve altered states of consciousness that lead us to our spirit guides and connects us with the universal flow of energy. The dance helps us transform not only ourselves, but the world around us. As I will reiterate throughout this book, we are interwoven with all of nature. We are a partner in the dance, if you will, that overlaps and intertwines our world with the otherworld, creating a beautiful tapestry that most people in our mundane lives are never really aware of.

Much of the work of shamanic healers involves movement and dance. It is used as a form of journey that opens the doorway to the world of spirits. Once in the other realm, the shaman acts as mediator for the needs of their community, be it assurance of a good hunt, a cure for disease, assisting the passing of a dying loved one, or even soul retrieval.

Heightening Consciousness through Dance

I'm sure most of us are familiar with the whirling dervishes of the Sufi Islamic tradition. Through their method of dance, in a ceremony called the *Sema*, practitioners become an instrument for Allah. The whirling opens their hearts and frees their souls in order to experience the words of the Qur'an—for God belongs in the east and west and wherever you turn is the face of God.

Dance may have been one of our earliest forms of ritual. Movements that emulated events in the stories of the gods of our ancient ancestors or mimicked the rhythms of nature were acted out in accompaniment to the music of pipes and harps. Dance was used to express celebration, ritual inauguration, or even grief by funerary mourners, as was the practice in ancient Egypt. It could be ecstatic and uninhibited, such as the frenzied dances performed by practitioners of the Dionysiac cults of ancient Greece, or it could be subtle and formalized, like the dances of Hindu priestesses whose stylized hand gestures are still being used in the classical Indian dance *Bharatanatyam*.

The thought of dancing, for some of us, can trigger some serious anxiety. But believe it or not, movement can empower us by allowing us to shake off lingering negative emotions that have built up over time—and just like exercise or sex, dancing releases neurotransmitters that help us feel good.

I find dance to be one of the most powerful tools in my Witchy bag of tricks. In my mundane life, I feel I have a pretty good intellectual understanding of the world that I live in. But how lovely it is to be able slip into dance, where I am free to shift and merge with the rhythm of the music until the barriers of my intellect are lowered and I can truly find an understanding, at a soul level, of my place in this world and know that I am not alone. Do you feel the rhythm call to you? Here are a few things to consider before adding dance to your craft:

Let Go of Ego: Relax—this isn't about worrying about what we look like or if someone will see us, so just move with the rhythm. Be it the driving beat of your favorite dance club music, a shamanic drum track played in the comfort of your living room, or the sound of nature's own earthbeat in the middle of your backyard, let go of everything and allow yourself the freedom to move without your ego getting in the way.

Treat Your Dance Area as if It's Sacred Space: Dance as ritual can be spontaneous and wild and create an intensely strong spiritual experience. But the ceremonial aspects of ritual and dance combined to release energy in your magical working can be incredibly powerful, so don't forget to take the time to establish your dance area as sacred space. That means removing negative energy (either by smudging or sweeping), setting up your altar or candles (somewhere where you won't accidently *dance* into them), and whatever else you would typically do to establish sacred space.

No Wrong Way: Yes, I did see the druids' dance on the first season of *Outlander*, and it was beautiful. If you want to try that, go for it! If jumping up and down wildly helps you shift consciousness, do that! That's the beauty about dance: you can shake, shimmy, jump, and spin in any way the spirit leads you.

Try Animistic Movements: Emulating the movements of birds, plants, or animals may help you tap into their spiritual medicine and help guide you to the answers you seek or help release spiritual dormancy. But to understand these movements, remember one must be familiar with the symbolism of the natural world. Go into nature and observe. How does nature speak to you? To help deepen your understanding even more, look to world myths, stories, and folklore. What messages weaved within these tales touch your soul? This way when you dance the dance of the spider (or whatever particular spirit calls to you), you will have a better understanding of its message and how it pertains to your life.

Power of the Drum

Rhythm is anything that repeats itself in time. Nature has a rhythm: the sun rises and sets, continuously guiding our passing days. The moon's monthly cycle of waxing and waning, the periodic rise and fall of large bodies of water, and the ever-turning Wheel of the Year's cycle of birth, death, and rebirth—all of these have a way of influencing the rhythms of our own bodies both physically and emotionally. They are key to feeling in sync with life.

And just as nature's rhythms affect our bodies, musical rhythms awaken our soul. As we move with the rhythm of the drum, the beat synchs with the sound of our heartbeat and it is within that synchronization that we feel our spirit unite with the rhythm of the earth.

For the Shaman, the most basic tools for entering an altered state are the drum and rattle. Through steady and repetitive sounds played at varying degrees of fervor and reserve, the shaman enters an altered state of consciousness allowing them to connect with the otherworld for healing, guidance, and problem-solving.

In many cultures, the shaman refers to the drum as the "horse" or "canoe" that transports them through the veil and into other realms.

The drum is as old as time itself and may have been the earliest instrument used by humans to keep rhythm. Some of the first drums used to keep a rhythmic beat were found in China and date to back to 5500 BCE. Small cylindrical drums excavated from Mesopotamian digs were dated to 3000 BCE, and drums of gourd and wood have also been excavated in the Americas and were used by ancient indigenous people for both ritual and celebratory practices.

Drums were also used as a form of long-distance communication for some of our ancient ancestors. Detailed messages could reach up to five miles away with the sounding of a drumbeat. Made from hollowed logs, talking drums had long, narrow openings that resonated deeply when they were struck. The longer the log, the louder the sound.

Ancient cultures had a good understanding of the effects of acoustics on the consciousness. A thunderous, driving beat would energize warriors and could be used to intimidate enemies during times of war. During times of celebration, a revelrous beat might play from dusk till dawn, calling community members to join together to sing in response to the rhythm. Even long, arduous hours of work could be eased with a beat that made mundane chores enjoyable. The shamanic beat associated with journey work is repetitive and consistent, with each drum containing its own voice matched to the intentions set by the user and keeping beat up to 220 beats per minute.

During a drum session, don't be surprised to discover that your heart rate speeds or slows until it is synched with the pounding rhythm of the drum. Afterward, the powerfully euphoric resonance of the drum may stay with you for several days. You might notice a harmonious energy and a better sense of balance.

Drum Circles

A great way to introduce yourself to the rhythm of shamanic drumming is by observing or participating in a drum circle. Drum circles are gatherings of people who play drums together. The drums that are most likely to be played are hand drums such as bongos, the djembe, and the conga. There are several types of drum circles you may want to investigate:

Informal Drum Circles: Social gatherings that may take place in a park or community center. Participants may bring any form of percussion instrument, and the drumming is typically improvised. It's a great way for beginners to pick up some tips and to blend in with more advanced drummers. If you don't have a drum, just come and enjoy the beat. I'll bet you can't keep yourself from dancing.

Facilitated Drum Circles: Used for education, healing, or community building and may be held at wellness or holistic centers, parks, or community centers. Drumming is led by an experienced drummer (usually the facilitator). Privately organized drum circles may require registration and include a small fee.

Drumming Lessons: Sometimes offered by skilled drummers in either a group or one-on-one classes. This gives you an opportunity to get hands-on experience from someone who has a lot of knowledge and to practice with others who are at the same skill level.

The best way to find a drum circle happening near you is to ask at your local holistic or wellness center or check online by typing in the keywords *drum circle* along with your location.

Finding Your Drum

For journey work, a drum is more than just a drum: it is a means of travel to the otherworld, as well as a magical companion with its own voice and personality. It is an extension of the practitioner, and great care should be taken when choosing your instrument. The most common drum used for shamanic journey work is a frame drum that is typically drummed with a beater.

When purchasing a drum, consider the animal skin and the wood used in the building of your instrument and how they resonate with you. Custom handcrafted drums made with animal hides average around $250. If you're on a budget, you can pick up a small ten-inch framework drum made with inorganic materials for as little as $20 and then personalize it by painting or decorating it yourself with symbols of power. Another option is to make your own, either through a workshop or by using an instructional manual or video. When you do get your drum home, cleanse it with smoke and play it often.

Get to know its voice, for you are building a relationship with the spirit of the drum, your partner on the journey.

If you really can't afford to spend any money on a drum, get creative. A pot and a wooden spoon will do, and if you have children, this is a great way to let them try out drumming without making an investment. Rattles can also be made easily by filling discarded vitamin or pill bottles with pebbles, dried legumes, or even small buttons.

Starting on Your Journey

Shamanic journeying is a technique used to attain healing and gain insight that may help us empower our daily lives. Remember, everyone who practices shamanic journeying imbues it with their own personal or cultural revelations, so your journey will be different from mine. But not to worry—there is no wrong way of entering the otherworld or gaining insight from the spirit realm. I do not consider myself a shaman, but I use shamanic journey work as part of my spiritual practice. I'm offering just a few tips that have helped me along my way. Listening or playing shamanic instruments can help guide you to the hidden realms of the otherworld. The beat is your transport that helps keep you focused and maintain clarity. I know how easy it is to slip back into the thoughts of our mundane world that can easily sneak into an unquiet mind: *I wonder if I need to pick up cat food tomorrow. Do I have bread to make sandwiches for lunches?* As the rhythm quiets the chatter, it also syncs us with the spirit of the land—drumbeat to heartbeat to earthbeat.

As you slip into the otherworld, you may feel that your conscious mind is set aside as you explore the hidden realms and engage with your spirit guides. If you have never tried this, do not be alarmed; you are not unconscious and can return from your journey anytime you choose. Remember, you are fully in control of your movements.

The one thing you are not in control of is who might appear in your journey. You may have entered the spirit realm in hopes of communicating with a particular animal guide, but a tree spirit or an ancestor may approach you. Listen to what they have to say. Pay attention to everything that is going on around you. I suggest you keep a journal to record every detail. There is symbolism in everything.

When you feel you are ready to return, thank your spirit helper, then retrace your steps back to where you first began. Remember, as with anything, practice makes perfect. You might start out with just glimpses into the otherworld (shapes or images may appear in flashes), but if you continue with the work, the otherworld will open itself to you.

Try this shamanic journeying exercise to get you started.

You will need:

Shamanic drumming music

Notebook and pen

Timer

Yoga mat or something comfortable to lay on

This is a great exercise to try in the evening after you've finished your day, but if you are doing this exercise during the day, I suggest closing curtains or placing a cloth to over your eyes to block out the light. Try to do this during a time when you will have no interruptions. Place your yoga mat or comfortable throw on the floor (or you can lie on a couch or on a bed). Set your timer for 15 minutes and turn on the shamanic drumbeat, making sure that it will loop for the entire 15 minutes. Lie down (with the cloth over your eyes, if needed). Breathe in and breathe out, focusing on the drumbeat. When mundane thoughts slip into your mind, push them aside. Do this for the entire 15 minutes. Don't kick yourself if nothing happens other than a feeling of total relaxation. This is just the beginning.

When the timer goes off, sit up and write down everything you felt. Continue to practice this as often as you like. Soon you will notice that it will become easier to push away your thoughts for longer and longer amounts of time. You might be one of those people who slip into the otherworld the very first time. Or maybe you'll be like me, and it'll take a bit of practice. No matter—continue to work at it, and soon you will find your way to your guides.

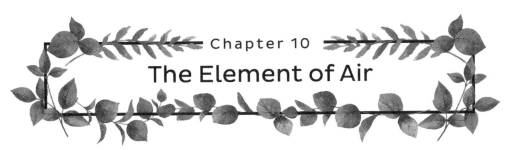

Chapter 10

The Element of Air

Is it there upon that mountaintop I will find you? Standing tall to the direction of knowing with your face raised into the wind? Spread your fingers wide as you embrace the power that moves through you, transforms your spirit, and reminds you that with change there is growth.

Air can be used to help guide us with the knowledge of new life and possibilities. It awakens our wanderlust—follow the cry of adventure if you dare. It lifts the veil and guides our divinatory practices, offering messages from the otherworld that prick our ears, longing to be heard. Magic involving air includes travel, divination, new possibilities, recovering lost objects, and transformation.

Experiencing this powerful element, you do not need to climb high peaks but only go outside, lift your face skyward, and allow the breeze to gently caress your skin. You invoke the power of air when you sing, chant, or yell your magic words into an inky night sky. Its power breathes life into your intentions as you blow gently onto your spells. The power of air infuses the music that gets your feet moving and is present in the wisps that rise from your sacred flame.

People born under the element of air are Libra, Aquarius, and Gemini. These curious, intelligent, and analytical folk see all sides of an equation, and balance is important to them. There is no prejudice with airy people. Magically, they may enjoy working with the energetic body or light beings. They may focus on balance and unification spells. They might be the Witch who incorporates technology into their craft as well.

Deities You May Like to Get to Know

Arianrhod: This Celtic Mother Goddess was sometimes depicted as a weaver of the tapestry of life. As the keeper of the circling silver wheel of stars, she presides over the fates of departed souls and nurtured their journey between lives. She may be invoked for spells concerning sexuality, fertility, beauty, past-life remembrances, reincarnation, and feminine powers.

Thoth: Endowed with complete knowledge and wisdom, this Egyptian god was credited with the invention of the arts and sciences. As scribe for the underworld, he keeps records of the verdicts of the deceased. Invoke him for wisdom, balance, knowledge, and divination.

Nut: One of the oldest-known deities, Nut is an Egyptian sky goddess. She helps Ra escape earth by transforming into a huge cow and lifting him to heaven. Becoming dizzy by her efforts, she is rescued by the four winds. She has been called upon for health, motherhood, sexuality, and fertility.

Cardea: Keeper of the four winds and Roman goddess of the hinge, she looks both forward and backward. She resides at the hinge of the universe behind the north wind. She has been invoked for her power in matters of the home and of children.

Correspondences for the Element of Air

Direction: East

Season: Spring

Hour: Dawn

Day of the Week: Wednesday

Magical Tools: Wand, staff, athame, sword, incense, feather, broom, scourge

Qualities: Hot, moist, dry, active

Magical Associations: Communication, travel, freedom, thinking instruction, knowledge, recovering lost items

Gender: Masculine, projective

Archangel: Raphael

Herbs, Flowers, and Trees: Agaric, agrimony, almond, anis, aspen, bean, benzoin, bergamot, bittersweet, borage, broom, chicory, citron, clover, dandelion, dock, endive, filbert, hazel, hops, lavender, lemongrass, mace, maple, marjoram, meadowsweet, mint, mistletoe, palm, parsley, pine, sage, slippery elm, star anise

Stones: Amethyst, azurite, blue lace agate, carnelian, diamond, fluorite, hematite, kyanite, mica, pumice, snow quartz, silver, blue topaz, turquoise

Colors: Yellow, pastels, sky blue

Elemental Being: Slyphs

Tarot Suit: Swords

Metals: Aluminum, tin

Runes: Ansuz, Raidho, Eihwaz, Tiwaz

Animals: Winged insects, spiders, bats, butterflies, most birds, including owl, hummingbird, hawk, and eagle

Part 3
DESERT
fire

Chapter 11
Desert Medicine

I was born with moss in my hair and rain in my veins. I worship the moon under a weeping sky and whisper my charms into the breeze that sweeps my intent through the rustling cathedral of trees that weave their way to the mountains that watch over us.

It is the mountains that are in part responsible for the unique environment that I call home. The North Cascade Mountain Range, often referred to as the American Alps because it is the most rugged mountain range in the contiguous United States, is what catches the storms that move in off the Pacific Ocean and holds them, severely limiting the amount of precipitation occurring in the eastern portion of our state and keeping our western portion temperate and wet.

Crossing over the mountains is like coming from beneath a protective mantle spun of cloud and moss and mist-filled valleys and being suddenly exposed to the wide-open regions of eastern Washington, where seas of grain roll golden under an endless sky and pine trees dot the periphery. It's shocking and thrilling all at once. I feel like Dorothy in the Wizard of Oz: "Toto, I've a feeling we're not in Washington anymore."

When I was a child, I had relatives who lived near the coulees around the Channeled Scablands in southeastern Washington. A desolate landscape of barren bedrock and strange rock formations, it was referred to as "scablands" by early settlers because it was unsuitable for farming and "channeled" because of the coulees (long crisscrossing channels) that were cut into the bedrock tens of thousands of years ago by a series of cataclysmic floods. As a child, I hated visiting there. I felt like an alien in a dry hostile land where the sky was too big and the trees too few. Every step in the arid landscape seemed to drain me of my energy, and I felt vulnerable without my beloved covering of trees, ferns, and moss.

"Why do we have to visit there? I hate it there. It's ugly," I would say, as if that explanation would sway my parents.

"Aw, come on, Monica," my mother would answer. "I thought you were my girl who saw the beauty in everything."

It wasn't until I was nineteen years old that I would come to appreciate the desert as a uniquely beautiful guise of Mother Gaia. It took working through an unraveling of my own sense of self to come to understand the power of strength and healing that is offered through its desolate beauty.

A naïve teen, I fell for the advances of a man who was fifteen years my senior through a work program at my high school. He was married with two children (his oldest was in my younger sister's class), and after months of awkward flirting, he finally approached me.

"You are an enchantress," he told me. "You take my breath away every time I see you, and I don't know if I can live without you."

Barely eighteen, I thought it the most romantic sentiment I had ever heard. Little did I know how quickly his seemingly small acts of humiliation would turn to total control and violence—and just how deeply those acts would affect me later in life.

A year into the relationship, we flew to Los Angeles and spent a couple of days exploring theme parks—his way of apologizing for some of his frivolous cruelties—then traveled by car south to California's largest state park, Anza-Borrego Desert State Park.

We arrived at our campsite just as the sun was setting and I wandered, as I usually do when in nature, to spend some time alone with the spirits of the land. I walked until I could no longer hear my partner's threats to stay close to the campsite echoing in my eardrum, until I could no longer feel the anxiety that pressed against my chest, until the serpents that had been coiling in my brain ceased their taunts and I no longer felt shame. I walked for what seemed like miles until a flat boulder presented itself to me. It looked out across a landscape that was beginning to glow under a sky set afire in way I had never seen before. Sitting on the rock, I held out my hands in order to somehow absorb the color's vibrations, as if all that red and pink could fill me up and help me to love myself again.

That year, which I refer to as my lost year, was the only time I can remember never shedding a tear. I had locked my shameful secret of abuse away in a little space in the back of my mind where no light was permitted, because everyone knows emotions cause fissures to form where light might seep in and allow secrets to be revealed.

As the color began to fade and shadows rose from the rock formations, I could hear footfall. I worried that it might be my partner looking for me. *Not now*, I thought. *I need this too much.* But as the shuffling grew louder, it was apparent that what was approaching was small and had four legs. I held my breath and sat very still, in hopes of not disrupting the creature's natural routine. The animal stopped and sniffed the air around me. *Silly, silly, girl*, I thought, *as if holding your breath could fool a child of the desert.*

I looked to where the creature stood. It was a coyote whose small outline was barely visible in the dimming light. "Hello," I whispered. It sniffed the air again then curled itself down in front of my rock. Not knowing what to do, I decided that maybe the coyote just appreciated the company and I would stay put.

The darkness had finally extinguished the last of the light as I lay back on the boulder. I cannot express to you in words the emotions that began to bubble up as I stared up into an inky sky like I have never seen before. It was if my whole world was being translated into vignettes that played out in the constellations that were the clearest I have ever seen—my childhood in the forest, my animals, my family, my friends, my downfall, my stupidity, my weakness, my shame, my secrets, my tragic fairy tale weaving amongst the stars. *What now? Silly, silly girl*, rang in my ears as all the unshed tears of that lost year gushed from my eyes, threatening to flood the entire Borrego Desert. *What now, young warrior? Time to reclaim your crown.*

"What was I thinking?!" I cried out into the stillness of that dark and lonely landscape. The coyote shifted and whined.

I cried myself to sleep on that boulder and dreamt I was walking out of the desert with the small coyote by my side. The next thing I remember was the brilliant glow of a flashlight and the voice of my boyfriend calling out my name.

"I'm right here," I answered.

"What were you thinking?" he barked, followed by a string of obscenities.

"Thinking that this is stupid and it's time to go home," I said calmly. I stretched and looked around for my coyote companion, but it was gone.

A few days later, I did go home—back to the home of my childhood where the scent of rain and conifer needles permeated my clothes, back to the arms of my parents and room of my youth. I went to college and, with a little help, regained my personal power.

Years later, I returned with my own family to the Channeled Scablands. As my husband and my sons were out exploring, my twelve-year-old daughter and I looked out across a chasm three and a half miles wide, the remnants of a now dormant waterfall that when active at the end of the last ice age was five times the width of Niagara Falls.

"You know why I like the desert?" my daughter asked.

"Why?" I smiled.

"Because it doesn't need a lot of frilly stuff. It just says, 'Here I am—accept me,' and that makes it more beautiful."

"You're right," I said. "It's raw and real and strong and beautiful."

"Like a warrior princess."

"I like that," I said.

My experience in the desert so very long ago helped me dig deep and find that warrior maiden who had been suppressed by humiliation and shame. I wondered about the coyote for the longest time. Was it just a coincidence that he chose to rest where I was sitting, or was he a guide there to help me find my truth? Upon researching this Trickster being of both foolishness and wisdom, I knew deep within my soul that he was there to help me to accept my mistakes, forgive my own self-loathing, and reclaim that warrior princess I had always been.

The desert is a symbol of beauty at its most extreme, as it is both simple and multifaceted. It is where we go to face our demons, to garner strength and call upon our deepest reserves. It is a source of wisdom and enlightenment, a land of prophets, seers, and creative visionaries. A holy land where nothing can obscure what is divine.

Embracing the Wise Fool

The Trickster is an archetype of liminality, that one who sits at the threshold with a mischievous air, calling us to question how our world is organized and revealing to us the possibilities that come with transformation. Both hero and villain, the Trickster embodies the world of both order and chaos.

This creature of typically questionable habits can be found in mythologies from all around the world. Loki is probably the most recognizable. He comes to us from the Norse myths, a shape-shifting god of chaos whose allegiance shifts so often that no one ever truly knows which side he is on.

Another familiar Trickster is Anansi, a spider known for his command of language, and according to one account, he became god of all stories by tricking and capturing a leopard, a python, and a hornet and delivering them to the sky god's home.

Coyote comes to us from the indigenous peoples of North America. His character varies widely from tribe to tribe, but typically he is known for making things more complicated than they need to be. But if we take another look at this Trickster, we will find that his cunning devices are not so much intended to misguide us but to demonstrate how ridiculous we often act in our own lives.

I don't know about you, but sometimes I'm my own worst enemy, and stepping back for a moment to reflect on my motivation helps me see my folly. Coyote is the wise fool who encourages us to stimulate our thinking and the metaphorical splash of cold water that wakes us up.

A Coyote Spell for Redirection

If Coyote is revealing itself to you, pay special attention to his messages. His is a message of discernment. He is an ally for navigating difficult situations and redirecting us so we can find the wisdom that was right in front of us all along.

You will need:
Incense blend (recipe follows)

Mirror

Picture of a coyote

Picture of yourself

White candle

Light your incense in a small cauldron or other fireproof container. Place a mirror (reflective side up) on a table or other flat surface. Place the picture of the coyote and the picture of yourself on top of the mirror. Light the white candle and place it at the head of the mirror (so it reflects the candle and the pictures) and turn off surrounding electric lighting.

Call upon Coyote spirit for guidance:

As I stand at the crossroads of my life
Help redirect my foolish ways
Coyote, Wise Fool, and cunning guide
Let me reflect upon myself through your eyes

Now take a seat in front of your setup. Breathe in and breathe out. Take in the scent of the incense. Close your eyes and imagine yourself watching the last years, months, days (or however long you need to go back) of your life. As you do this, see yourself through the eyes of Coyote. How do the implications of your past decisions look from another perspective? What changes can you make that might help improve your quality of life? Are you following the right path, one that truly makes you satisfied? These are all things you want to meditate on.

When you are done, move the candle to a safe position and let it burn out on its own. Repeat this spell several times and don't be surprised if Coyote starts to appear in your dreams. Keep a journal by your bedside and record your reflections as soon you wake up. Use them the next time you perform this spell.

Incense Blend for Wisdom and Reflection
    2 parts sage for wisdom
    1 part lavender for balance
    1 part sandalwood for inner strength
    ½ part frankincense for reflection and meditation

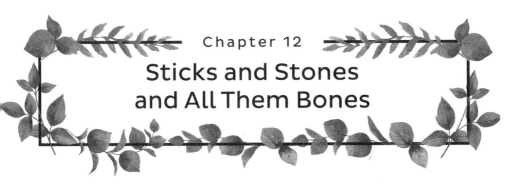

Chapter 12
Sticks and Stones
and All Them Bones

She empowered the bones and her sticks and stones, gifted by nature, under the light of the moon. Skulls were reddened with ochre and symbols of empowerment were drawn upon them. Used in ritual, they housed the spirit of the animal and provided a potent magic. She was my friend, my mentor, and a powerful Witch who taught me about gardening and magic when I was in my early twenties.

Upon first glance, my friend's cottage might have seemed innocent and charming. While visiting, one might have spied garden beds of old-fashioned perennials and heirloom vegetables, beautiful containers of herbs, and swaths of wildflowers, all framing her little cottage with the mismatched shingles coated in moss. Hanging off the eaves were homemade chimes that rattled in the wind. If poked around inside, you'd find her treasures that she collected on walks tucked on shelves and in cupboards. Aw, looks like Grandma's house.

But if you had looked closer, you would have seen that the whimsical decorative pieces that dangled in the breeze were protective amulets made of animal bones and hagstones. All those lovely plantings not only were there to provide food and beauty but were both medicine and magic, as well. And those eccentric collections of skulls, skin, and teeth that could be found tucked in cupboards and lining windowsills were her magical tools, gathered lovingly and cleaned with reverence and ritual. Grandma's house, indeed. "No need to buy expensive trinkets from a metaphysical store," she would say and point to the window. "Everything we need is right out there."

Our ancestors didn't have access to the latest perfectly polished stones, dyed feathers, or resin representations of spirit animals or deities. Tools, both mundane and magical, were gathered from what was available to them. The bones, antlers, claws, or feathers from animal waste were fashioned into utilitarian pieces for household use or could be crafted into tools or weapons, but they could also be used as decorative pieces for ritual clothing or jewelry and for divination and sympathetic magic.

The use of bones seems to have gone out of fashion with our clean and tidy Instagram-ready take on Witchcraft these days, but I'm here to encourage you, if at all possible, to incorporate those things of nature into the Craft as long as they can be collected in an ethical way. That goes not only for bones, feathers, fur, and claws but also for twigs, herbs, and stones. It's time to get your hands dirty, Witch.

Bone Collecting

Do not fear the soul who is wild, the one who is not afraid to get her hands dirty as she gathers from the earth herbs and bone. It is the antlered one who whispers to her the secret places where they lie. It is her job to honor the spirit of everything she gathers. This is how I feel as I go into nature and gather the tools of my craft. Upon my return, with stained hands and unkept hair, I clean and empower my magical offerings. This is not a romantic act, as it can be gruesome, but is to be done in reverence and quiet as I honor the creatures that I take.

Recently, as I worked my mundane job as a mail carrier, I delivered a package to an affluent family whose luxury home sits uncomfortably within the confines of the forest. They have a paved drive that leads to two garages. As I placed their packages at the entrance of the largest garage that housed a motorhome and several ATVs, I saw a perfectly pressed humming bird seemingly glued to the pavement. "Oh, honey," I said. "Somebody really ran you over."

What I didn't see was the lady of the manor staring at me from the opening of the other garage, watching as I peeled the hummingbird from the driveway. "Can I help you?" she asked.

"No." I suddenly felt like I was four years old. "I was just picking this bird up off your drive."

We stood awkwardly staring for what felt like years but was only a second or two, and then I scurried as fast as I could back down the drive to my car.

Upon my return to the post office, I warned the clerks that they might be getting a call.

Sometimes this is how I find bones, feathers, or other treasures—while out and about doing my daily activities. Typically, if you find a dead animal on someone's property, though, I suggest you ask before collecting it. I know it feels weird, but all they can say is no.

If you find bones while out on a walk or if someone gives them to you, before using them in magic, make sure you know what kind of animal they came from. What messages do they convey? Also research the folklore and mythology concerning your animal or bird to get a better sense of its spirit. Cleanse them by using hydrogen peroxide and water, and then once again with a good smudging. The hydrogen peroxide not only sterilizes them but works as a bleaching agent that isn't harmful to the bones. Don't be tempted to use chlorine bleach, as it degrades the bone material. You can also empower your bones under the full moon.

If you find a deceased bird or small mammal that still has some skin or flesh attached, I suggest using exposure as the method to allow the completion of the decomposition. It works efficiently, and you are less likely to break delicate bones than if you were to use maceration. Maceration is the easiest and fastest way to clean bones, but it's not for the faint of heart. I suggest using this method if there is still a lot of fleshy material on the animal or if it's a larger animal. Both methods follow.

Once you have cleaned your bones, it's up to you how you want to use them in your practice. Mine are used as sacred vessels of the animal spirit, whose energy I connect with in ritual. Use bones on your altar to honor an animal guide's spirit or for divination. Use pieces of bone in medicine or charm bags or piece into ritual jewelry. By wearing the bones, feathers, fur, or claws of a power animal in ritual wear, some practitioners are able to take on the animal's attributes and use their power to shift between worlds.

Cleaning Bones by Exposure
You will need:

    Lidded container large enough to hold your animal

    Sharp object for poking holes (screwdriver or hammer and large nail)

If you choose something like a plastic-lidded compost bucket, use a screwdriver to punch holes all around the sides for ventilation. If you are using a small metal garbage can, use a hammer and a nail to punch out ventilation holes. When ready, put your small carcass in the container and secure the lid. Place it somewhere on your property or in a shed or garage where it can remain undisturbed for several weeks or more, depending on the state of decomposition and your climate. Also remember to secure the lid if there is a chance wildlife or the neighbor's dog or cat may disturb it. There will be a slight odor, so it's probably not best to keep it in the hall closet. The bones are ready when the odor has subsided and they are free of flesh; sterilize them with hydrogen peroxide and rinse with water.

Cleaning Bones by Maceration
You will need:

> 2 containers that are large enough to allow for complete immersion (storage tubs work nicely)
>
> Close access to water
>
> Hydrogen peroxide

First, you will need to remove as much of the remaining fur or feathers and tissue as you can from the bones. Place what is left in the container and completely cover it in plain tap water.

Replace the water every couple of days, pouring the used water into your compost or straight into the garden (warning: it will be gross and kind of smelly). Repeat this every couple of days until the water is clear—this means that the bacteria have finished breaking down the flesh.

Place the bones in the second container and pour over enough hydrogen peroxide to cover completely for sterilization. As hydrogen peroxide is also a bleaching agent, allow the bones to stay in until they have reached the shade of white you desire. This can take as long as 6 to 8 hours if you are bleaching a skull.

Give them a final rinse in water.

Reddening the Bones

You may want to empower your bones with sigils, with symbols, or by reddening them with a paste made with brick dust, madder, beet powder, ochre (or another naturally red plant or mineral), red wine, or a little blood. This is a tradition used by cultures who practice ancestor worship, and it was traditionally done using a red ochre paste to symbolize blood or the "life force" being returned.

You will need:

Brick dust or ochre powder

Red wine (or moon water; see recipe on page 229)

A few drops of your own blood (optional)

Plastic wrap

Mix enough ochre powder or brick dust and red wine (you may also add drops of blood) to create enough of a thick paste to cover your bones. Use your hands (you may want to wear protective gloves) to completely coat your bones. Wrap them in plastic wrap and let them sit overnight, allowing them to stay moist. Remove the wrap and allow them to air dry. When completely dry, brush off the remaining dust.

While holding your bones, take a deep breath. Now slowly blow out across your bones, ritually breathing life into them.

Messages in the Bones: Bone Divination

Have you ever gazed into the dying embers of a fire and seen shapes or symbols? What images come to mind when you stare at the flickering of a candle flame? What comes to mind as ghostly shapes appear in the smoke of your incense? How about the popping and cracking of coals? Pyromancy is a form of divination using fire used by many magical practitioners, but did you know that oracle bones were once tossed into the fire as a way of divination? Pyroosteomancy is a form of divination using fire and bone and is thought to go back to the Shang dynasty in China. Omens and prophecies lay hidden in the cracks that formed on inscribed oxen scapula and turtle shells when they were exposed to extreme heat. Good or bad fortune for the coming year could be established, and meteorological and even military events could be predicted by the burning of the bones.

Pyro-Osteomancy

If you're using small bones, they can be placed against a charcoal tab in a fire-safe container instead of a fire pit. I've done this while divining with small chicken bones in a cast-iron pan.

I recommend using larger bones (from a roast or turkey leg for example) in a proper fire pit. If you are making one for the first time, remember to pick a spot away from trees and shrubbery. Dig a hole that is approximately two feet deep and four feet wide, and keep the leftover soil nearby. In case the fire gets out of control, it can be used to smother the flames. Line your pit with stone or brick. It really doesn't matter what kind of wood your fire is made of, but consider adding one or more of the nine sacred woods to add a little more enchantment: birch, oak, hazel, rowan, hawthorn, willow, fir, apple, and vine. When you are done with the fire, use a bucket of water to drown out the coals.

You will need:

Permanent marker

Cleaned, dry bones, ethically gathered (dinner is a good place to start)

Fire pit, charcoal barbecue, or charcoal tab in a fireproof dish

With your permanent marker, write *yes* on one end and *no* on the other end of the bones. You're going to want to let the fire burn down until you have a nice bed of coals before placing the bones near the fire. If you are using a charcoal barbecue or a charcoal tab in a fireproof dish, let the coals get nice and red before placing your bones beside them.

Hold your bone and ask a yes-or-no question out loud. Place the bone near the hot coals and listen for the crack. You will know the answer to your question by looking to see if the crack formed closer to the *yes* or to the *no*.

Throwing the Bones

Many cultures have used bones as a way of divining the future, and there are many different approaches and techniques to reading them. Some readers rely on ancestor wisdom, while others study the placement and configuration on a cloth or animal hide or a circle drawn in the dirt. While some readers use traditional methods of only using chicken or opossum bones for their readings, many use a combination of bones, wood, found objects, roots, dice, stones, and so on.

It is traditional to keep the bones in a basket or bag or near your altar when not in use. In some traditions, each bone has a specific meaning, while others note the bones that are grouped together to obtain yes or no answers. The pattern in which the bones are thrown also holds significance. An easy way to introduce yourself to the art of bone divination is by using the chicken bones from a roasted chicken and tossing them onto a circle drawn onto a large piece of paper.

You will need:

Permanent marker

One 11-by-14-inch piece of paper or poster board

Cleaned bones from a whole roasted chicken

Carefully clean the following bones that are left from a roasted chicken. Each bone signifies the following:

Whole Wing Bone: Movement

Broken Wing Bone: Slow progress

Neck Bone: Poverty

Wish Bone: Good fortune

Rib Bone: Limitations

Thigh Bone: Spirituality or spiritual trials

Breast Bone: The heart's desire

Whole Leg Bone: Travel by land

Broken Leg Bone: Setbacks

With the marker, draw a large circle on the piece of paper and then draw two more lines to divide your circle into four quarters (this represents the crossroads). To each quarter assign an aspect of your life (finances, love, health, etc.). Toss your bones onto the paper. The bones that land near the center reveal issues of prevalence to the seeker, while the bones that are dispersed to the edges could indicate past or future events. Remember, as with any divinatory practice, follow your intuition and listen to your guides.

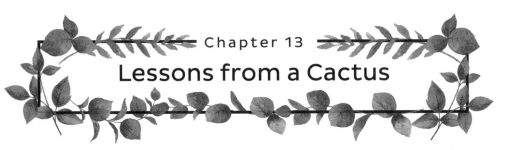

Chapter 13

Lessons from a Cactus

As do most natural Witches, I spend as much time as I can in my outdoor sanctuaries. For me that means dew-kissed mornings in my garden gathering herbs or tending to my flowers. Afternoons might be spent under a favorite tree in quiet meditation, and evenings take me to the riverbank, where the silky threads of the otherworld are tangible and my magical workings seem to flow the most smoothly. I am at my most comfortable in my temperate rain forest surroundings. For me, it almost seems strange to visit a location whose trees aren't coated with club moss and licorice fern or the ground isn't slightly saturated with rain. But the earth has many beautiful faces, and within the lines etched into the land, there are lessons.

The forest is calm and reminds me to keep steadfast and grounded in my beliefs, the mountain reminds me that it's okay to cry out and that my words have value, and the ocean with her roaring undulation reminds me that our Earth Mother is alive and we are not alone. But the desert...the desert has a stark, quiet beauty that teaches us to take a step outside of our ego and just be.

Some of the most delicate and beautiful plants I have ever seen have been in the desert. Wildflowers like the golden suncup, California poppy, mariposa lily, and sand verbena add vibrancy to the desert's landscape and teach us that we're never too old to appreciate surprises. And the cactus, the most regal of all desert plants, teaches us about resiliency. The cactus collects water over a large root system, with small, thin roots near the surface to collect rainwater as quickly as possible. They also have a taproot that grows much deeper to reach water in times of drought, not to mention that their stems work as holding tanks for water. Their tough skin and spiny tips, which are modified leaves, protect them from predators.

So step back and take another look at that cactus sitting in your windowsill. What is it speaking to you? You might hear wisdom like this:

- Learn to grow a thick skin so you can tackle the tough challenges with strength and grace.
- When you are faced with obstacles, think about the big picture (in magic and life).
- Use your energy to be proactive about situations you may face—no one ever got anywhere feeling sorry for themselves.
- Fill your soul with strength and confidence and know you can take on anything.

Magical Correspondences for Desert Plants

Here's a list of beautiful desert plants that bloom and thrive despite their extreme conditions. They can not only show us the beauty of resilience but also add enchantment to your spellwork.

Agave (*Agave americana*)

Planet: Sun

Element: Fire

Energy: Masculine

Agave is also known as century plant, though it typically lives only ten to thirty years. This succulent boasts three-to-five-foot gray-green leaves that have a prickly margin and an impressive spike at the tip. This plant only blooms once at the end of its life, and the stalks may reach upward of twenty-five feet, laden with yellow blossoms. In Mexico, agaves are called *mezcales,* and it is from the extraction and distillation of the sugar from *Agave americana* that we get *mezcal*; tequila comes from *Agave tequilana.* Use agave in magic for strength and endurance or to add a little sweetness to your spellwork.

◀ Aloe (*Aloe vera*, *A.* spp.)

Planet: Moon

Element: Water

Energy: Feminine

A popular household plant, aloe is a succulent that can grow up to forty inches tall with gray-green fleshy leaves that have serrated margins. The excretions from the leaves are used widely in cosmetics and as an anti-irritant to soothe chafed or sunburned skin. Hang the leaves in your home for luck and protection. Use the plant in spells for protection, money, and luck.

◀ Brittlebush (*Encelia* spp.)

Planet: Sun

Element: Earth

Energy: Masculine

Used as incense by early Spanish missions, the brittlebush is also called *incienso*. Commonly found throughout the North American Southwest and northern Mexico, brittlebush is a shrub used in magic for healing, luck, protection, banishing, cleansing, and empathy.

◀ Cactus (*Cactaceae* spp.)

Planet: Mars

Element: Fire

Energy: Masculine

Though the cactus has the reputation of being a prickly desert plant, there are actually many different kinds of cacti that can grow in a variety of conditions both indoors and outdoors. Cacti come in a wide range of shapes and sizes, and most can be found in regions that are subject to drought. Cacti are a part of a group known as succulents, meaning instead of leaves, they have thickened fleshy stems adapted to store water. In order for a succulent to be a true cactus, the plant must have areoles. These are small, round, cushion-like mounds where spines, leaves, or flowers can grow. In magic, the cactus is a protective plant whose spines can be used in Witch jars or for inscribing candles and other magical tools. Plant cactuses at each corner of your home to protect the property.

I have listed four of the most common desert cacti along with a tropical cactus found in the rain forest of Mexico:

Barrel Cactus (*Echinocactus grusonii*)

Planet: Mars

Element: Fire

Energy: Masculine

This striking cactus, sometimes known as golden ball cactus or mother-in-law's cushion, has a large bulbous shape and yellow spines. It bears yellow to orange and sometimes purple flowers. Use it in magic for growth and prosperity.

Cholla Cactus (*Cylindropuntia fulgida*)

Planet: Mars

Element: Fire

Energy: Masculine

Also known as a jumping cholla because of the stems' easy detachment when brushed against, this tree-like branching cactus is an important food and water source during heavy drought for many desert animals, including bighorn sheep and deer. Use cholla in magic for curses and protection.

Saguaro Cactus (*Carnegiea gigantea*)

Planet: Mars

Element: Fire

Energy: Masculine

This impressive slow-growing cactus can reach up to forty feet tall and can take up to seventy years before growing its first arm. Though not an endangered species, this classic cactus only grows in the Sonoran Desert region, and therefore it is illegal to cut down.

The saguaro was sacred to the Pima people, who thought of the plants as a tribe deserving respect. It was believed that when a Pima man died, he was reincarnated as a saguaro and that the arms that grew from the stems were his wives. Wives that had been good in their human life grew straight up, and the bad wives pointed down. Perfect for light construction, these cacti were once used for constructing sweat lodges, cots, and drying racks. The fruit of the cactus has a very delicate flavor, and its juice can be fermented into wine. The internal structure, when dried, was used as splint for broken bones. Use saguaro in magic to connect with your higher self, wisdom, patience, strength, and facing challenges.

Prickly Pear (*Opuntia phaeacantha*)

Planet: Mars

Element: Fire

Energy: Masculine

Also called desert prickly pear or tulip prickly pear, this cactus is one of a group of paddle segmented cacti with flattened, spined pads that bear brightly colored purple, pink, or reddish flowers. The fruits of the prickly pear can be peeled and eaten. Medicinally, the fruit was used as a diuretic. Stems were also used as folk remedies to treat wounds, aches and pains, and diarrhea. Use prickly pear in magic for protection and endurance.

◀ Queen of the Night (*Epiphyllum oxypetalum*)

Planet: Moon

Element: Water

Energy: Feminine

Queen of the night is an epiphytic cactus native to the tropical rain forests of Mexico, which means it grows not in soil but on other plants, absorbing water and nutrients from the air. I added this plant because it's a fairly common cactus for indoor plant lovers. It has white, circular, sweet-smelling flowers that bloom from dusk till dawn. If it looks familiar, it is because it is in the same family, Cactaceae, as the very popular

Christmas cactus. Use queen of the night in magic for intuition, self-love, transformation, and psychic abilities.

❧ Cayenne (*Capsicum annuum*)

Planet: Mars

Element: Fire

Energy: Masculine

These peppers have a rating of thirty to fifty thousand units on the Scoville scale, which gives them just enough spice to kick things up just a bit. Use cayenne to kick up your spellwork for exorcism and protection and to dispel evil.

❧ Chuparosa (*Justicia californica*)

Planet: Venus

Element: Fire

Energy: Feminine

A favorite of hummingbirds, chuparosa is a flowering bush native to the deserts of Southern California, Arizona, and northern Mexico and produces succulent leaves followed by brilliant red (or sometimes yellow) tubular flowers. Use this plant in magic for beauty, self-love, sexuality, new beginnings, and positivity.

❧ Creosote Bush (*Larrea tridentata*)

Planet: Saturn

Element: Water

Energy: Masculine

Creosote bush grows throughout the desert southwest in North America, its range including the Sonoran, Mojave, and Chihuahuan deserts. This evergreen shrub can grow nine feet tall and bears resinous stems, dark green leaves, and five-petaled yellow flowers. It exhibits the characteristic scent of creosote, from which its name derives. Use the bush in magic for longevity, health, overcoming challenges, and knowledge.

❦ Desert Lavender (*Hyptis emoryi*)

Planet: Mercury

Element: Air

Energy: Masculine

Desert lavender is found in Nevada, California, Arizona, and northwestern Mexico and is an aromatic perennial shrub of the mint family. It produces tiny blue-violet flowers that grow along a main stem and is a favorite of bees and hummingbirds. The seeds have been used as a folk remedy for gastral problems, and the petals were used for hemorrhaging. Desert tribes also used it for spiritually cleansing and protection from malevolent forces. Use it in magic for protection, banishing, purification, and healing.

❦ Distant Scorpionweed (*Phacelia distans*)

Planet: Mars

Element: Fire

Energy: Masculine

Also known as wild heliotrope, this annual shrub can grow from one to three feet in height. Finely haired, fern-like leaves and coiled, scorpion-like arrangement of the flowers give this plant its name. It is native to the Sonoran and Mojave deserts of the southwestern US. Use desert scorpionweed in magic to overcome fear, for strength, and for protection.

❦ Honey Mesquite Tree (*Prosopis glandulosa*)

Planet: Moon

Element: Water, earth

Energy: Feminine

Honey mesquite is a medium-size thorny tree in the legume family that can grow between twenty and fifty feet in height depending on moisture. Mesquite is known for the ability to access water deeper than most trees can. Use it in magic for healing, protection, and cleansing.

❧ Milkweed (*Asclepias linaria*)

Planet: Moon

Element: Air

Energy: Feminine

This desert variety of milkweed known as pineneedle is rare in most of the United States but is common in the desert areas of the southwest. It has needle-like leaves with tiny clusters of white or pink flowers that are great for attracting butterflies. Use this plant in magic for divination, working with the Fae, protection, and wishes.

❧ Mullein (*Verbascum thapus*)

Planet: Saturn

Element: Fire

Energy: Feminine

This biennial grows a rosette of large, velvety leaves up to twelve inches in height in its first year. The second year boasts a beautiful velvety spike that can grow up to eight feet in height and is clustered with small yellow flowers. Use mullein in dream pillows to guard against nightmares. Use it in magic for divination, love, courage, health, and protection.

❧ Palo Verde (*Parkinsonia florida*)

Planet: Venus

Element: Earth

Energy: Feminine

This beautiful desert tree, blue palo verde, is known for its bright yellow flowers and striking green trunk. Because of the high presence of chlorophyll in the trunk, most of the photosynthesis occurs there. This tree is also a nurse plant for the slow-growing saguaro cactus—the vulnerable cacti seedlings can be found growing under its protective cover. Use palo verde in spellwork for growth, family, and protection.

❧ Rose of Jericho (*Anastatica hierochuntica*)

Planet: Mars

Element: Air

Energy: Masculine

A small tumbleweed of the Middle East and Sahara Desert, rose of Jericho rarely grows more than six inches in height. This plant has the ability to hibernate during times of drought by curling into a ball, protecting any seeds and preventing them from scattering prematurely. During the rainy season, it will unfurl and turn gray-green within hours. This is great to use in spells for transformation, money, blessings, and protection.

❧ Sacred Datura (*Datura wrightii*)

Planet: Saturn

Element: Water

Energy: Feminine

With its creamy white trumpeted flowers, this ground-loving perennial of northern Mexico and the Desert Southwest opens its blooms in the morning and evening and stays closed during the heat of day. Sacred datura has been used in ritual ceremonies and rites of passage among various Native American tribes. Datura is extremely poisonous and may cause skin irritation, so handle carefully. Use the plant in magic for protection and hex breaking.

❧ Sagebrush (*Artemisia tridentata*)

Planet: Venus

Element: Earth

Energy: Feminine

Sagebrush, a silver-gray-leafed shrub that has a pungent odor, is common across the Plains and into the Desert Southwest. When attacked by predatory insects, sagebrush emits volatile organic compounds that neighboring sagebrush shrubs can sense and react to by producing their own chemicals to ward away the predators. Use it in spells for purification, negativity, and warding evil.

❧ Yellow Bells (*Tecoma stans*)

Planet: Sun

Element: Earth

Energy: Masculine

The official flower of the US Virgin Islands, this ornamental vine boasts evergreen leaves and large yellow trumpeted flowers that attract pollinators. Use yellow bells in spells for strength, healing, and resilience.

❧ Yucca (*Yucca* spp.)

Planet: Mars

Element: Fire

Energy: Masculine

The yucca has dense rosettes of long, narrow leaves with a spine at the tip. The white flowers are bell-shaped and grow in clusters along a short stalk. Boil yucca roots to add to your bathwater before ritual. Use it in spells for protection, transformation, and purification.

Aloe Money Charm Bag

Feeling the need to bring a little prosperity into your life? Working with aloe is extremely simple. In fact, you don't even need to have the plant for this little spell.

You will need:

Small green drawstring bag

A few coins

Aloe vera gel

Rub a little of the aloe vera on a few coins while focusing on bringing wealth into your life. Place the coins in a green drawstring bag and tie three knots. As you tie the last knot, say,

Prosperity, find your way to me
Soon enough, I'll be in the green
As I wish it, so mote it be

Rose of Jericho Blessing Water

Rose of Jericho plants are easily obtained through many online metaphysical or garden supply shops. When you receive it, it will look like a little dried-up tumbleweed. The magic happens when you place it in a bowl of water! Here's an easy way to make your own blessing water.

You will need:

1 rose of Jericho

Bowl

Water

1 sunstone

During a waxing moon phase, fill a bowl with water and place the sunstone in it. Carefully place the dormant rose of Jericho on top (roots to the water). Now wake your plant up with these words of power:

Arise, arise, sweet desert rose
I release you from your sleep
Blessing true, I ask of you

Let the tumbleweed sit in the water overnight (it can take anywhere from two to twenty-four hours for your rose of Jericho to fully awaken). When your plant has unfurled and color has returned to its leaves, it will be fully awake. Remove the plant and place it somewhere safe for it to return to dormancy.

Remove the sunstone and pour the water into a bottle to be used in your spellwork. Sprinkle it around your home, add it to a floor wash to bless your home, use it as you would holy water in spells to exorcise negativity or to reverse bad luck, rub it on coins for money spells, or use it to bless your magical tools.

Chapter 14
A Warrior's Instinct: Protection Magic

I love that I live in the middle of a rain forest, whose cleansing vibrations feed my soul daily. Magic is palatable within the cover of giant conifers, whose weeping branches hold within them ancient wisdom that rides on silky threads straight to my willing hands, which I use to cast spells. But the downside to living in a semi-remote area is that we fall prey to people who are looking for an easy home to burglarize. They are a brazen lot, those who come in the middle of the day and walk right up on your porch or into your shed and grab whatever they can with no regard to sentimentality or value. They're quick, cunning, and ruthless.

It was February and a cool steady drizzle had been falling for the better part of the month—it's the kind of rain that causes joints to ache and hair to frizz. The kind of rain that, if you're not careful, tears at your spirit.

I stood out on the porch and as I looked up at the thick, gray clouds that showed no sign of breaking, I heard someone clear their throat. "Hello," I said. "Is there someone out here?"

A young man with a dark beard and tattered hickory shirt stepped from behind one of my emerald greens. I held in the complete and utter shock that was coursing through my veins and calmly asked, "What are you doing here?"

"Sorry, ma'am." He straightened his shirt. "I didn't mean to scare you. It's just that my car broke down up on Caskey and I had to hike out." He walked closer to the porch and I stepped back and took hold of the door handle.

"Did you need to call someone?" I asked.

"Yeah, if you don't mind." He smiled. I looked to his eyes, which were soft and brown. He seemed harmless. He seemed like a guy who was having a bad day and needed a little help, so I did something stupid ... I invited him in.

"Why don't you sit by the fire," I said and picked up the cat crowding the chair. He sat and I handed him my telephone. As he punched out a number and held the phone to his ear, I went into the kitchen and poured him a cup of coffee. "Black okay?" I asked and handed him the cup.

"Thank you, so much," he said. "You have no idea how much I appreciate this."

"Not a problem," I said. "I'll bet you're hungry." I smiled.

"Well, yeah." He hesitated. "A little."

"Eggs okay?" I asked, as I went back to the kitchen.

"That would great," he said, then punched out another number on my phone.

When I returned with scrambled eggs and toast, he was petting my cat who had tried to reclaim the chair by the fire. "Sorry about Wren," I said. "Trade you." I exchanged the plate of food for an irritated black cat. "So, did you get ahold of anyone?"

"Afraid not," he said between bites, "I guess I'll just walk the rest of the way to town." He put down the plate. "But, thanks I really, really appreciate what you did for me."

"I feel bad. That's a fifteen-mile walk and I'm carless today or I'd take you."

"You've done enough, really." He smiled and stood up.

"I've got an idea." I picked up the phone. "I'm going to call a sheriff to come and pick you up. They could take you home and maybe even help arrange for a tow for your car."

It's crazy how a word can become a trigger for some people. As soon as the word *sheriff* fell from my lips, his demeanor changed.

"I said I'm fine." His eyes hardened and brow furrowed.

"Okay." I realized at that moment something was wrong. And as I watched him slam out my door and jump off my porch, ripping a wind chime my oldest son had made me when he was five years old from an eave, I knew I had been made an ass out of. I ran after him yelling, "Give me back my wind chime!"

From my yard, I heard him start his vehicle that was parked along the road conveniently hidden from our view. He sped off, along with my wind chime, some gas, a few miscellaneous tools, and a chainsaw. Apparently, my stepping out on the porch had interrupted his second trip to my husband's small shop. And I made him breakfast!

I quickly called the sheriff and reported what happened. I even checked my phone to see who the violator had called so I could at least know who he was associated with, but he had pushed random numbers and held a dead phone up to his ear. He had played me well for free food. I was mortified and cried a lot, especially over the loss of the wind chime, which held no monetary value for him but was priceless to me.

After a few days of feeling sorry for myself (and maybe a little ashamed), I picked myself up and got down to some serious warding plans for our property.

"I don't know why we've never done this before," I said to my husband.

"Probably because we've never had a reason to. We live in a pristine area with amazing energy. Why would we feel the need to shield ourselves?"

"You're right." I felt a little better. "But now this jerk has gone and pissed me off. He took my wind chime!"

Steve hugged me. "I know."

I and each of my three children, who were fourteen, eleven, and seven, at the time, painted protective symbols coinciding with each of the elements on stones we had collected from the riverbank. It seemed fitting to me that all the components for our ritual either came from our property or were created by our own hands. I used a smudge made from the needles of a cedar tree that stood stately in our yard and lavender from my herb bed to represent air, a red candle I had made especially for the ritual to represent fire, a wooden bowl my husband had made in high school filled with soil from our garden to represent earth, and last, another one of Steve's bowls filled with water from our pond to represent water.

The morning we chose to perform our little family ritual was clear and unusually warm for late February, which brightened our spirits and had the kids convinced it was a sign from the God and Goddess that they were on our side. I had to agree with them. "Yes, I do believe we're in their favor today."

Beginning at our front door, I led our family, my wand in hand, and drew a banishing pentagram. I stated, "We sanctify this property with fire and air!" Then we all walked in single file around the perimeter of the property, each of us taking a turn to repeat the phrase. Steve smudged and my oldest son,

Joshua, held the candle until we made our way back to the house. This process was repeated for earth and water.

When we were done, we planted our warding stones, invoking the element represented on each by tapping the stone with my wand and chanting the phrase, "No baneful presence shall disrupt our peace. Only love is welcome here."

That was eleven years ago, and we haven't had any problems since. Coincidence? I don't know. But I can tell you that every vacation cabin and the other two permanent residences that sit within a ten-mile radius of us have had several break-ins each, including a spree that happened last summer where everyone but us was hit. Makes you think…

A Few Words of Advice

Use your energy well, wild one. Eat healthy foods that fill you up and make you strong. Quit denying yourself those wonderful meals that warm your soul (a carb or two isn't going to kill you). Sleep well and meditate often under leafy trees, on sandy beaches, or on cool grassy lawns. Keep your chakras in balance. Go to nature and walk briskly, taking in every sound that nature has to offer up. Try to identify birds by their call; take in the rhythmic sound of the ocean's pounding surf; listen for messages tangled in the breeze.

Serve yourself well, dear one. Surround yourself with beautiful things— favorite books and cozy blankets. Splurge on crystals, candles, and incense (you're worth it). Soak away anxiety in ritual baths filled with magical herbs and scented oils. Take time for healing, whether that means a weekend alone or gatherings with friends, family, and lots of laughter.

Accept yourself, magical one. Don't be afraid to speak your truth. Reclaim that untamed part of your spirit that burns with passion and knows your power. You are strong; don't deny yourself an adventure from time to time. Hike that trail or swim as far out as you feel safe. Set attainable goals for yourself and relish in your victories. Surprise yourself with bold gestures and be confident because you are divine. Celebrate the ever-turning Wheel of the Year with ritual, laughter, and praise.

These are things one must do to maintain a healthy vibration. Your physical, emotional, and spiritual health are all intertwined, and someone who is rundown, anxiety ridden, and emotionally drained cannot perform protection magic efficiently. In fact, being in a state of self-loathing or other emotional turmoil can make you more susceptible to a psychic attack. Exercising, eating healthy foods, and taking time for yourself are all ways of making you a more powerful practitioner. So, before you begin, make sure you are the best you can be.

Warding

A protection spell is anything that is meant to avert negativity, turn away harm, or shield you, your loved ones, or your property from a psychic or magical attack. A ward is categorized as a type of apotropaic magic (meaning to turn away) that acts as a magical barrier, shield, or deflector. You may not realize it, but you have most likely been around wards throughout your entire life. That horseshoe above the threshold of your grandparent's home—that was a ward. How about that hex sign you admired on the old barn? That was a ward. And what about that pretty chime your parents may have hung outside of your window to keep the ghosts a bay? That too was a type of ward. While these are amazing techniques meant to protect thresholds from negativity entering, we're going to talk about another type of ward, created by you and infused with your personal power and charged using the energy of the elements.

Wards, when placed at the four directions, can be used as guardians to protect your home or property. We used stones with protective symbols and placed them at the four directions of our property, but anything that you want to charge with your power can be used. One great idea is to plant trees, flowers, or shrubs that correspond with each element in the four directions of your property. Or how about using crystals to place on sills or shelves in the four directions of your home? Warding bottles are also a great way to add a protective punch, and the great thing about them is that they can be modified to suit your needs.

When protecting your property, keep in mind that neither wards nor protection spells are meant to replace locks on your doors, alarms, or other security devices. They are only meant to enhance your protection and throw off would-be criminals.

Warding Bottles

For this warding technique, we are going to make warding bottles, one for each of the four directions. We will be filling them with protective stones and herbs (most of what I chose can be found in the pantry) that correspond to each element.

Element	Herbs	Stones
Earth	Oats, barley, alfalfa, buckwheat, corn, wheat, fern, cotton, potato	Jade, jasper, jet, onyx, obsidian, hematite, quartz
Air	Almond, bean, clover, dandelion, rice, sage, pine, parsley, lavender	Citrine, agate, tiger's eye, turquoise, zircon, fluorite
Fire	Garlic, cinnamon, clove, bay, basil, tobacco, tea, sunflower, ginger	Sunstone, garnet, red tourmaline, carnelian, amber
Water	Avocado, aloe, chamomile, chickweed, lemon, thyme, yarrow, peach, poppy	Moonstone, lapis lazuli, aquamarine, amethyst, blue tourmaline

You will need:

Protective herbs and stones

4 pint-sized canning jars (or decorative jars of your choice)

Paint pens with colors corresponding to each element (or black marker)

Sealing wax (optional)

Choose several of each of the herbs and layer them into each jar with a few stones. As you do this, imbue your jars with your personal power. Imagine as you handle the herbs and stones that they are taking with them your protective energy and filling the jars. After the jars have been filled, secure the lids and use the paint pens or marker to draw protective symbols or sigils on the jars. If you would like, use sealing wax to complete the jars.

When you're done, line them up and charge each one with these words:

Guardian of the (fill in with appropriate direction)
Protect my home and all that abides within
Let no baneful energy nor negative power break through the barrier
Only love may enter here—so mote it be

Now carry the jars to the four corners of your home, room, or property, and as you place each one in place, say something like this:

No baneful presence shall disrupt our peace
Only love is welcome here.

As you do this, visualize a shield (or bubble) forming from each bottle and coming together to envelope your home, room, or property.

Besom Threshold Ward

Did I ever mention that my husband makes traditional brooms (or besoms)? After he suffered a stroke a few years ago, he needed something to help him improve his strength and dexterity. Broom making was not only great therapy but also an opportunity to revive a dying art, and it allowed him to create items that are relevant to the Pagan community.

Classically, a ritual besom is made from birch or heather twigs attached to a willow, ash, or hazel handle. Besoms can be seen as having both masculine (the handle) and feminine (the bristles) energies and are used in many traditions as a means of cleansing a space and in handfasting ceremonies, as a couple "jumps the broom," a symbolization of fertility and the crossing from one's old life into a new one.

Just as hanging a horseshoe above a threshold was said to protect the inhabitants of a household, hanging a besom above your threshold is a way to keep unwanted energies out of the home as well. Let's revive this old practice by imbuing a craft besom with protective herbs and add a little protective color magic with a bright red ribbon.

You will need:

Craft broom 12 to 15 inches long (cinnamon scented—even better!)

Birch or oak twigs

Hot glue gun

3 bulbs of garlic

Sprigs of 1 or more of the following: rosemary, sage, yarrow, holly, marjoram, and ivy

Red ribbon

Lay your craft broom in front of you with the bristles facing down. Gather your twigs and artistically arrange them (starting at the top of the bristles) to lie with the natural shape of the broom, then attach them using your hot glue gun. Add your herb sprigs and garlic bulbs in the same manner. Use the red ribbon to add a bow or to wrap around the handle and attach with hot glue. When you're done, use this charm to charge your protective besom:

> *May your presence be a protective charm*
> *To keep all inhabitants safe from harm*
> *All baneful energies will stay clear*
> *Only peace and love are welcome here*

Make Your Own Traditional Besom

If you feel like you would like to try your hand at making a traditional besom, here's how to do it. These instructions are for the smaller and simpler "cobweb" broom, a great introductory project to the art of broom making that still maintains the look of a traditional witch's broom.

You will need:

Large handful of broomcorn with stalks, enough to go around the broom without overlapping (can be purchased online—try Caddy Supply Company)

Interesting found or gifted stick approximately 4 feet long and ¾ to 1 inch in diameter for the handle

Tarred nylon braided twine #18 in your choice of color

Scissors

Wood tying block (2 × 2 × 15 inches long, used under your feet to help tightly secure your broomcorn)

5-gallon bucket

Drill with ³⁄₁₆ drill bit

Drill a hole in the center of the tying block. Knot the twine through the hole and wrap approximately 15 feet around it in the center, leaving room for your feet at both ends.

Fill the 5-gallon bucket with enough warm water to cover your broom corn (stalks down) and let soften for a minimum of 20 minutes.

Drill a ³⁄₁₆ inch hole 3 inches from the end of your stick.

Lay the broomcorn to one side of you within easy distance of reaching while keeping tension on your tie block with your feet.

Tie your twine (from the tie block) through the hole in your broom handle. Using your feet to pull, roll and pull tightly several layers of twine around your handle toward you. Keep the tension tight.

Begin adding your broomcorn one at a time under the twine. Keep adding side by side without overlapping. As you pull on the handle, the twine should make a slight dent in the broomcorn stalks. When the stalks have been added all the way around the broom, wrap the twine three to four more times tightly around your broom, stopping at the back of your broom.

We are now ready to weave the twine in and out of the stalks to give the top of your bristle end a plaited look. To make this aesthetically pleasing we need an odd number of stalks. If you have an even number, use a sharp knife to split one of your stalks.

Try to start your weaving as close to the first three wraps as possible. Weave the twine over and under, continuing around the broom; it will naturally spiral on its own. At the end of approximately six turns around the broom, your plait will be complete. Create a loop with the twine, then wrap the twine completely around the broom handle tightly over the loop three to four times. Cut the twine and tie the loose end into a secured loop. Trim the twine. Use scissors to trim the tops of the stalks to about an inch above the plaited design.

Banishing, Shielding, and Cleansing—Oh My!

Here are a few other simple ways of protecting yourself from negative psychic energy:

The Banishing Pentagram

The upright five-pointed star wrapped by a circle that is worn by Witches and used in spellwork and ritual has a long history. The five-pointed star in symbology goes back thousands of years. In ancient Sumerian cuneiform, the pentagram was a glyph for the word *ub*, meaning "corner" or "nook." In ancient China the pentagram represented the five elements of water, earth, wood, metal, and fire. In ancient Judaism, the star represented the five books of the Torah, and Christians used it to represent the five wounds Jesus had suffered while on the cross.

In sacred geometry, scientific constants can communicate as examples and cycles in nature, the pentagram is a prime example of this. The golden ratio, which is equal to 1.618 and is symbolized by the Greek letter phi, presents itself throughout the angles that make up the five-pointed star.

For modern practitioners, the star's five points represent earth, air, fire, and water, with the top point representing spirit. Depending on who you ask, the circle that surrounds the star represents the continuation of life and rebirth, divine wisdom, or the binding by spirit of the four terrestrial elements. I like to believe it represents all those things. During ritual, practitioners may use a sword, athame, or wand to trace a pentagram in the air. Depending how it is drawn, it can be used to either banish or invoke energies.

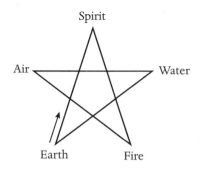

Banishing Pentagram

To draw the banishing pentagram, you begin in the lower left corner, at the earth point, then draw upward to the spirit point, and then on around in a clockwise fashion until the star is complete. When I draw a banishing pentagram, it's as if I am putting a key into a lock between dimensions and letting that unwanted energy know, "You are not welcome here!"

Clean Away Negativity Times Three: House Cleaning Ritual

Negative energy can build up fast in a home. And though you may not see it, just like those dust bunnies hidden under the couch, it's there. The way we feel, act, and live causes a release of energy into our homes and its buildup can influence our thinking and our emotions. Think about it: if there has been illness, toxic visitors, or problems with familial relations, all the negative gunk, such as anger, resentment, self-loathing, and mental or physical violence, mounds up. It can intensify or cause uneasiness, anxiety, and financial or relationship problems.

The vast majority of homes are never cleared of psychic residue, so remember you're dealing with not only your own buildup of energy but most likely the energy of every past resident as well.

This house cleansing is done in three parts.

You will need:

Ritual besom or broom

Stick of palo santo

Small natural bowl or shell

Water

1 teaspoon salt

Sprig of basil

First, undertake a good physical cleaning and organization of your home.

Second, we're going to sweep away that negativity with our ritual besom (a regular broom will do). Start at the front door, and working your way deosil, sweep away that negative energy. As you sweep, repeat something like this:

Baneful energy, you are not welcome here—only love and peace reside

Make your way all the way around your home and back to the front door and give it a good push out.

Last, we will consecrate the home with the four elements. Take your lit palo santo stick, which represents both fire and air, to the front door and open it. Drawing a banishing pentagram, state,

By fire and air, I consecrate this home

Repeat the clockwise circuit you had done earlier with the broom, smudging and repeating,

By fire and air, I consecrate this home

When you arrive back at the front door, visualize all of the negativity being blown out the door. Now state,

Only love resides here

Fill a small bowl or shell with water and add the salt. Once again start at the front door and draw your banishing pentagram using the basil sprig dunked in the water. State,

By earth and water, I consecrate this home

Repeat the clockwise circuit, repeating your blessing. End at the front door, once again visualizing all the baneful energy being blown away, and say,

Only love resides here

Now that your house has been cleaned times three, you'll only have to go through it once in a while with a smudge or a besom to give it quick cleansing upkeeps.

Shielding

I don't know about you, but I am a sensitive soul. A child of the moon, I feel everything to an extreme. I can walk into a room and immediately absorb the stressful energy of those around me. I'm easily overstimulated in public places, causing me to become overwhelmed and exhausted. Sound familiar?

One thing that helps empaths and other sensitive souls is a technique known as shielding. Think of it as a protective bubble that surrounds you, allowing all that toxic energy to bounce off while still allowing you to take in positive vibes. With a little practice, you can put up a shield quickly and easily. Once you learn to master this technique, you'll be able to shield not only yourself, but your home, property, and ritual space as well.

Take a few deep cleansing breaths. Imagine a shield of protective fabric (or water, net, bubble, etc.) completely surrounding your body and extending a few inches beyond it. This is your armor, and within it, feel yourself centered and energized. To take down your shield, take a deep breath, and as you exhale, imagine the fabric around you disappear.

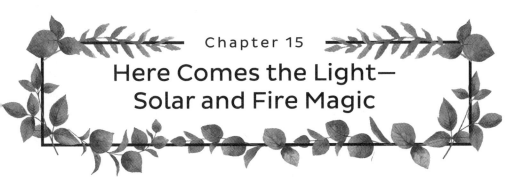

Chapter 15
Here Comes the Light— Solar and Fire Magic

Darkness falls on the Pacific Northwest in November as the Cailleach strikes the ground with her staff, causing the icy waves of winter to ripple across the terrain. She stirs the tempests and shapes the land and dances freely atop the mountains—and I swear sometimes I hear her laughter mixed with the rain and sleet that seem to fall nonstop. The dark crone's mantle falls heavy across our landscape, and by Yule we only experience about eight hours of light, glowing dimly behind a thick covering of gray cloud.

January can be tricky. Some years it can remain crisp and clear, turning our homestead into a strange sugar-frosted fairyland where every twig on every tree sparkles under moonlight, coaxing even the faintest of souls into the cold just to breathe in a little of its magic. But it can also be the dreariest of months, and I remember many a January when it rained nonstop from New Year's Day straight through February.

I vividly remember waking up one morning in March a few years back. As I looked out my window to the valley shrouded in clouds that press up against the mountains, I realized I hadn't seen even the tiniest glimpse of blue sky since before Samhain. And though I try my hardest to appreciate the beauty that is tangled up in all that gray, I also long for just one single ray of sun to stretch its fingers through the warbled glass of my home and caress my cheek.

With spring, the rain turns warm and a green fire bursts through the valley, igniting my world and brightening my soul with the hope of sunnier days to come. There have been times when I worried that April's constant weeping skies would have me repeat something I do not like to say: "I haven't seen the sun for over six months." The most optimistic of Pacific Northwesterners reply something lame, like "April showers bring May flowers" or "This is Washington—what'd you expect?" I just want to punch them right in the face.

But then it happens! That special morning when I am stirred by birdsong and slender streaks of golden light. My heart quickens as I throw on boots and run to find my world anew.

And as I stand in all the beauty that nature has to offer me, crowned majestically by the glorious rays of the Sun King, deep in my soul I know that it would be worth 364 more days of rain to experience the bliss of that one day over again. Blessed be the Sun King.

The Magical Powers of the Sun

To our ancient ancestors the sun was a living being who had a great share in shaping man's destiny. Some thought of our galaxy's only star as an all-seeing eye—no deed would go unseen—and whose rays were strong enough to reach the underworld. To cultures whose ideology included sun worship, the sun was thought to bestow light, life, and wisdom to the totality of the cosmos. Kings ruled by the power of the sun and even claimed descendancy from the sun. But though almost every culture uses solar motifs, sun worship was only prevalent in Egyptian, Indo-European, and Mesoamerican cultures.

It's obviously no surprise why our ancestors venerated that powerful golden orb: there's nothing more important to us on earth than the sun. Without its heat and light, the earth would be just another lifeless ice-coated rock. It is the sun that warms our seas and stirs our atmosphere. It is the sun that gives energy to everything that grows, from the trees that absorb the carbon dioxide and give us oxygen to the sprouts we plant every spring that provide us with nourishment.

Harnessing the power of the sun for spellwork is simple and to the point, and like the moon, the sun has phases.

Dawn: The newborn sun reaches out to you. This is a sun of new beginnings and unchartered territories. The dawn encourages us with bright blessings and a wild abandon that reminds us that anything is possible if only we believe. Use the dawn for magic concerning new beginnings, new relationships, love, transition, renewal, rejuvenation, joy, health, and energy.

Morning Sun: As the sun builds strength, it becomes a glorious presence in the sky that can add power and heat to spells concerning growth, expansion, resolution, courage, hearth and home, relationships, love, garden and plant magic, romance, and sex.

Noon Sun: At his peak, the sun is the eternal flame whose power can be harnessed for magic concerning justice, finances, charging magical tools, health, strength, power, and knowledge.

Afternoon Sun: As the sun begins to slip, his light becomes both wisdom and strength and can be used in spells for clarity, communication, exploration, inner self, knowledge, and strength.

Sunset: As the last embers fade behind the western hills and the sky turns a brilliant scarlet, we can use his waning light for spells concerning, cleansing, divination, banishing negativity, bad habits, release, and simplification.

To make solar-charged water, set out a bowl filled with water, a sun stone, and a few sprigs of lemon balm or another citrusy herb and let it charge in the noon sun. This sun water is great for incorporating into your solar magic or for charging magical tools.

Sunset Tea Divinatory Spell

Teacup

Hot water

Sunset tea blend (recipe follows)

Place a ½ teaspoon of the tea blend in a teacup and heated water. Let steep for at least 5 minutes while sitting in a comfortable spot in view of the setting sun. Before drinking, ask the sun in your own way to lend his knowledge and warming energy to your divinatory practices. Now relax and enjoy your tea. Leave a little liquid with the herbal mix at the bottom of your cup and enjoy divining your future with the power of the setting sun.

Sunset Tea Blend

2 parts chamomile

1 part calendula

1 part mugwort

½ part lavender

Harness the warming power of the waning Sun King with this relaxing tea blend.

Harnessing Fire: Candle Magic

The importance of harnessing fire is apparent throughout humanity's mythology and folklore. For the Greeks, it was Prometheus who stole fire from the sun for mankind to survive. For the Cherokee, Grandmother Spider snuck into the land of light using her web to secure fire and keep it in a jar. In Maori mythology, it is the hero Maui who tricked the fire goddess Mahuika to obtain the secrets of fire.

In harnessing the magical aspects of fire, we can utilize its transformative powers in spells to garner strength and confidence and for empowerment and freedom. We can use it for purification and to ritually destroy bad habits. An easy way to harness the power of fire is through candle magic.

The ancient art of candle burning often marks the beginning of a ritual, just as snuffing them out marks the end. Candles are lit to honor deity and used in sympathetic magic, serving as a representation of something, not to mention they create an enchanting atmosphere. I'm a busy Witch who doesn't always have time to set up complicated rituals, so candles are a favorite magical vehicle for me because they are portable, are available in a huge array of colors for incorporating color magic, absorb personal power easily, and release energy slowly.

Hand-Dipped Taper Candles

I always try to push any practitioner to create as many of their magical tools as possible. By imbuing your tools with your personal power, your magic will be all that more powerful. Taper candles are relatively easy to make. Try a craft that hasn't changed since ancient times.

You will need:

Beeswax (A nice choice because it burns slow and layers onto the wicking thicker than paraffin.)

Wax dye pellets (optional)

Double boiler (The pot needs to be tall enough to accommodate the length of candle you wish to make.)

Cold water

Wicking

Scissors

Metal nuts to use as wick end weights

Candy or kitchen laser thermometer

Broom

Melt the wax (and optional wax dye pellets) in a double boiler over high heat. Turn down the temperature when it reaches 165 degrees Fahrenheit. Do not let it rise above 200 degrees.

Set up your cold water in a container close to your melted wax.

While the wax is melting, prepare your wick by cutting a length of wicking that will leave enough room for dipping a candle on each end. Tie a metal nut to each wick end.

Holding the wicking at its midpoint, seal the wick by dipping the ends into the melted wax up to the desired candle length. It should harden within a few seconds.

Dip again into the hot wax, followed by plunging the wick into the cold water. Repeat this until your candles are at their desired thickness. About halfway through the dipping and plunging process, use the scissors to clip off your metal nuts.

Hang your finished candles over a broom balanced between two chairs (make sure the candles aren't touching) for at least 24 hours.

Adding Color Magic

Color is a manifestation of vibration and each color vibrates at a different speed. A high vibrating color like red has a stimulating effect, yellow produces feelings of joy, green is quiet and soothing, and the lower vibrating colors such as blue or purple are cooling and suggest vastness. Color can have both a physical and psychological effect upon the mind and have been utilized by humans for healing, meditation, and magic.

Adding color magic helps the practitioner tap into the vibrations associated to each color and adds another layer that can greatly enhance your spell crafting.

Here is a list of colors and their correspondences that can add a little boost of magical energy to your candle magic.

Red: Strength, courage, lust, passion, love, courage, protection, fire

Orange: Success, attraction, goals, business endeavors, legal matters, ambition, real estate, invitation and welcome, drawing warmth

Yellow: Communication, blessing, balance, happiness, travel, intelligence, clarity

Pink: Romance, friendship, healing, peace, femininity, relaxation, nurturing, caring

Green: Hope, environment, fertility, earth, tranquility, money, abundance, achieving goals, plants and trees, promises

Blue: Water, cleansing, messages, clarity, patience, spiritual inspiration, creativity, calm

Purple: Spirituality, awareness, higher self, power, third eye, psychic, hidden knowledge, inner self

Gray: Neutrality, respect, acceptance, change, endurance

Black: Banishing, removing negative influences, protection, binding, shape-shifting

White: All-purpose, the Goddess, higher self, protection, purification, summoning

Silver: Money, the moon, open hearts, possibilities

Gold: The sun, radiance, health, healing, success, higher self

A Simple Candle Blessing

White or yellow candle

Blessing oil (recipe follows)

Picture of and/or items from the person you want to bless

Dress candle with blessing oil and place it in an appropriate candle holder. Set the picture and items around the candle, making sure they are a safe distance from the flame. Light the candle. Take a cleansing breath and say something like this:

May you be blessed, dear (insert name)
May you walk in light
May your health be sound
May you have peace of mind
May you experience joy
Blessed be

Allow the candle to burn out on its own.

BLESSING OIL

2 ounces carrier oil (grapeseed, olive, or fractionated coconut oil)

4 drops rose oil

2 drops lavender oil

1 drop rosemary oil

Reading the Flames with the Salamander

What questions can be answered from within the flames? Can you see your future within the wisps of smoke? Using the power of the salamander, we can interpret what messages lie within the dying embers just as our ancestors did. Pyromancy is a scrying method using fire. Next time you're sitting in front of your fireplace or an outdoor fire pit, invoke the fire elemental, the salamander whose gifts include the psychic ability of "sight" to help you read the flames.

Invoke the salamander by looking to the flames and saying,

Salamander of the dancing flame
What is it that I have to gain
Reveal the answer for me to see
In the name of spark, ember, and flame, so mote it be

Then engage in one of these forms of pyromancy:

Scrying the Open Flame: You can add herbs, twigs, nuts, or leaves (laurel leaves are traditional) and ask your question. Then divine using your own interpretation of the images you see in the flames, or you can look at the color of the flames. Bright red flames can indicate courage, deep red corresponds to your desire, orange flames may indicate the incentive to keep trying, and yellow flames may correspond to a lightening of spirit.

Symbols within the Smoke: Smoke that rises straight up is a positive sign. Smoke that hangs low around your fire is unfavorable. If the smoke is touching the earth, a new direction should be taken.

Interpreting the Coals: Another way to practice pyromancy is to wait for the fire to die down and throw a handful of salt at the coals. Watch the patterns while allowing your eyes to unfocus naturally. What do you see? A windmill, indicating change for the better? How about a flower, which represents disappointment may be in your future? A house is said to indicate prosperity, while a horseshoe is a sign that good luck is in your future. Are you wondering if there is anything about an adventure in the plans for you? Look for a ship or a horse in the coals.

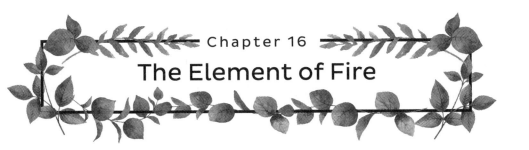

Chapter 16
The Element of Fire

Is that you dancing to the primordial rhythm of your soul, entranced by the fire that stirs sultry and willful within you? Your fire energy is that which ignites your desire and encourages the development of your personal power. It draws you, like a moth to the flame, toward growth and transformation. It is the power that feeds visionaries and thrill seekers. It is the pulse that throbs within the minds of creative thinkers and the spark of their inspiration. It's the fire within us that, when stirred, allows us to act courageously. It demands nothing more from you than complete determination to get through life's pitfalls.

Fire, unlike the other elements, is born through a chemical reaction requiring heat, air, and fuel. Just as fire can be a ravenous and destructive force in nature, too much fire energy may let you become compulsive and reckless. But when harnessed correctly, the power of fire can bring true spiritual evolution into your life.

The power of fire can be experienced when you light a candle and cast your spell. It is what feeds your intentions. When you step outside and face the sun, it is the energy that ignites within you and gives you the strength to conquer any obstacle that is holding you back. And it can be experienced in the bonfire where you leave your fear and self-doubt to be exhumed by the flames of purification.

Leo, Aries, and Sagittarius are all ruled by the element of fire. Natural-born leaders, their passion for life can be infectious. These people are your visionaries and your adventure seekers. Magically, these Witches take pride in their magic and it shows. They may be performing fire magic in a theatrical style.

And though they are not afraid to dabble with the dark side of the craft, they also excel in spells for love and passion.

Deities You May Like to Get to Know

Brighid: Daughter of the Dagda, she is a Celtic triple goddess who ruled over the hearth, poetry, and childbirth. Her holy temple was at Kildare, where nineteen virgins tended a perpetual flame. With the onset of Christianity, this beloved goddess was turned into a saint. Brighid has been used in magic for the hearth and home, clarity, creativity, transformation, and fertility.

Vesta: Roman goddess of the hearth, home, fire, and state, she had a temple at the Forum Romanum, where priestesses, known as the Vestal Virgins, kept her eternal flame lit. She has been called upon for legal matters, strength, hearth and home, healing, and change.

Frigg: This Norse goddess spun the clouds of fate upon a spinning wheel that represented female wisdom. She was the goddess of the hearth, home, childbirth, marriage, and destiny and was known as Bertha or Holda in Germany. Her sacred animal was the goose, and she later became the inspiration for Mother Goose. Frigg has been invoked in magic for parenting, wisdom, fate, hearth and home, and childbirth.

Lugh: This Celtic solar deity is associated with Lughnasadh (meaning the "assembly of Lugh" in Irish) for inaugurating the day as an assembly in memory of his foster mother, Tailtiu, who died from exhaustion while clearing forest land for planting. He was inventor of the arts, patron of commerce, and hero to the Tuatha Dé Danann for securing the secrets of ploughing and planting. Lugh has been called upon for legal matters, courage, strength, art, and athleticism.

Ra: This Egyptian sun god represented the power of the sun to his people, as he brought the sun with him while he traveled across the sky in his chariot. He was depicted sometimes as a falcon but always with a solar disc above his head. Eventually, pharaohs came to be seen as embodiments of this solar deity, gaining absolute power. Ra has been invoked for strength, passion, success, and energy.

Correspondences for the Element of Fire

Direction: South

Season: Summer

Hour: Noon

Day of the Week: Sunday

Magical Tools: Candle, censer, sword

Qualities: Hot, dry, light, active

Magical Associations: Lust, sex, action, will, energy, strength, protection, purification, banishing, courage

Gender: Masculine, projective

Archangel: Michael

Herbs, Flowers, and Trees: Alder, allspice, angelica, basil, bay, betony, cinnamon, clove, copal, cumin, dragon's blood, cactus, chili pepper, frankincense, ginger, hawthorn, lovage, mandrake, marigold, mullein, pine, nutmeg, rosemary, St. John's wort, sunflower, thistle, pineapple, tobacco, walnut, witch hazel, yucca

Stones: Amber, bloodstone, carnelian, coal, diamond, flint, red jasper, ruby, smoky quartz, sunstone, topaz

Color: Red, orange, gold, yellow

Elemental Being: Salamander

Tarot Suit: Wands

Metals: Brass, gold, steel

Runes: Thurisaz, Kenaz, Naudhiz, Sowilo, Ingwaz

Animals: Lizard, lion, tiger, horse

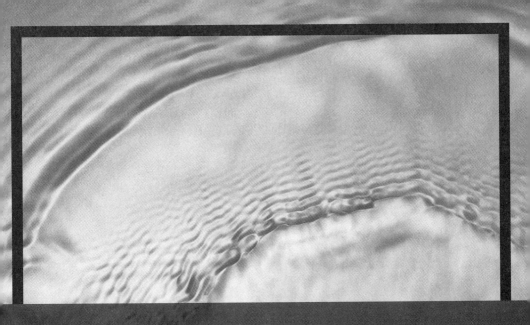

Part 4
OCEAN
w a t e r

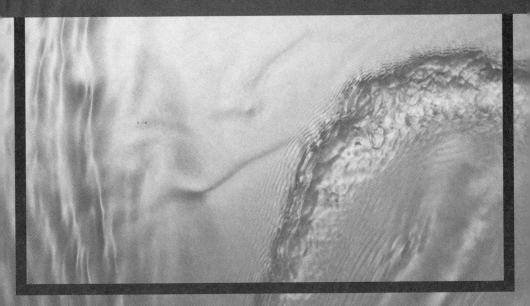

Chapter 17
Conjurings from the Sea

As you all know, I am a forest dweller. A child of dark, shadowy trees, dripping in moss and at home along the creek side, where elves mingle with the deer amongst the sword fern. And though I wouldn't trade our home in its enchanted forest setting, there are times when spring clouds boil and churn around the mountains that guard our tight valley that my family and I feel the tug of the ocean's tide. A siren's cry mingled with mountain song leads us on a one-and-a-half-hour car ride to the Salish Sea. As we drive out of the forest and into the open wide farmlands of the Skagit Valley, I always look back. The branches of large conifers are still swaying as if waving goodbye. *We understand*, they seem to say, *and we'll be here when you return.*

My husband, more than any of us, is drawn to the Salish Sea because he was raised near its rocky shores by fishermen who worked with and against the sea's fickle moods to scratch out a living. My children always like the change of scenery—for them it is an adventure. For only in such a place can they sift the sand for lost treasure and scout the horizon for sea serpents.

As I walk the windswept beach, a sweater pulled tight, I close my eyes and allow the sound of the Mother's churning waters fill my head: *Hush, girl.* The words roll in with every wave. *Let me teach you something of yourself.*

I hold out my arms to her and welcome her message of transformation. Tiny salt crystals gather at my lips and the wind stings my face. Unlike the green Goddess energy of shady forests with babbling streams and soft soil that smells of earth and gathers dark and moist beneath my nails, this energy is raw and beautiful and ever changing and abundant. Here the Goddess is powerful and holy and mysterious, and I am humbled in her presence.

Let There Be Water

Before there was breath, there was water. We all began in the womb where we are warm, nurtured, and in sync with our mother's gentle rhythms. We are born through water and we enter the world gasping, naked, and vulnerable. Some, like my husband, quickly find their way back to the water. Drawn to the sea's ever-shifting presence, they pursue hobbies or occupations that keep them in her mysterious hold throughout their lives. I chuckle at my husband's excitement as he excitedly prepares his boat for an adventure or researches new fish for one of his aquariums. He will drive an hour and a half to watch the sun set over the harbor in Anacortes, and he is always the last one in from the pool.

"You must have been merfolk in another life," I often tease.

"Merman," he always answers, mimicking a line from the movie *Zoolander*.

Others, like me, have to be coaxed back—her presence too demanding, her constant change unsettling. It took me twenty-six years to find my way back to the Mother's womb. I still remember my intake of air upon seeing the open ocean for the first time as her briny breath stung my face. She roared, and I stumbled back against an outcropping of rocks unable to process the flow of emotion.

"Are you okay?" my husband asked.

"Yes," I said. "Is it weird to feel terror and calm at the exact same moment?"

"Not if it's you." He chuckled.

Magical Bodies: Oceans

She is constantly shifting and changing, all at once terrifyingly wild and mysteriously alluring. Water covers 70 percent of the earth's surface, and 98 percent of that water is oceanic. And though we tend to think in terms of five separate oceans, there is actually only one world ocean that covers some 142 million square miles. It is the relation in which she is positioned around and between continental land masses that has given the ocean her five distinct forms:

The Arctic Ocean

The smallest of the five oceans, the Arctic Ocean is also the shallowest and home to one of the planet's most endangered animals, polar bears. Surrounding the north polar region, icy land masses that once dominated this quiet ocean realm are melting, which takes a toll on the creatures who call this crystalline world their home.

Magical Arctic: This is a land of peaceful assurance. Working with the energy of the Artic, we can tap into our empathetic selves. Let her icy waters open your heart to the needs of the vulnerable and be reassured that if we can all do our part, there will be healing.

The Atlantic Ocean

The youngest of the five ocean bodies, she is also the most diverse. Her energetic waters stretch from the eastern edge of the Americas to the coasts of Europe and Africa. Winter storms have been known to raise waves upward of thirty feet. If the Atlantic Ocean were drained, it would reveal the Mid-Atlantic Ridge, which is twice as wide as the Andes mountain range.

Magical Atlantic: Stand upon her rocky shore with your arms raised out and take in her passionate energy. Let her briny fervor instill you with freedom and rebellion. Connect with her when you need a good boost of vitality and motivation.

The Indian Ocean

The warmest ocean in the world, making it less conducive to marine life as compared to the other oceans, stretches from the western edges of Australia to the Indian subcontinent and across the coast of East Africa and was home to the world's earliest civilizations. Sadly, this stunningly beautiful ocean, known in Sanskrit as *Ratnakara,* meaning "creator of jewels," has been heavily mined. In fact, 40 percent of the world's offshore crude oil comes from the Indian Ocean.

Magical Indian: Let the warm breezes and shimmering light that catches on azure waves remind you that you are a sensual being. The energy from this exotic and beautiful ocean can ignite your inner goddess or god. Be empowered and know that you are beautiful just the way you are.

The Pacific Ocean

The oldest, largest, and deepest of the five oceans, the Pacific Ocean spreads from the western edge of the Americas to the eastern coast of Asia and Australia and includes all the Pacific Islands and New Zealand. Surrounded by 75 percent of the world's volcanoes and shifting tectonic plates, the Pacific Ocean basin is known as the Ring of Fire. This area has the highest occurrence of volcanic disturbances and earthquakes.

Magical Pacific: The veil (as in all liminal places) is very thin along her sandy shore. Her waters provide primordial wisdom. Look into her waves as they break around your feet. What inner truths does she reveal?

The Southern Ocean

Also known as the Antarctic Ocean, South Polar Ocean, or Austral Ocean, the Southern Ocean is made of water merging from the Atlantic, Pacific, and Indian oceans at the southern hemisphere surrounding Antarctica. This is the coldest of the five oceans and its crystalline waters contain many icebergs that can reach hundreds of feet in height. The Southern Ocean is home to over 100 million birds who nest on its rocky shores. It is also home to whales, penguins, seals, and the largest invertebrate in the world, the giant squid, which grows up to forty-nine feet long. The Southern Ocean has been deemed a whale sanctuary, though whaling does happen within the boundaries under the guise of "scientific research."

Magical Southern: Look out over the vastness of this ruggedly serene ocean landscape and take in the energy that expresses personal boundaries and respect. Work with the energy of the Southern Ocean for balance and karmic action.

Spell to Connect with the Spirit of the Ocean

On the Oregon Coast there is a small cottage with creaky floors and a stone fireplace that sits precariously atop Cape Foulweather, overlooking the wild churning sea. It was converted into a shop that provides tourists a menagerie of shell-created trinkets, Witches' balls, linens, and historical books to take home as a memento. We always stopped when my husband fished the Oregon Coast, not because their shell-encrusted ornamental boxes are better than another shop's, but for the aesthetic.

As I stepped inside, I wouldn't see the display cases filled with imported resin lighthouses or scallop shell tree ornaments—I saw lantern light and a crackling fire, polished wood floors, and baskets filled with yarn or medicinal plants. If I closed my eyes, I could imagine there were offerings from the sea: abalone for healing, clam shells for prosperity, and cowrie shells for fertility and divination. I could just make out the misty edges of the lady of the cottage humming as she looked out over the cape, untying knots along a rope to ensure the winds brought her lover home safely.

I knew that this cottage was actually built as a home and coffee shop (long before there was Starbucks) by entrepreneurs in the early part of the twentieth century, but I am a romantic at heart who wants to see the magic in the everyday—and at times wishes she could be whisked away to a lighthouse or cottage looking out across the ocean. A Sea Witch at heart, I suppose, who longs to stand as close to the waves as I dare on a stormy night, my hair lashing the sky and my arms stretched out as I yell my charms to the moon.

Here's a spell for all of you who seek the craft of the Sea Witch but don't live near the coast. This is a way to soulfully connect with the spirit of the ocean.

You will need:

Sea conjuror's bath salts (recipe follows)

Blue, green, or white candles

Shells, sea glass, and/or figures that represent the sea

Recording of ocean sounds

Bathtub (preferably) or a large pan or tub for soaking your feet

The night of the full moon is a wonderful night to perform this spell, but it can be done anytime you feel you need to connect to the spirit of the ocean.

Fill your bathtub (or footbath) with nice warm water. As the tub fills, place your candles, shells, sea glass, and/or figures around your tub in a way that is aesthetically appealing to you. Light the candles and start the recording of the sounds of the ocean. Dissolve a couple of tablespoons of the bath salts into the bathwater. When you are ready, get into your briny bath and enjoy the sensation of being enveloped by the sea. Call upon our Ocean Mother (out loud or silently to yourself):

The moon is high
And I call to you
Goddess of the sea
I will rise from your watery womb
Sea Witch, priestess, and ruler
Of my own destiny

As you relax, take in the scent of the bath salts, the comfort of the water, and the sounds of the sea. Imagine yourself beneath the waves (go ahead and dunk if you're comfortable). You are once again in the Mother's womb, warm and content. When you are ready, imagine yourself rising from the ocean (you can go ahead and rise from the tub if you wish). As you do this, know that you are a Sea Witch, intrinsically connected to the cauldron from where life emerged. You are wild and rebellious and ready to conjure storms!

Sea Conjuror's Bath Salts

3 parts Epsom salts

2 parts sea salt

1 part baking soda

1 part kelp powder

10–20 drops rosemary oil

5–10 drops eucalyptus oil

Moonstone

Put all ingredients in a bowl and use your fingers to mix. Place in an airtight container with the moonstone. Place in a window that faces the full moon and let charge overnight.

Beachcombing for Magical Tools

Because of their ties to the fishing industry, my husband's family has always lived on, or near, a body of water. Even after his parent's retirement, they couldn't pull themselves from the rolling surf, the call of seagulls, and the scent of creosoted pilings, so for the past decade they have lived in a little cabin just a short distance from the Pacific Ocean in a tiny town in southwestern Washington. Sadly, for us, it's a five-hour drive from our home tucked in the Cascade Mountain foothills to their seaside cottage, so the visits are few and far between. During my in-laws' first year in Tokeland, Chloe and I went to stay with them for a long weekend, and though we had taken her to the Oregon Coast several times as a wee Witchling, she had little memory of it and was excited to greet the open ocean with upstretched hands and a mermaid's heart.

"Mama!" Chloe cried, as she stood with her bare feet in the sand facing the majesty of our Ocean Mother. "It's so amazing! I think I want to cry or something!"

Unlike the bright and sandy beaches of California, the Washington coastline is rugged and wild. It's rubber boots and gray skies, slickers and windswept conifers. It's the kind of place you'd expect to find a wild-haired Witch attempting to turn the winds. And on that day, I felt as if I were that Witch, as I was excited to beachcomb for new magical treasures and maybe try out a spell or two.

"I said the same thing the first time I met her too!" I yelled back, trying madly to keep my long hair from thrashing my face. Chloe laughed at the sight of me.

The sky was turbulent; it moved with the pounding of the surf and rumbled to us threats of rain. We explored rocky outcrops and built sandcastles that cold October afternoon. We gathered shells and driftwood and seagrass that we later wove into Brighid's crosses. Even as the rain began to fall, and the wind stung our cheeks, we continued to play and explore in that liminal place, so beautiful and so unlike our forested landscape, until twilight seeped through stormy clouds and Chloe couldn't stop yawning.

After we ate dinner in the quiet home my in-laws kept, Chloe drifted off to sleep and I went back to the ocean with a bag of our collected shells, a candle, and a few small battery-operated lanterns I had brought along with us. I used driftwood to carve out a circle in the sand and placed a battery-operated lantern at each quarter. I laid out the shells I had collected to make a spiral in the middle of the circle and called to the elements, who answered my request with all the fervor of a storm. As I knelt and lit the single candle in the middle of my spiral, I called out to the Sea Mother, who spoke to me with lulling that was both raw and soothingly rhythmic.

Though I am a Witch who happens to be madly in love with trees and could never leave my enchanted wood, the purpose of my small ritual was simple: an introduction as one of her own. I released the elements and picked up my lanterns. The shells and the driftwood I left for the tide to take back to the sea.

I am only at the wild, open Pacific once every couple of years now, but I do visit the Sea Mother in her more passive form, the Salish Sea, coastal waterways that weave throughout the islands of the Puget Sound region, on a regular basis and work with the healing, quiet energy she provides.

The Earth Speaks in Symbols: Shell Magic

One of the first magical experiences I think most of us have as children is holding a seashell to our ear to hear the sound of the sea. I was probably four or five when my grandfather handed me a big conch shell he had picked up on a vacation and told me to listen. I remember standing open-mouthed as the shell whispered the mysteries of the sea in my ear; I was mesmerized. There is something about shells that still mesmerizes me, and though our Washington coast beaches aren't known for the most exotic shells, I get very excited when I find that perfect clam shell that is still hinged or an unbroken sand dollar.

These gifts found between land and sea and created by both earth and water have been sacred in many cultures for over fifty thousand years. Ancient societies used them as tools, currency, ornaments, and spiritual objects. Cowrie shells were so precious on the Fiji islands that they were forbidden to be worn by anyone other than a chieftain and were used as currency in many cultures. Due to its resemblance to female genitalia, it was also used in fertility magic.

The shell is associated with the Greek goddess Aphrodite and her Roman counterpart Venus, whose image was immortalized by Botticelli in his circa 1484 painting, *The Birth of Venus*, showing her being lifted from the sea on a scallop shell. Tyrian purple, or royal purple, was a dye that was first produced in the Phoenician city of Tyre during the Bronze Age by extracting the secretions of murex shellfish. Because of its difficulty in manufacturing, it was highly desirable, expensive, and sought after as a symbol of imperial authority and status throughout the Mediterranean.

Around the seventeenth century, wealthy European collectors prized the exotic shells that were brought back from trade expeditions from Australia and the Far East. Shell collecting is still popular to this day. The beauty, proportion, and symmetry of the seashell have also inspired numerous designs by many architects, furniture makers, and artists.

Shells are a reminder that the earth speaks to us in symbols, and they are a powerful tool for transformation. Natural objects such as shells are infused with spiritual energy that we can harness for our own use in spells and charms. Shells are associated with the element of water and with the moon, both having strong feminine energies that are receptive in nature, so use shells to draw things you desire into your life.

The following are some common shells and their correspondences:

Abalone: These shells are nicknamed sea ears or ear shells because of their flattened oval shape, and there are over a hundred species of abalone worldwide. Abalone are commonly used in jewelry and inlay because of their iridescent interiors. Commonly used as smudge bowls for cleansing negativity, they can also be used in magic for abundance, empowerment, and inner beauty.

Auger: With over three hundred species worldwide, augers are the lovely spired shells of predatory gastropods. These beautifully phallic shells can be used as wands or attached to decorative headdress. Use augers in magic for protection, fertility, courage, focus, and power.

Cerith: There are over a hundred species of these marine gastropods, whose shells, often referred to as horned shells, are banded and spired, which makes them great as adornment for magical tools or for focusing your magic. Also use ceriths in magic for protection and fertility.

Clam: Clam is a common name for a wide range of species of two-shelled mollusks which can be circular, oval, or triangular and their colors may range from white to shades of brown. Use clams in magic for love, friendship, purification, grounding, and communication.

Cockle: Over two hundred species of this edible bivalve of the Cardiidae family can be found the world over. Sometimes called heart clams because they resemble a heart when on their side, cockles have been used as currency, as food, and for ornamentation as far back as 3000 BCE. Use them in magic for love, friendship, rebirth, and grounding.

Conch: Of the many species identified as conch, the group known as "true conchs" refers to gastropod mollusks in the Strombidae family. Conch shells are large with a spiraling shape. By taking the tip off the shell and blowing, conchs have been used as instruments to call spirits or to open the heavens in ritual. Use them in magic for strength, wisdom, freedom, communication, and clearing energy.

Cone: Cone shells come from a large group of venomous and predatory sea snails that range in size and reside in tropical ocean waters. Because the sting of the larger cone snails can be fatal to humans, you should never handle one that is alive. Their shells are shaped like a geometric cone and boast beautiful color and intricate patterns. Use these shells in magic for protection, transformation, and courage.

Cowrie: With over two hundred species worldwide, cowrie shells have appeared as currency and been used as ornamentation and in ritual by a wide range of cultures. With a rounded belly-like side and a flat side with a serrated opening, cowry shells have represented both the vulva and the pregnant belly and can be used in spells for abundance, fertility, and women's mysteries. Also use them for divination and spells for growth, prosperity, and grounding.

Helmet: Helmet shells come from medium- to large-size sea snails of the Cassidae family and are sometimes mistaken for conch shells. They are heavy and rounded with short spires and wide whorls, and several of the larger species resemble the human heart. Use them in spells for protection, affairs of the heart, grounding, and strength.

Jingle Shells: Also known as mermaid's toenail or saddle oysters, jingles are part of the Anomiidae family, related to oysters. The shells are thin, often take shape of the object they lie on, and may be white to gold in color. Jingle shells got their name because of the bell-like sound they created when shaken together. Use these shells in magic for transformation and prosperity.

Limpet: With slightly conical, oval, or irregularly shaped shells, limpets are aquatic snails that eat algae from rocks and other hard surfaces. They attach themselves to hard surfaces by using mucus and a muscular foot. Use in magic for strength, confidence, and courage.

Moon Shell: With snail-like globular shaped shells that have a tightly coiled spiral, these members of the Naticidea family are predatory sea snails that range widely in size. Use moon shells in lunar magic, for psychic awareness, and in spells for harmony, peace, rebirth and protection.

Mussel: Found attached to rocks and piers or in muddy or sandy shallow water in both salt and fresh water, these bivalve mollusks of several families share the common name of mussel. About seventeen species of mussels are edible, the most common being the blue mussel (*Mytilus edulis*). They are pear-shaped and range in color from blue to blue-black to brown. Use mussel shells in magic for stability, inner strength, and community building.

Nautilus: Often called a living fossil, the nautilus is the only cephalopod that produces a shell. Its shell is an example of mathematical exactness in nature and is often associated with the golden ratio. The shell is creamy white with brown markings with an interior of pearly iridescent and separate chambers that are created as the animal grows. Use nautilus shells in spells for balance, growth, wisdom, ancestors, cycles of life, and harmony.

Olives: Olive shells come from medium- to large-size predatory sea snails in the family of Olividae. The oblong shells with muted coloring are popularly used in jewelry making and for decoration. Use them in magic for beauty, reflection, friendship and abundance.

Oyster: Oyster is a common name for saltwater bivalve mollusks from varying families. Oysters will attach to hard surfaces in intertidal zones that are often referred to as oyster reefs or beds. Pearls are produced as a means of protecting the mollusk from an irritant, such as a grain of sand. Oysters have an irregular, rounded shape in varying colors. Use their shells in magic for transformation, community building, fertility, lunar magic, beauty, and love.

Sand Dollar: This is not a shell but a type of sea urchin. Sand dollars are very common on the beaches near me and to find one whole is a treasure. Sand dollars are round and flat, and their colors vary between white, gray, and tan. The five-petaled shape that is etched onto both the common sand dollar (*Echinarachnius parma*) and the keyhole urchin (*Mellita quinquiesperforata*) are reminiscent of the pentagram and make a nice edition to your altar. Use sand dollars in magic for prosperity, balance, wisdom, hidden secrets, and transformation.

Scallop: With more than four hundred species of this member of the Pectinidae family found worldwide, it has been used to symbolize fertility and divinity throughout many cultures. The shell, with its beautiful fanned shape and varying colors, is said to resemble the setting sun. Use scallops in magic for fertility, the divine feminine, strength, rebirth, travel, lunar magic, and beauty.

Sundial: This unique snail of the Architectonicidae family gets its name from its circular shell that is flattened on one side with whorls leading to a spired top. Use in magic for strength, vitality, hope, cycles, and encouragement.

Tulip Shell: The tulip shell and spindle shell are the common names for the shells of two or three species of large predatory sea snails of the Fasciolariidae family. They get their common names from their similarities to closed tulips or a yarn spindle. Ranging from white to multicolored, their shells have large bodies that whorl to a high spire. Use in magic for fate, new beginnings, change, and karma.

Whelk: Whelk is a common name for over fifty species of predatory marine mollusks with a heavy, pointed spiral shell that can be found in temperate, boreal, and tropical seas. Whelks have been used for consumption, in dye making, and as currency. The lightning whelk (*Sinistrofulgur perversum*) is one of the very few shells that coil to the left. Use in magic for wisdom, creativity, stability, and change.

Charging Seashells

Not all of us have access to ocean beaches to pick up seashells for our magical workings. I have several nice shells that I use that came from my husband's family, and the rest of my magical shells are ones that I collected myself. If you are looking for seashells to use in Sea Witchery, I suggest you do a little research before you make your purchase.

Most mollusks that are harvested for the souvenir trade still have living animals inside of them and are left out to dry up before being immersed in vats of oil and acid for cleaning. Some mollusks are harvested for their meat and their decorative shells, while others, like the nautilus, are harvested for only their decorative purposes. According to a 2018 *National Geographic* article, one plant in India processes from thirty to a hundred tons of shells per month, including species that are listed under India's Wildlife Protection Act.[14]

This doesn't paint a very enchanting picture, so before you are tempted to pick up that beautiful conch at the gift shop, ask the shopkeeper or cashier where their shells came from and how they were harvested. If they don't know (or if they do and it's clearly unethical), don't purchase them.

If you have seashells that have been passed down to you or were picked up at a garage sale or thrift shop, or are ones that you collected yourself that need to be recharged, here's a simple way to do that:

Place your seashells or sea glass in a large container filled with water that has a little sea salt added and let them sit in the moonlight for a couple of hours. That's it!

Jingle All the Way to the Bank Prosperity Charm Bag

Many cultures used shells as currency. Cowry shells were the most widely used worldwide, but other shells, such as whelk, tusk and olive shells, were also used. This makes shells great for prosperity spells. We are going to be using jingle shells for this spell because the little bell-like sound they make when shaken will help keep your intention fresh in your mind, but any shell will do.

You will need:

A few jingle shells (or shells of your choice)

1 bay leaf

1 coin

Green draw-string bag

Patchouli oil

---

14. Tina Deines, "Seashell Souvenirs Are Killing Protected Wildlife," *National Geographic,* July 16, 2018, https://www.nationalgeographic.com/animals/2018/07/wildlife-watch-seashells-illegal-trade-handicrafts/.

Put the shells, bay leaf, and coin in the draw string bag and anoint the bag with a drop of patchouli oil. Now shake the bag, and as the shells jingle, imagine that sound as your money increasing. Place your charm bag somewhere that you will see it, and every once in a while, give it a good shake.

Correspondences and Uses for Other Sea Treasures

Driftwood: Use driftwood to create enchantingly beautiful wands to work your ocean magic. Collect it and use it in spell crafting. Use it to create balefires for sabbat celebrations on the beach.

Sand: To reduce rock to sand is a process that takes ages of turbulence and weathering. Sand carries with it the energies of the cycles of the seasons and the tides. It reminds us of the shift and flow that occurs throughout our lives. It imbues ancestral wisdom. Use a bowl of sand as a representation of earth on your altar. If you are casting spells on a beach, mark out your circle, runes, magical symbols pentacles, and so on in the sand. As the tide becomes higher, draw a symbol of something you would like to banish and watch as the sea washes it away. Use sand in magic for wisdom, ancestral knowledge, and transformation. Here are some correspondences for different sand textures:

Fine: Creativity, psychic awareness, prosperity

Medium: Purification, cleansing, love

Coarse: Protection, healing, banishing

Seaweed: A marine algae that has been used as food, medicine, agricultural fertilizer, and filtration for thousands of years. Use seaweed to create symbols during a seaside ritual or use in knot magic. Here are a few common seaweeds and their correspondences for spell crafting:

Carrageen Moss (Irish Moss): Psychic awareness, clarity, and cycles of life

Coralline: Joy, new beginnings, and success

Dulse: Love Magic

Japanese Wireweed: Banishing and binding

Kelp: Prosperity and balance

Mermaid's Tresses: Clarity, balance, and inner knowledge

Sea Lettuce: Peace, calm, and happiness

Rope: Every once in a while, pieces of rope, cord, or netting that have escaped from a boat or a piling wash up on the beach, and they work wonderfully for knot magic. In sea magic, it is the knots that hold the wind and stir up storms. It is said that if a Witch wanted to protect a certain boat, she would use a rope from it and bind her intention within each knot she tied. Traditionally, she would tie in the power of the winds, releasing them as she felt necessary.

Knot Magic for "Smooth Sailing"

Metaphorically, we all want smooth sailing as we move through our lives. Use knot magic to help you get through the little storms that stir us up from time to time.

You will need:

3-foot piece of rope, twine, or string

For this spell, we will be tying knots into a length of rope and untying them to release our intentions. On the night of a full moon sit quietly somewhere that you are comfortable and take the rope in your hands. Think about all the little things you need to release from your life that will make your life feel easier. Maybe you're having problems with organization, maybe it's bad eating habits, maybe you have a hard time saying no, and now you're stressed out. Whatever it is you would like to banish, work it all up as you rub your hands together.

Now that all that negative energy is in your hands, tie your knots, focusing on one problem area for each knot you tie. Get angry as you do this and say with each knot,

Knot of (fill in blank), has no hold on me

When you are done tying your knots, say,

So mote it be

Hang your rope somewhere you will not see it until the dark of the moon. On the dark of the moon, take the knotted rope and as you sit comfortably, set it in front of you. Now begin to rub your hands together, focusing on your own personal power. When you have built up enough energy, use that power to untie the knots. As you do this say,

Knot of (fill in the blank), I banish you from me

When you are done untying your knots, say,

So mote it be

Mermaid's Tears: The Magic of Sea Glass

I first started my meager collection of sea glass as a young teen when, on a family outing to West Beach along the Salish Sea, I had inadvertently come upon a green gem. I picked it up and admired it in the sunlight.

"Looks like you found yourself a mermaid's tear," said a beautiful older woman with long gray hair that lashed at the air.

I smiled. "It's so pretty," I said. "Why are they called that?"

"Well," she said, "did you know that when a mermaid falls in love with a sailor, she swims alongside his ship in order to protect him?"

"No," I answered and shrugged.

"It's true," she said. "Mermaids become very attached to the men they love." She looked out at the rolling surf. I remember a longing in her eyes that made me think that maybe she was herself a mermaid who had somehow been cursed with legs, unable to swim near the ship of the sailor that she once loved. "But you see, my dear," she continued, "the mermaid's love of another made Neptune very angry. For he was a jealous god, who insisted that he could be the only one to whom the mermaids showed their affection."

"So what'd he do?" I asked.

"He banished the poor mermaids to the bottom of the sea." She reached for my treasure. "May I?"

"Sure," I said, and handed her the sea glass.

She rolled it around in her palm, then said, "The poor mermaid, banished and with a broken heart, would cry. Her tears would crystallize and wash ashore as these." She handed my treasure back to me. "Enjoy your sea glass," she said and winked before walking away.

Of course, in actuality, sea glass is a product of human pollution, mostly glass containers and tableware that have accumulated in our oceans as part of refuse dumps or shipwrecks. The broken pieces are washed and tumbled by the churning seas, a process that takes decades, before washing up onto the shore transformed into beautiful rounded, frosted gems.

Serious collectors grade sea glass according to its size and shape, color, pitting, frosted appearance, and flaws (such as chips). Jewelry-grade sea glass will be thick with rounded edges and have more pitting and a more frosted appearance than craft-grade sea glass, which is typically thinner, less frosted and may have sharper edges. Craft-grade sea glass can be used to create mosaics, stained glass, and other decorative pieces. Most beachcombers collect pieces for the sheer enjoyment, displaying them in glass jars or bowls. I collect them not only for the beauty and stories held with each frosted gem but also for spellwork. Sea glass obviously represents the element of water but can also be a representation of fire.

I find it amazing and truly beautiful that the Sea Mother has taken into her womb the trash of humankind and tumbled it into enchanting treasures. Some ways you may want to use sea glass in your Craft include in color magic, in charm bags, engraved as rune stones, in mermaid magic, as decoration for your magical tools or jewelry, and for dream catchers. I have found a couple of pieces that had a hole all the way through them, and I used them as I would a hagstone. Sea glass can be used in spells for transformation and (especially with the rarer colors) luck. Also use it in magic for strength, inner beauty, environmental issues, mermaid magic, and for sorrow.

Here is a list from the most common to some of the rarest color finds along with their color correspondences for spellwork:

White: Most sea glass found today will come from broken or discarded clear glass—anything from a soda bottle tossed overboard a ship, to the old warbled glass windows of a lighthouse keeper's cottage, long taken by the sea. White sea glass is an all-purpose magical piece that can be used in magic for the divine feminine, mysticism, higher self, and invoking the Sea Mother.

Brown: If you find a piece of brown sea glass, it may have been the remnant of a beer bottle left behind from a beach party, or maybe an early twentieth-century Lysol bottle or Clorox bleach jug. Use it in spells for grounding, earth, introspection, health, strength, focus, and security.

Kelly Green: This is a common color for wine bottles and some beer bottles. If you're lucky, though, you may find a piece with bubbles or an embossed texture that could indicate it came from a pharmacy bottle dating from the nineteenth and early twentieth centuries. Use Kelly green glass in magic for prosperity, luck, creativity, courage, success, hope, fertility, earth, harmony, and rebirth.

Seafoam Green: If you find a piece that is this beautiful shade of light green, it more likely than not started out as a mid-twentieth-century Coca-Cola bottle. Or it may have started out as a wine bottle set adrift accidently by lovers on a romantic midnight sail. If bubbles are present, it could be something much older. Use seafoam green glass in magic for ancestors, calming, ocean magic, lunar, divination, and psychic awareness.

Cobalt Blue: Approximately one in every 250 pieces are this rich shade of blue. A common color for pharmaceutical containers, this jewel-like blue stone may have started as a holder for medicine, poison, Vicks VapoRub, milk of magnesia, or even perfume. Use in magic for leadership, growth, intellect, peace, truth, happiness, travel, environmental (ocean) spellwork, and calming.

Lime Green: Lime green pieces may have started out as beer or lemon-lime soda bottles or perhaps as decorative glass pieces that had ended up on a garbage barge. Use it in spells for new endeavors or opportunities, vitality, clarity, and enthusiasm.

Lavender: Lavender glass is easy to date because it was produced with manganese, used to neutralize the natural green tint of raw glass in America until just after WWI. The lovely color is the result of sun exposure. Most common lavender glass began life as a pre-WWI canning jar. Use it in spells for tranquility, mermaid magic, clairvoyance, calm, psychic powers, spirituality, lunar magic, and inner beauty.

Pink: These pretty finds were most likely a part of Depression-era glass collections. This affordable glassware was often given as gifts with purchases at gas stations and movie theaters or as incentive pieces by cereal and laundry companies in the 1930s. Use pink sea glass in magic for harmony, peace, friendship, romance and femininity, loving vibes, sexuality, and compassion.

Yellow: Another rare and lovely find that may have originated from Depression-era glass or old glass insulators made with selenium. Use this in spells for vitality, healing, friendship, clarity, happiness, creativity, and wisdom.

Gray: If you find a piece of gray sea glass, you most likely have found a treasure whose previous life was a television screen, leaded glass tableware, or Depression-era glass. Use it in magic for neutrality, invisibility, lunar magic, and psychic awareness.

Black: At first glance, you might mistake a piece of black sea glass for just another beach pebble. But hold it up to the sun—see that deep green translucent glow? Black sea glass originated as very dark olive-green bottles or jugs that were widely used in the mid-nineteenth-century for housing ale or beer. Use in magic for banishing, protection, divination, karma, establishing boundaries, absorbing, creation, rebirth, and invisibility.

Red: This lovely rarity (about one in every ten thousand pieces) could have started its life as a 1950s Schlitz Beer bottle or as decorative ruby glass collected lovingly by a lighthouse keeper. Use in magic for strength, lust, sex, health, ambition, and courage.

Teal: These rare beauties are usually from older sources. If you're lucky enough to find a teal (or turquoise) piece of sea glass, it may have come from a canning jar that once lined the pantry of a cottage near the shore. It could have been an insulator from an early twentieth-century electric pole or an old seltzer bottle. Use in spells for inner strength, healing, and protection.

Orange: If you find one of these elusive treasures, it could have originated from a modern automobile's warning light or a vintage decorative glassware or art glass piece. Orange is believed to be one of hardest and rarest to acquire because it wasn't a very popular color for mass production. Use orange sea glass in spells for happiness, confidence, alertness, strength, breaking barriers, and enthusiasm.

Sea Glass Spell for Sorrow

There are times in everyone's life when we must face sorrow. And though no one wants to feel sad, it is an emotional response that heralds the healing process—and healing is the seed of growth. Though this spell is not a quick fix, it can help ease your sorrow and promote calm and healing.

You will need:

Mostly clear glass dish

Water

Several pieces of lavender or seafoam green sea glass (white works too)

This is a very simple spell that uses symbolism and color to promote calm and ease sorrow. As you do this spell, I suggest you play calming music or sounds of the sea and light a few candles. First, you need to fill a glass dish about two-thirds full of water. Place it in front of you somewhere you can sit comfortably. The water represents our Sea Mother's womb, that place where we feel contentment and calm and the cauldron where transformation begins. The sea glass represents our tears of sorrow; their colors represent calm and healing.

Take each teardrop (sea glass) and hold it. Rub it around in the palm of your hand and imagine its healing vibe from decades of our Sea Mother's transformative power releasing itself into you. Look at the tear, and as you do this, do not think about what "could have been." Do not ask, "Why me?" This is about accepting what has occurred, letting go of pain, and encouraging the healing process to begin.

Now drop the sea glass pieces, one at a time, into the water, and as you do so, focus on the release of emotion as you give your sorrows back to the Sea Mother to transform and reshape your sorrow into healing.

Drop one piece of sea glass for each spoken line:

Goddess Mother, I release to you my sorrow
Take from me my despair
My hurt
My anger
My pain
(Etc.) ...

Continue until you have run out of sea glass. When you have finished dropping all your pieces into the water, focus on the healing. Imagine the water washing away your sorrow.

When you are done, thank the Mother Goddess in your own way. Leave the sea glass in the water for a full moon cycle, then gently poor the water onto the earth.

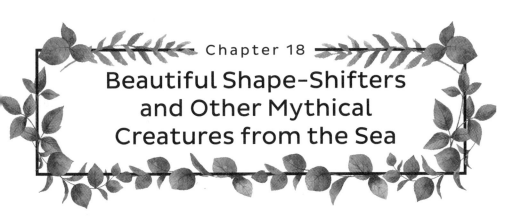

Chapter 18

Beautiful Shape–Shifters and Other Mythical Creatures from the Sea

"You are different and that's okay," I said to my twelve-year-old daughter, who sat before me with swollen eyes and tear-streaked cheeks.

It was early September, and the sun peeked between giant maple trees, creating lacy shadows that wove across my yard. "Why can't the kids accept me for who I am?" Her voice trembled as she spoke.

Because those kids are asinine and ignorant little … ran through my head before I paused and took a deep, cleansing breath. I didn't want to come across as small-minded to my daughter, whose only sin was that she was acting … well, like a twelve-year-old girl. "Because they're just as confused by you as you are by them," I said. "And that girl who made fun of you for using your dragon mark on your paper was testing you. It's like she drew her sword to see if the dragon bites."

"Well, I didn't bite. I ran to the bathroom and cried, Mama." I pulled my daughter close to me as she began to sob.

We primarily homeschooled our children, but there were times that, either by their own choice or due to financial circumstances, they were put into the public school system. This was my daughter's choice. She wanted to experience junior high, and I wanted my children to have a say in their education.

Chloe was by no means immature for her age. She was (and still is) highly organized and self-motivated. By the age of twelve, she was already experienced at goat husbandry and made a pretty good income from the sales of her Nigerian Dwarf goats. Our family was a squeamish lot, so Chloe was the one we went to for medical needs that can occur on a small farm. She administered all the shots and took care of the worming. When one of our goats tore her udder open on a sharp branch, I almost passed out. It was Chloe who lovingly cleaned the wound, sprayed it with antibacterial spray, and monitored it carefully throughout the healing process. It was Chloe who was up all night with birthing does and who, on more than one occasion, I would find up to her elbows in amniotic fluid because she had to turn a breached kid.

On the other hand, my daughter was raised in a family of magical practitioners, and the use of sigils (magical symbols) was as commonplace to her as peanut butter on bread. The "dragon mark" that she was made fun of for was her sigil for courage that she had been using since she was six. It didn't occur to her that others didn't use them or that they would think of her as a silly child for doing so. "Let's see you fly, Dragon Girl," she would hear as she walked between classes.

As November approached, Chloe and I walked down a trail that weaved through ghostly alder trees and black cottonwood. A few leaves clung to their branches, refusing to acknowledge the cool breath of the approaching winter.

"I've decided that I am a shape-shifter, Mom," she announced.

"Like a werewolf?" I asked and nudged her with my elbow. I thought this was a game.

"No." She snapped the tip off a broken branch and nervously played with it. "Kinda like a selkie," she said.

I was beginning to understand. "You mean at school?"

"Is that wrong?"

The first thing I wanted to say was *Yes! Never disguise who you are to fit in,* but I didn't. I thought of the many times I had transformed myself in order to appease someone or to ease a situation. "No, I get it." I said. "It's hard enough to fit into this world and it makes sense that you would want to be like the others." I grabbed her hand. "It's a small school."

"No, Mama," she said. "You don't get it."

"What do you mean?"

She stopped and pulled at a couple of decaying maple leaves that were caught up in the shrubby branches of a salmonberry bush. "I shape-shift into a dragon when I go to school. Watch." She put her hands together as if in prayer and lifted them until her forearms and elbows touched. She closed her eyes and took a breath, then pulled her arms quickly apart. "There. If you use your imagination, you can see my scales and my beautiful wings."

I smiled. "Yes, I can."

She repeated the action to metaphorically shift back into my Chloe. "It helps me to feel braver around the kids who call me Dragon Girl. I didn't want you to be mad."

"Why would I be mad?"

She shrugged and gave me a crooked smile. "I don't know."

We walked in silence for a while. The leaves crunched, releasing an earthy scent that reminded me of my own childhood tromping through the deciduous forest along the river's edge communing with nature spirits. "Dragon Girl, huh," I finally said. "That's kind of a cool name."

"Yeah, I actually like it. But I don't tell them that."

"Good plan."

That was over six years ago. And my daughter still uses the same dragon sigil she came up with when she was just a little girl. In fact, as I write this, she is getting it tattooed on her arm as a permanent reminder that she is a shape-shifter. A strong woman who has the power to transform into a dragon when times get tough.

Spread your wings, Dragon Girl, and fly!

Here Be Dragons: A Charm Bag for Courage

Early people grouped along the ocean's coastlines and tributaries, as water provided sustenance, a way to irrigate crops, and drinking water. Waterways provided a means of travel long before roads were cut through primeval forests and carved out of mountains. When early cartographers charted maps, they drew dragons or other mythological beasts in areas that were unexplored. What areas have been left unexplored in your life? Those little insecurities, habits, or things set aside because we just don't want to deal with them?

Being courageous in your abilities, actions, and thinking will help uncage the power that is hidden within you.

You will need:

Red drawstring bag

Paper

Red marker

Bloodstone

Dragon's blood

Dragon charm

You will need to create your own symbol for courage and activate it in a way that holds power for you. For example, after creating your dragon symbol, you could activate it by holding your hands over it and repeating the word *courage* three times, followed by *so mote it be*.

On a piece of paper, write a list of things that you have not wanted to deal with, be they finances, toxic friends or family members, dealings at work, and so on. Take the red marker and draw your symbol of power over the completed list. As you draw it, imagine yourself metaphorically shape-shifting into the powerful dragon spirit that resides within you. Place all ingredients in your drawstring bag and activate your charm bag with these words:

With courage and control, I take a stand
Authority of the dragon is within my hand
Imbued with the power of three times three
Let the magic hold—so mote it be

Sea Tales: Romance and Folklore from the Sea

It is beside my woodstove, where the heat radiates dry and comforting, that I curl up in an oversized armchair with a mug of tea. My black Labrador retriever sits at my feet with sad, watery eyes and sighs every once in a while to remind me that it's unfair that I should make her sit on the floor instead of on my lap. Outside, the rain hits the roof in a pounding rhythm that seems to beat in time with cold northerly gusts that tear through the trees and topple garden statuary (much to my chagrin). These are the nights that I lose myself in worn books whose romantic tragedies tell of mythical lovers who are both predator and prey—they are the seekers of the lonely and heartbroken that on stormy nights seem the perfect touch of melancholy for my romantic soul.

The stories can be heart-wrenching in their telling. So many times the rules of magic, meant to bind two lovers, are broken—sometimes out of betrayal and sometimes for love's sake. The creatures that enchant these tales are something between a god and a mere mortal. Some are gentle souls who want nothing more than to dance in the moonlight and are somehow tricked into a desperate situation, while others are the tricksters who find humor in toying with human sensibilities. What they all have in common is the sea.

Stories of selkies and merfolk, of sea dragons and of water faeries, reflect the human imagination and attempt to explain the unknown. Maybe it is because the nature of the ocean is so unpredictable that many mythological sea creatures were portrayed as volatile and sometimes deadly. Sea serpents, sea monsters, and dragons of all kinds can be found in myths from all around the world. Their appearance usually foretold an impending doom or was used to illustrate chaos. Chinese mythology was the exception, wherein dragons represented good fortune or generosity.

Though most mythical sea creatures may be considered malevolent, the sweet, mournful gazes of seals and sea lions may have inspired the legends of the shy shape-shifters, known as selkies or seal-faeries (or roane in Ireland), who can shed their seal skins and come to shore in a human form. And though they may marry and even have children, the ocean's song can prove too strong a draw, resulting in their inevitable return to their watery home.

Mermaids

The quintessential mythical sea creature, the mermaid, is usually thought of as seated on a rock, combing out her hair with a fishbone, which symbolized power over storms. In some tales this lovely creature would guide sailors to safe harbor, but she could also be seen as a sirenesque being that was more than happy to drag men into the inky-black depths of the sea.

The earliest mermaid figure may have been the Syrian fertility goddess Atargatis, whose temple was adorned with a pool of sacred fish. Atargatis loved a shepherd but accidentally killed him. She was so full of sorrow and guilt that she jumped into a lake and transformed into a fish. The waters could not conceal her divine beauty, so she remained in a human form from the waist up.

With the upper body of a woman and the lower body of a fish, these lovely creatures appear in folklore and mythology from cultures worldwide. Mermaids could appear as friend or foe and were commonly seen holding a fishbone comb or a mirror. Mermaids have been called upon in magic for sexuality, fertility, freedom, mirror magic, vitality, lunar magic, liminal magic, and play-fulness.

The following deities are associated with mermaids:

Jūratė: Jūratė is a Lithuanian sea goddess/mermaid and consort of Perkunas, god of thunder.

Sirena: From Guam folklore, Sirena is a mermaid who could only be caught with a net of human hair.

Yemanja: A Mother Goddess who is considered queen of the ocean and mother of all, this goddess has African origins but was brought to the New World with the African diaspora. In Santería and Haitian Voudou, she is considered the mother of all living things and owner of the water. She is the spirit of motherhood and protector of children. She is sometimes depicted as a mer-maid and given offerings that include combs, shells, flowers, watches, and mirrors. In some legends, it is said that she will take followers down to her underwater realm, to return imbued with spiritual wisdom.

Nā-maka-o-Kahaʻi: Hawaiian goddess of the sea who fought with her sister, Pele, who had seduced her husband. Their battle continues to this day as Pele spews fire from her mountain and it rushes down to meet the sea.

Mama Cocha: Incan sea Mother Goddess who ruled over fishing and provided nourishment for her people.

Spirits of the Sea

In British folklore, mermaids were considered unlucky omens and were some-times depicted as speaking to doomed ships. Other tales tell of mermaids who treated humans with favor, as in a folktale from the Isle of Man where it is said a fisherman once carried a stranded mermaid back to the sea and was re-warded with the location of a wonderous treasure.

Interestingly, mermen predated their feminine counterparts. The Mesopo-tamian sea god Ea, who had the upper body of a human and the lower body of a fish, is one of the earliest representations of a half-human, half-fish being. He was associated with wisdom, arts and crafts, divination, and exorcism, and as told in the *Epic of Gilgamesh*, he was responsible for the saving of humanity from a devasting flood sent by the supreme god, Enlil, who was tired of humans' never-ending noise. Ea foresaw his plan and quickly instructed a sage to build an ark so humanity could escape destruction.

Unlike their female equivalents, mermen were typically described as monstrous with seaweed hair and green skin and teeth. Mermen could be responsible for violent storms and for the sinking of ships. In Cornish folklore, offerings to vengeful sea spirits were left on beaches by fishermen. In Finland, the merman known as *vetehinen* could cure sickness or lift curses—but one had to be careful, because if one of these water spirits became too curious, he may cause unintentional harm.

In general, water spirits, faeries, and other creatures from the deep epitomized the mysteries of the ocean realm. So if you are one of those watery souls who feels they must answer the call of this seductively mysterious element—or maybe you feel a connection with the merfolk or suspect you share lineage with a selkie—the water spirits listed below may help you in your magical practice. But as with any natural spirit, never demand their assistance and always treat them with respect.

Lake Faeries in Folklore

Imagine yourself as you walk along a gentle lakeside. Out of the corner of your eye, you glimpse movement—a trick of the sunlight, perhaps, or is it more? A breeze picks up, scented of the trees that stir in its wake, and draws you to the lake's silky shoreline. You hear a splash and you feel a quickening in your chest. Another splash and you turn. There she is, smiling, beguiling you, and motioning you to come near. She is the Lady of the Lake, and some say to see her brings misfortune, while in other tales she has been taken as a faerie bride.

In Wales, near the edge of Llyn y Fan Fach, the faerie woman of the lake captured the heart of a young man, whom she agreed to marry, warning him that if she were ever to receive three blows from her husband, she would return to her kingdom along with her cattle dowry. The couple was happy and prospered on their farm, and together they had three beautiful children.

A playful swishing of a glove too near her shoulder provided the first blow, after which she warned him to be more careful. The second blow came at a wedding, when he tapped her on the shoulder to ask why she wept so for the couple. She told how she wept for their troubles that lie ahead, then warned, "And for you, unless you take care, for you have offered a second blow."

Years passed, and the couple continued to live in comfort and joy. Their children grew to be happy, contented adults. The husband almost forgot how one accidental blow could destroy his happiness. But, when attending a funeral together, his faerie wife filled the somber room with a burst of laughter. Embarrassed, he nudged his wife and said, "Hush." To this she answered, "The last blow has been struck and the marriage contract is broken." She returned to the lake with her cattle and other stock and disappeared beneath the water.

The most famous Lady of the Lake is from the Arthurian legends. She is the mysterious faerie queen who inhabits the lake surrounding Avalon. Her elegant hand raises above the water to give Arthur his sword, Excalibur. Upon Arthur's death, she, along with three other faerie queens, takes Arthur by boat back to Avalon. She has also been connected to the faerie woman who was Lancelot's foster mother and to Viviane, the enchantress who refused Merlin her love until he revealed to her all his secrets. She is a strong archetype who, as a sword bearer, is a great symbol for feminine power.

Rediscovering Self-Love with the Lady of the Lake

What is it that you see when you look into that mirror? If you ask me, I would probably say, "What mirror?" because I usually avoid them at all costs. Appreciating my own beauty has been tough. As a child I was taunted for being thin. Already socially awkward, it didn't help me make social connections when being called *bones* or *scarecrow* by the children on the playground as the dodgeball was being thrown at my head. High school wasn't any better. I have a very vivid memory of myself coming off of the track field and being stopped by a young man who said, "You know, you have a pretty face. You'd be hot if you gained a little weight."

But the comment that has truly haunted me for the majority of my adult life was one made by my own mother, the very person I trusted to be my advocate and to protect me when words were used as weapons against me. When I was fifteen, we had driven over the North Cascades Highway to camp on the banks of the third deepest lake in the United States. But before Lake Chelan was a summer destination place for wine tastings and weddings, it offered quiet camping areas with a few family-orientated amusement facilities near town.

We always went to the water slide park, where we awkwardly donned new swimming suits and splashed about in the wake of too many other tourists.

I remember standing in line for one of the taller slides. I was wearing a two-piece swimming suit that was a little baggy in the breasts, while riding slightly in the seat. I uncomfortably shifted the material while looking over the sea of women whose larger breasts bulged from their cups and whose torsos were much shorter and curvier than my own. Suddenly there was a breath in my ear that startled me, and I turned. It was my mother.

"You know..." It seemed as if she hissed in my ear. "You strut around in that suit like you're something, when there are a hundred more girls who fill that out better than you." She pulled at the strings of my bikini then walked back to her lounge chair.

I went back to the locker room and slowly put on my clothes. After the sting of her statement finally settled, I went into a bathroom stall where I cried for a good ten minutes.

Throughout the rest of my teen years, she was mostly the supportive mother who would do anything for her girl, but every once in a while, she would strike me with jealous comments that cut at my psyche and left scars deep into my adulthood. In fact, to this day, I am more comfortable completely nude than I am in a two-piece swimming suit.

I'm not going to tell you that after doing this ritual, I mystically fell back in love with my body. No, that took time and some therapy. It took someone telling me that maternal envy was an actual thing and that the disdain I felt for my physical appearance was partly a byproduct of my mother's own insecurity.

One day when the sky was warm and the riverside beckoned, I went to the body of water that knows me best. I went, robed and with a long sword I used in ritual at times, to the Sauk River, where I have drawn down the moon and danced abashedly on her banks. That place where I had gathered with my family and friends and where laughter and love have permeated the landscape for over twenty years. I dropped my robe, revealing to the river the reflection of a woman whose lined face told the story of the hard work, laughter, and tears that have shaped her into a strong multifaceted human being. The glistening water reflected back a particularly deep cesarean scar carved into her abdomen—the battle scar of the bearing of her precious children. Every fold and lump and every line and crease were taken in and relished that day. I was reminded of my strength and capabilities and of the unique splendor that is me.

It was that day that I ritually took the sword and raised it up as a symbol of my shift in self-perception. I am beautiful, I have worth, I am strong, and I am capable of creating positive change. I am a warrior. I am divine.

Here are a few ways to remind yourself of your beauty daily:

Positive Self-Talk: Don't tell yourself that you're stupid, ugly, or a failure or use any other negative talk with yourself. Remind yourself daily of your wonderful, amazing, and unique traits that make you beautiful. If you must, write down positive words on pieces of paper and place them around your house where you will see them.

Explore New Interests: Learning to love ourselves demands that we allow ourselves time for fun and relaxation. What wild and fun activity is waiting for you? What crazy skill have you always wanted to learn? I really wanted to learn to wield a sword. I know! It's not the kind of activity you think of a middle-aged woman doing on a Sunday afternoon, right? But I love it, and to tell you the truth, I have never felt stronger. So go and have some fun.

Pamper Yourself: Take an exquisite bath in a tub scented with oils and the glow of candlelight. Buy the chocolates or, better yet, buy yourself a bouquet of flowers and the chocolates. These are little ways of reminding yourself that you are worthy.

Speak Up: No more holding back your opinions to make others feel comfortable. Allow yourself to be heard.

Don't Be Afraid to Seek Help: Sometimes the pain is so deep that all the positive words we tell ourselves aren't enough. Don't feel like a failure if you decide you need to seek help from a counselor, life coach, or a support group. This is a brave and loving act, worthy of a warrior, that will ultimately help you find your worth.

Beautiful Warrior: A Ritual of Self-Discovery

To be beautiful doesn't mean you have to look like a supermodel. And if you're older, it doesn't mean to attempt to recapture how you looked at eighteen.

Being beautiful is accepting yourself as you are now—never mind how others think of you, never mind what the latest trends are, never mind what your status is. This ritual is designed for you to see yourself with fresh eyes as the beautiful warrior you are. And in turn, you can be the light for others to do the same.

If you can do this by a body of water (lake, stream, ocean, river, pool, tub, etc.) that would be great, but you can always do this in front of a mirror.

You will need:

Private access to a body of water or a full-length mirror

Decorated staff (directions follow) or sword (if you happen to have one)

Begin with a few moments of meditation outdoors, if possible. Use this quiet time to focus on forgiveness. Forgive yourself for judging yourself for so many years. When you are ready, stand in front of the mirror or body of water and disrobe. Look closely at your beautiful form and thank your body for its strength and wholeness. Thank your body for honoring you. When you feel ready, raise your staff or sword high into the air and in your own words take back your sovereignty. You are a warrior and no one (not even yourself) can make you believe that you are not worthy, strong, or beautiful.

Decorated Staff of Power

This is a great representation of your own self-worth. After you use it in ritual, place it somewhere you will see it daily as a reminder of your warrior spirit.

You will need:

Found or gifted 4–5-foot stick, branch, or piece of straight driftwood (a dowel that can be purchased at any DIY store works fine too)

Permanent markers or craft paint in your choice of colors

Ribbons, yarn, or decorative lace in a color that is empowering to you

First, prepare your staff for paint by removing any loose bark and wiping it down with a damp cloth. Paint the wood with colors that are an expression of you. After the paint dries, use the permanent marker to write words of empowerment and to draw symbols that have meaning to you on your staff. Wrap ribbon, yarn, or lace around the top of your staff and tie it off, leaving 12 to 14 inches to hang freely.

The Siren

If you happen to be aboard a ship whose sails billow upon the tossing and churning sea, be careful of the song that weaves through the blistering winds and rises above the waves. Plug your ears with wax and tie yourself to the mast, because that intoxicating voice that beckons you and fills your head with unabashed sexuality will lead you to your doom.

The sea could be seen as a dangerous place for ancient mariners: whirlpools, jagged coastlines, shallow reefs, and storms, and the endless fickle sea took with it many a ship. For the Greek sailors who faced these dangers, the personification of the allure of the unknown and the danger of the sea was beautiful winged sea spirits who sat amongst the rocks, singing haunting songs that lured mesmerized men, or whole ships, to a gruesome end. Sometimes the hapless victims were drowned or led to high cliffs, where they threw themselves to the rocky outcrops below, but other times they were eaten by the very beings who drew them in. In other words, sex equals death, or at least betrayal.

According to mythology, sirens were the daughters of Achelous, a river god who lived amongst the small islands called *Sirenum scopuli*. In some of the stories, the sirens were created as companions for Demeter's daughter Persephone. After Persephone's abduction, they were given wings by Demeter to assist in locating her missing child but were later cursed for failing to intervene with the kidnapping.

The idea of the siren in our modern world brings to mind the classic femme fatale, that dangerous man-eater of noir novels popularized in the 1940s and '50s and used primarily as a plot device to prove the hero worthy. And as much as the stereotyping pisses me off, I have to admit I am drawn to the siren archetype. The siren is unabashedly sensual and confident in her manner. She is intelligent and provocative, exudes sexuality, and oozes an undefinable allure that draws people in. Yeah. I want to be her. Here's a lovers' ritual for all of us souls out there wearing yoga pants and too busy to cook real food, let alone release our hair from its hairband.

Siren's Song Lovers' Ritual

For this ritual we will employ some tantric sexual practices to interlace your physical and spiritual energies through slow and explorative lovemaking.

You will need:

> Besom or smudge bundle
>
> As many candles as can fill a room without burning it down (electric candles give a nice glow too)
>
> Siren's song enchanted oil (recipe follows)

Start by cleansing the room of all negativity with either a besom or a sage and lavender smudge bundle. Light your candles and turn out the lights. Disrobe and apply the siren song oil slowly and purposefully on your body. As you do this, visualize yourself as the siren. You are the one everyone is drawn to. You are the most alluring person in the room. You are intelligent and provocative. You are a sensual being.

When you are ready, face your lover in your candlelit sanctuary both dressed only in robes. Look into one another's eyes. Drink each other in. Synchronize your breathing: as they inhale, you exhale, and as they exhale, you inhale. Do this for as long as *you* choose (you are the siren—you are in control). When you feel ready, begin to disrobe one another. Slowly caress one another, wrap yourselves around each other, and add kissing, but continue to breathe in sync with each other. Take the time to explore one another. Make your lover *want* you.

At this point, it's up to you to take this where you want it to go. Enjoy the evening, you siren, you.

Siren's Song Enchanted Oil

> 8 ounces of your favorite carrier oil (fractionated coconut oil, sweet almond oil, or grapeseed oil are nice choices)
>
> 10 drops rosemary oil
>
> 3–4 drops tuberose
>
> 2–3 drops vanilla
>
> Small red aventurine stone
>
> Pretty glass bottle

Mix in all ingredients, pour the oil into the glass bottle with a small red aventurine stone, and charge with the following charm:

Power of the siren's song
Let arouse within me desire
I am Witch, I am temptress
I am femme fatale, I am a siren

A Selkie for My Bathroom

I work part time as a rural delivery carrier for the post office in the sleepy town of Concrete, situated approximately fifteen miles from my forest home. It's not a fulfilling job by any stretch of the imagination, but it does help keep us living indoors with the added benefit of modern luxuries like electricity and internet service. One morning, as I stumbled in late (as usual) and not quite caffeinated enough to hold a proper conversation, I found a painting propped against the case where I put up the mail for my route's daily deliveries.

"Who put this here?" I asked.

"That was me." Sheena, a clerk with dark curls and an infectious smile, poked her head from around a cage, holding trays of mail.

"Oh, Sheena. Thank you." The painting was of a woman who sat on the seashore, looking longingly to the sea. In the direction the young lady was looking, perched on a rock was a seal.

"I don't know what the picture's about," she said, "but I saw it at a yard sale, and it reminded me of the things you've been getting for your bathroom."

I had been ordering a lot of things for my bathroom, and because I work at the post office, I'm able to show off my finds to my work family. Steve had put a saltwater aquarium in a wall in our bathroom some time before. At first, I was annoyed because it didn't go with the forest grotto theme I had put together, but instead of knocking him over the head and burying him in the backyard, I decided to just roll with it and added mermaids and seashells. I will never admit it to him, but I really liked the way it turned out. "I know what this picture is about." I smiled. "She's a selkie, and she's looking to the sea. She wants to go home," I said and could almost feel her heartache.

"Oh, that sounds so sad." Sheena, who was now standing beside me, added. "And I don't even know what you're talking about."

"Well, let me tell you all about them." I smiled and, of course, used that as an opportunity to educate the entire office about the folklore of selkies.

Selkies in Folklore

Of all the sea faeries, selkies of Scotland, Scandinavia, and Ireland are by far the gentlest of legendary creatures, but there is debate about the origin of the legends of these beings who could remove their sealskin and mingle with humankind. Some say they were started when Spaniards who had shipwrecked along the coast of the northern Atlantic came ashore, and their dark hair reminded the inhabitants of seals. Another tale says that the Spaniards saw the Finns or Sami people traveling in kayaks wearing sealskin coats. There have even been suggestions that selkies were fallen angels or condemned souls. But like many myths from all cultures, tales of the selkies were most likely created as a way of explaining the unexplainable.

In the myths, selkies were sea faeries who appeared as seals. They shed their sealskins on special nights when the moon was full to dance under its silvery glow. According to the legends, if someone were to take their seal coat, the selkie was bound to them. Many a selkie married and even had children. It is said that selkies were loving wives and loving mothers to their children, but once a selkie recovered her sealskin, she immediately returned to the sea. Ironically, there are some tales that depict a selkie's half-human children finding their lost or hidden skin and returning it to their parent without realizing the consequences.

Male selkies were known to be very good-looking and sought after by women who were disappointed in their lives. If a woman had a husband who'd become unbearable or perhaps even out too long to sea, all she need do was shed seven tears into the sea to beckon a selkie man to her. Of course, he could only be with her for a short time before returning to his watery home, unable to revisit her until seven years had passed.

Dance of the Selkie: Full Moon Dance Party

Liminal or between times are when the veil between this world and the otherworld thins, and one can reach through the threshold and connect with the silky threads that make communication with the spirit world easier, allowing shadows of the future to lighten. Magic during these times takes on a deeper connotation.

Between spaces can include borders such as tree lines, marking the border between tame and wild; shorelines or other watery edges, which designate the space between land and sea, river, or stream; bridges; thresholds; windows; cemeteries; crossroads; marshes; and volcanic craters. In modern times, places such as hospitals, hotels, airports, and train and bus stations may all be considered between spaces because they are passed through, but never lived in.

Time can be liminal: dawn is not quite morning nor still night, noon is between daybreak and evening, dusk is neither day nor night, and midnight is not light nor shadow. As the Wheel of the Year turns slowly around, we have many "between times" that are celebrated by modern Pagans. Those most noted for their thinning veil are Beltane (between winter and summer for the ancient Celts) and Samhain (between summer and winter), but the equinoxes and solstices are between times as well.

Humankind share many between-time experiences. Think of coming of age ceremonies like bar mitzvahs or quinceañera celebrations; new beginnings, such as first jobs, weddings, or birthdays; and endings, such as divorce, death, or retirement. These liminal passages have been dealt with by ritual or ceremony since ancient times.

There are also times in our personal lives that we find ourselves in transition. And even if we know that stepping through that boundary is the best thing for us, it can be hard to push through the anxiety of the unknown and believe that, in the end, the change will lead to something far better. For this simple spell, we are going to peel off the layers of apprehension and unease. We are going to dance under the full moon with those who love and support us the most and embrace the beauty of transition.

You will need:

As many white candles as you want to light (safely)

A few of your best friends or family members

Some of your favorite dishes to share

You can set up this ritual on a beach or in the backyard or even in the living room—anywhere that is comfortable and provides ample space for dancing. This is all about support and embracing change. Set up the candles in firesafe containers and out of the way of moving bodies (we don't want to start a fire). If you're outdoors and have a fire pit you'd like to light, that would be really nice too.

First, gather friends in a circle around the person who is going through the transition. Each person in the circle will say words of advice or encouragement to the one in transition. End the circle with everyone laying their hands on the person in transition and then raising them all together with an excited whoop or cry that sends your positive energy into the universe.

When ready, cue the music! Whether you have live music or are playing tunes from a favorite playlist, crank it up and dance. Enjoy this time and feel the apprehension melt away under the milky glow of moonlight. When you're done dancing, share a midnight meal or favorite cocktails.

Chapter 19
Moon Magic

How did I know her? That beautiful celestial body whose phases fed my ever-transforming soul? I don't know, but somehow, even as a small child, I knew instinctively of her nourishing essence and of her rhythms that internalized within my body. I was drawn to her pallid glow and would have to be led gently back indoors on nights when she shined full and round above me.

"No, you have to come in, sweetie. It's time for bed," my mother would say after I promised to clean my room and be good forever, if only I could watch the moon for just a little while longer. "School comes early," she would remind me before tucking me in and turning out the lights.

I was a willful child, though, and when the beams of moonlight reached through my window, splashing me with silver light, it triggered something in my wild heart that tore me from the safety of my room and led me to sneak out through an open window with a blanket in tow to a favorite apple tree to gaze skyward as droplets of moonlight hung from the branches around me.

I consider myself a true moon child. I was born on a Monday in late June. Both my sun and moon signs are in Cancer, and even my name, which means woman of wisdom, is connected to that shining orb that illuminates the night. I have come to know her well—her every movement as she cycles through the year, the exact moment of any given month where she will rise above our hillside. During winter months she shines high through the warbled glass of my home and floods my darkened spirit with soft glowing light. In the summer, I must go to her, for she rides low upon the tree line during the sun's reign. It is within the woodland that her silver streaks the greenwood and bathes me in her speckled moonglow.

The moon is the largest and brightest object in the night sky and radiates an air of mystery that has long inspired wonder and curiosity. Lady Luna does not present us with the same face every day, but waxes and wanes in an endless cycle that reflects the constant alternation of birth, life, and rebirth every twenty-nine and a half days.

Luna's Many Faces

The moon and other celestial bodies have been used for tens of thousands of years to determine the seasons, months, and years. Activities done by our ancient ancestors, whether for work, celebration, or rest, were in harmony with the flow of the rhythms of nature, the rising and setting of the sun and moon, and the phases she passed through every cycle. All these observations became the blueprints for myths and legends for cultures worldwide, and the moon played a starring role in many.

Female lunar deities are a feature of many well-known mythologies. For Polynesians, the moon was Hina, a creator goddess who presides over healing, fertility, childbirth, and wisdom. She is the bringer of life, death, and renewal. Connected to the element of water, she is also a goddess of the sea, and in some myths, she leaves her undersea home with a coconut gourd containing the moon and stars and places them in the heavens.

The Greek goddess Selene drove her moon chariot pulled by two white horses, or sometimes bulls, across the heavens each night. She is the personification of the moon and fell in love with a shepherd called Endymion, who slept in eternal youth. Chang'e is a Chinese lunar deity who does not personify the moon, but only lives on the moon along with a jade rabbit who makes elixirs. Human events were associated with the phases of the moon for the Mayans. Their goddess Ix Chel was a moon goddess who was associated with both fertility and death.

Not all deities attached to the moon were female. The Hindu god Soma is a moon god personified as a fermented drink of the same name and who is sometimes represented as a bull. In Norse mythology, Máni is a moon deity and brother to the sun goddess, Sól. They ride the sky in horse-drawn chariots pursued by the wolves Sköll and Hati.

Moonstruck

Superstitions abound about the effect that moonlight has on human behavior. We all know the words *lunatic* and *lunacy* derive from the Latin word for moon (*luna*). This comes from an old idea that mania, or any behavior considered odd, was connected directly to the moon. Everything from sleepwalking to violent activity could be explained away as being "moonstruck." Of course, there's my favorite, lycanthropy, a condition that turns the sufferer into a werewolf during three days of the full moon.

Other popular superstitions included these:

- It is unlucky to be born in moonlight.
- To give a newborn baby strength, expose it to the waxing moon.
- It is unlucky to see the first silver crescent of a new moon through your window.
- A full moon on a Sunday is unlucky, but one on a Monday is lucky.
- Holding a moonstone in your mouth during a full moon will reveal your future.
- To be moonstruck is to be chosen by the Goddess.

I feel blessed to be among the magical souls whose moonstruck ways lead us through ancient lands—enfolded by the earth, enlivened by fire, and enraptured by the sea, we know the mysteries that can be heard entangled in the breeze. We are deeply and uniquely connected to the natural world. To those who think of us as mad, we just smile. Our celebration of life and freedom of spirit set us apart and we are better for it.

Working with the Moon Phases

Learning to work with the moon's powerful energy is a very important part of spell crafting. As the moon waxes and wanes in a continuous cycle, we can harness its different qualities and transform it into soulful wisdom by surrendering to the moon's natural phases. In this section, I offer ways to work with and honor those phases in hopes that it will inspire you to better know the healing power of lunar energy.

New Moon

Low on the horizon she sits, that first sliver of light sometimes called the crescent moon. Work with new moon energy in magic for new beginnings, creating positive change, inner harmony, growth and potential, peace, cleansing rituals, and designating a new sacred space. Goddesses associated with the new moon include Artemis, Diane, Athena, and Bast.

New Moon Spell for a New Business Venture

We all have those ideas—seeds of creativity that we store somewhere in the back of our mind. Maybe it's an idea for a business venture you've been kicking around for years or taking that hobby to the next level. This simple spell is intended to help those seeds take root.

You will need:

Small pot filled with potting soil

Citrine (a great stone for manifesting what inspires you)

3 legume seeds (any bean or pea will do)

3 green tealights

On the night of a new moon, set your small pot filled with soil in front of you. Take the citrine and hold it. As you do this, imagine yourself successful, happy, and content in your new venture. When you feel ready, lay the stone in front of the pot. Pick up your first seed and poke it gently into the soil (about ½ inch). Pick up the first green tealight, and as you light it, say,

I plant the seeds of creativity
I plant the seeds of prosperity
I plant the seeds of drive
In the name of the Goddess three times three
My dreams are now alive

Repeat this with the remaining seeds and candles. Let the tealights burn out on their own and place your potted seeds in a sunny window as a reminder that your dreams grow.

Waxing Moon

She grows and gains strength as she rises upon the skyline. This is a good time to practice magic for increase. Perform spells or rituals for money, communication, pregnancy, new jobs, legal matters, and healing. Goddesses associated with the waxing moon include Aphrodite and Freya.

Waxing Moon Spell for Well-Being

Have the blues and want to add a bit of harmony and well-being to your life? This is a great spell to help fill you with joyous and loving energy.

If you can do this outside (on a deck, patio, or porch) in the moonlight, that would be really great. Indoors near a window that receives moonlight would be nice too, but of course any place you are comfortable works fine.

For this spell you want to be in a relaxing environment with a little soft music playing in the background. Before the spell, pamper yourself with a soak in the tub with a little bergamot essential oil added.

You will need:

Rose quartz, citrine, or yellow jasper (any or all of these stones for loving and joyous energy)

White tealight

Bergamot essential oil

Incense blend for well-being (recipe follows)

Sit yourself somewhere you feel comfortable and light your incense. Place your white candle in front of you. Rub a little of the essential oil around the wick, and as you light it, focus on the simple pleasures that your life offers. Now place your stones around the candle and imagine the increase of joy, happiness, love, and well-being filling your being. If you are sitting where the moonlight touches you, close your eyes, and absorb the brilliant lunar energy. Do this as long as you feel is needed. Let the candle burn out on its own.

Incense Blend for Well-Being

2 parts sandalwood

1 part sweet marjoram

1 part lavender

A few drops bergamot oil
Small citrine stone

Blend using mortar and pestle and store with a citrine stone for a little added energy. Remove citrine before burning.

Full Moon

She is lovely when she is full of face, illuminating all she touches. Work with full moon energy in magic for psychic abilities, spiritual development, personal growth, celebration, intuition, and renewal. Goddesses associated with the full moon include Selene and Luna.

FULL MOON SPELL FOR PSYCHIC AWARENESS

The full moon is a great time to work spells for fullness. This spell is meant to help open your mind and help you find a deeper understanding of your own psychic power.

You will need:

Incense blend for psychic awareness (recipe follows)
Moon water (instructions on page 229)
Amethyst crystal or quartz crystal

Find a place where you are in contact with moonlight, such as a patio, deck, or balcony, or somewhere you are comfortable in a natural setting. Light your incense and hold the moon water in front of you. Take your crystal and touch it to your third eye, then drop it into the moon water. Hold the bowl up toward the moon and say,

With this water consecrated by the moon
My higher power I will attune
I invoke this power by sacred moonlight
I've heard the call and I claim this spell right

Set the bowl down and with your index finger dab the water on your third eye and say,

I possess the power to see

You will do this action two more times. The second time you touch the moon water to your third eye, say,

I possess the power to know

The third time say,

I possess the power

When you are finished, remove the crystals from the water and thank the Goddess in your own way. You may also want to use the bowl of moon water to do a little scrying.

INCENSE BLEND FOR PSYCHIC AWARENESS
2 parts bay leaf
1 part star anise
1 part mugwort
½ part cinnamon
A few drops orange oil
1 small clear quartz

Blend the herbs using a mortar and pestle and store with a clear quartz crystal for a little added energy. Remove the quartz before burning.

MOON WATER
Moon water is great for giving a little extra enchantment to your magical herbs, spell crafting, or cleansing and charging your magical tools, stones, and so on. During the gardening season, I make this stuff with every full moon by the gallons.

You will need:
Large bowl
Rainwater (Easy for me to say—I live in Washington state. If you can't collect it, tap water is fine.)
Moonstones or quartz crystals (optional)

On the night of the full moon, place your bowl of water outside (you may add moonstones or quartz crystals if you'd like). Make sure you can see the moon's reflection in the water. Place your hands over it and say,

> *Mother Moon, your light does shine*
> *Charge this water with energy divine*
> *With the power of three times three*
> *As I wish it, so mote it be*

Let the water charge for at least an hour, or you can leave it overnight.

Waning Moon

She begins to decrease as she journeys back to her original position. This is a good time to practice magic for release, letting go, and breaking bad habits. Goddesses associated with the waning moon include Cerridwen and the Morrigan.

WANING MOON RITUAL FOR LETTING GO

Is there something you just can't seem to let go of? I'm not talking about the dress you swear you're going to fit into again or the stack of magazines filled with recipes you'll never make—I'm talking about regret. You know, the one that got away, the diet you didn't stick to, the money you didn't save, and the words left unsaid. A little bit of regret isn't necessarily bad; in some cases it can help spur positive change. But sometimes too many regrets can become monstrous and materialize a feeling of worthlessness.

For this spell, we are going to release those regrets and turn our attention onto how we can better enjoy today.

You will need:

Scrap paper (as many pieces as you have regrets)

2 scrap pieces of black natural fiber fabric (cotton, linen etc.), 4 x 4 inches in size

Rosemary, garlic, vervain, bay leaf, nettle, and/or thyme

Needle and thread

Fireproof container or fire pit

Several days before your ritual, write out all your regrets onto pieces of scrap paper and set them aside. Sew the scrap fabric (right sides together) either by hand or by machine, leaving a small opening. Turn the fabric right-side out and begin to stuff the paper and the chosen banishing herbs into your poppet. As you do this go ahead and get mad; be mad at yourself, cry, or whatever, because this is the last time you get to mourn what you should have or could have done in the past. When you have finished, stitch the opening closed.

On the night of your ritual, prepare your fire outdoors if at all possible. This can also be done indoors if you have a fireplace or wood-burning stove.

Take your square poppet, hold it above the fire, and say,

I release these regrets to the fire
To bring me the relief that I desire
No longer to possess power over me
As I will it, I am set free

Throw the fabric square into the fire. As you watch it burn, imagine all your regret dissipating with the smoke as it rises.

Dark Moon

Her face is in shadow and so we contemplate. The dark moon is a good time for planning and going within. Some practitioners choose not to work magic during the dark phase of the moon, but if you do, use this phase for magic concerning self-knowledge, shadow work, divination, banishing, protection, and insight. Goddesses associated with the dark moon include Kali and Hecate.

Shadow Walk with the Dark Goddess
You will need:
Lit candle (battery-operated is a safe option)

Alone you will walk with the Goddess to banish whatever you wish from your life. Before you begin your shadow walk, make sure the area is clear of debris or any tripping hazards for you will be doing this with only the light of one candle to guide you.

On the dark of the moon, go to your predesignated spot. If it is indoors, turn off the lights. If you are outdoors, do this as late in the evening as possible. Light your candle. You will walk in a circle widdershins (counterclockwise), starting at an eastern point and continuing in a circle until you come back to the east. As you walk, imagine yourself safe under the mantle of the Dark Goddess as she guides you through this cleansing process.

As you begin past the eastern quarter, allow her to cleanse your mind of unhealthy thoughts. As you continue past the northern quarter, feel the grounding energy as it flows through your body. As you turn west, allow the Dark Goddess to cleanse you of emotional strife. As you come to the southern quarter, be filled with renewed spiritual strength.

Once back at the eastern quarter, step into the middle of your circle and lift your candle skyward. Thank the Dark Goddess for her regenerative power and know that you are cleansed.

Weaving Dreams

While writing this book, my youngest sister called me and said, "Monica, I had the weirdest dream."

My baby sister has had several dreams throughout her life that have come true, and as she took me through the details, which included her running through a forest that is now a well-developed neighborhood behind our small town's only gas station, a chill ran up my spine.

"I came upon a tombstone," she said, "that read 'Rest in Peace, Tim' along with the word *found*." She paused. "Well, that's what I think it said, the tombstone was a little muddy because it was raining in my dream."

"Wow, wouldn't it be cool if someone named Tim died?" A twinge of guilt struck me just as the words escaped. "I don't mean I want someone to *die*," I quickly added. "It's just that it would be weird."

"Yeah, I know, right?" she concluded.

Three days later, I receive another call. This time my sister was frantic as she described a strange event that had happened the evening before. She told me that she and her kids and a friend of one of her daughters, who was staying with them while her mother was on vacation, were getting ready for a church event when they received a phone call from the parent of a young woman who was needing a ride to the same event. It was the friend of my niece who volunteered to pick up the young woman, who just so happened to live near the neighborhood my sister had dreamt about.

To make a long story short, the seventeen-year-old girl who went to pick up the other friend had seen what looked to be someone lying in the mud beside a truck in an obstructed driveway. When she got out to check on the person, he was face down in the mud, surrounded by strewn papers, and very much dead.

The coroner's report stated the victim had had a heart attack while getting into his truck. The name of the victim was not Tim but Jim, and his house was situated exactly where my sister saw the tombstone in her dream.

Dream a Little Dream

Dreams are stories that weave our emotions, feelings, bits of memory, and elements from our waking lives throughout our unconscious mind while we sleep. They have a bizarre way of reflecting aspects of ourselves that we might find surprising. Through the scenarios that play out in our dreamworld, many truths can be uncovered, problems solved, and clues discovered that may help lead to a better understanding of our authentic selves.

Dreaming is a universal human experience that the average person will spend two or more hours per night doing. While some of us are very good at recalling our dreams, the majority of us only have hazy recollections of the themes that sift through our unconscious mind. One way of using your dreams to access information or spiritual messages is by practicing lucid dreaming.

When you are having a lucid dream, you are basically aware of your dreaming state and, with practice, may be able to manipulate your dream state as well as tap into wisdom that is imparted to you during slumber.

Here are a few tips to help you experience and gain insight from lucid dreaming:

- Shut off your electronic devices an hour before bed. Artificial light slows down the release of the sleep hormone melatonin.
- Try meditation before sleep with the use of one or more of the crystals listed next. I like to keep quartz crystals on my bedside table as well. I also recommend slipping a crystal into a dream pillow filled with herbs to enhance specific dreams.
- Keep a dream journal near your bed and record your dreams as soon as you wake up.

Use these crystals to aid in magic related to dreams:

Quartz: Helps promote lucid dreaming

Lodolite: Helps promote lucid dreaming

Moldavite: Helps with dream recollection

Moonstone: Promotes lucid dreaming, wisdom, and insight

Amethyst: Activates third eye

Ametrine: For wisdom, insight, and dream recall

Azurite: Helps you open yourself up to the meaning of your dreams

Herkimer Diamond: For psychic dreams

Herbal Sleep and Dream Pillows

Dream pillows have been used to induce peaceful sleep, enhance dreams, encourage dream memory, and protect against nightmares for centuries. No matter the reason, herbal pillows are beneficial for anyone.

To prepare an herbal pillow, select a piece of fabric, preferably cotton or other natural fiber. Wash and dry the fabric. Don't use scented detergent or fabric softener; it will take away from your herbal mix. Now cut the fabric into whatever shape you wish. Of course, squares and rectangles are easiest, but go ahead and get creative. Moon and star shapes are fun and relatively easy.

Next, create a blend of sleep or dream-inducing botanicals from the mixes I have included or craft your own mixture with fragrant herbs you find pleasing. With the right sides of the fabric together, stitch along the edges, leaving a ¼-inch seam allowance and making sure to leave an open space along one side. Once finished stitching, flip the pillow out through the open space and fill with your herbal blend. Finish the pillow by hand stitching the area shut. You may add embellishments, such as buttons, lace, or embroidery—you decide. Remember, be creative.

If you like, bless your finished pillow with this charm:

Weaver of dreams, I ask of thee
To bless my sleep three times three

Usher me to the land of dreams
With herbs and stardust and moonlit gleam

Dream Pillow Blends

Whether you want to protect against nightmares or enhance your dreams, blend any of the following:

Anise: Prevents nightmares and ensures pleasant dreams

Bay: Induces prophetic dreams

Catnip: Helps dream of love, promotes relaxing, and induces sleep

Cedar: Used to dream of love

Chamomile: Calm, relaxing, and keeps bad dreams away

Cinquefoil: Used for a restful sleep or to dream of a new lover

Clove: Brings warmth and an exotic feeling to dreams

Jasmine: Brings pleasant dreams and restful sleep

Marigold: Induces prophetic dreams and protection against black magic

Mistletoe: Prevents nightmares and insomnia

Morning Glory: Safeguards against nightmares

Mugwort: Induces prophetic dreams, enhances lucid dreaming, and helps with dream remembrance

Peppermint: Enhances dream clarity and vividness, enhances prophetic dreams

Rose: Evokes romantic dreams

Rosemary: Encourages a deep, restful sleep and keeps away bad dreams

Sage: Helps make dreams come true

Sweet Woodruff: Offers protection from nightmares

Thyme: Drives away nightmares and ensures restful sleep

Valerian: Used to prevent nightmares

Wooly Betony: Keeps negativity at bay and prevents nightmares from interfering with sleep

Yarrow: Induces prophetic dreams

Below are combinations that have worked well for me:

Lucid Dreams: Encourages active dreaming
1 part peppermint
½ part yarrow
½ part mugwort

Dream Remembrance: Encourages dream recall and restful sleep
1 part mugwort
¼ part lavender

Romance Blend: To stir your sensual nature
1 cup rose petals
2–3 whole cloves
¼ cup peppermint
¼ cup catnip

Nightmares Be Gone: Great for kids
¼ cup rose petals
¼ cup rosemary
⅛ cup lavender
⅛ cup hops

Sleep Pillow Blends

Sleep pillows are great for anyone who has difficulty falling asleep. For a blend that supports a deep, peaceful sleep, blend any of the following:

Balsam Fir Needles: Relaxing and soothing

Catnip: Relaxing and helps bring deep sleep

Chamomile: Calm, relaxing, and keeps bad dreams away

Cinquefoil: Offers a restful sleep or a dream of a new lover

Hops: Brings relaxation and peacefulness

Lavender: Soothing, relaxing, induces sleep and relieves headaches

Lemon Balm: Eases stress, anxiousness, and nervous feeling and is good for insomnia and headaches

Linden: Promotes sleep

Rose Petals: Brings warmth and love

Rosemary: Encourages a deep, restful sleep and keeps away bad dreams

Thyme: Ensures pleasant sleep and drives away nightmares

Marjoram: Calms restlessness and nervousness

Here are a few blends that have worked well for me:

Stress Tamer: Takes the edge off a stressful day
½ cup hops
½ cup mugwort
⅛ cup sweet marjoram

Blues Blend: Helps ease melancholy
½ cup sweet marjoram
¼ cup rose petals
¼ cup mint
1–2 whole cloves

Out Like a Light: For deep, restful sleep
½ cup lavender
¼ cup hops
¼ cup mugwort

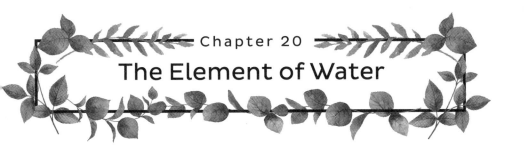

Chapter 20
The Element of Water

Is it in the mysterious depths of open water dotted with drops of moonlight that I will find you? Water is the most mysterious of all elements. Its power speaks of the unknown and invites you to shape-shift. What is it you will become? Are you brave enough to tap into its transformative powers? In the twilight, when the sky begins to transform to a sea of stars, we must open our third eye and allow the knowledge we seek from this feminine element to emerge. It speaks to us in dreams and through divination. The power of water tugs at our spirit and reminds us that there are some mysteries worth seeking.

The element of water is symbolized by the cauldron and brings to mind tales of regeneration and transformation. For many of us, to be in a body of water is transformative and may invoke a spiritual experience—it charges us, it cleanses us, it purifies us. The sound of the river as it cuts through my tiny valley is the rhythm that I set my magical workings to. A soft gurgling siren call that draws me to her emerald waters daily. What are we without water? It covers about 70 percent of the earth's surface and is essential for our human bodies to function.

The power of water is attributed to emotions, creativity, psychic abilities, transformation, intuition, and dreams. It is associated with the signs of Cancer, Scorpio, and Pisces. These are our sensitive souls who are intuitive and nurturing. Magically, you may find them making use of a scrying bowl under a full moon or reading tarot. They may perform dreamwork and past-life regression. They are great healers and Hedge Witches.

Deities You May Like to Get to Know

Anuket: As the personification of the Nile, this Egyptian goddess was sometimes known as "nourisher of the fields" and is sometimes depicted as a gazelle or as a woman wearing a tall headdress made of reeds or ostrich feathers. In magic, she has been invoked for protection, abundance, growth, childbirth, and fertility.

Boann: Boann is the Celtic goddess of the River Boyne, which is said to spring up at the mythical Well of Segais. She is also known as "White Cow" because of the importance of both milk and water to the ancients. She was called upon in magic for eloquence, knowledge, the arts, creativity, family, fertility, inspiration, and abundance.

Lady of the Lake: Thought to be the voice of the Great Goddess, she was the head of nine priestesses of the Isle of Avalon. She has been known by many names, including Vivienne, Nineve, and Nimue. She is the sword bearer to Arthur and guide to Merlin in the Arthurian legends. She has been called upon for healing, purification, knowledge, the Great Rite, and feminism.

Akheloios: Greek god of the river Aitolia, he fought Herakles for the love of the princess Deianeira. Herakles tore off one of Akheloios's horns and formed the horn of plenty. Akheloios has been called upon for abundance, fertility, wealth, and creativity.

Correspondences for the Element of Water

Direction: West

Season: Autumn

Hour: Twilight

Day of the Week: Monday

Magical Tools: Cauldron, chalice

Qualities: Moist, cold, heavy, passive

Magical Associations: Emotions, compassion, dreams, sleep, psychic awareness, purification, astral travel

Gender: Feminine, receptive

Archangel: Gabriel

Herbs, Flowers, and Trees: Aloe, apple, balm of Gilead, belladonna, birch, blackberry, bleeding heart, cabbage, catnip, columbine, comfrey, daisy, datura, elder, hemlock, iris, lilac, mallow, orchid, plum, poppy, ragwort, sandalwood, spearmint, thyme, valerian, violet, willow, yarrow, yew

Stones: Alexandrite, aqua aura quartz, calcite, emerald, jade, lapis lazuli, moonstone, obsidian, rose quartz, river rock, pearl, turquoise

Colors: Blue, sea green, gray, silver

Elemental Being: Undines

Tarot Suit: Cups

Metals: Silver, copper

Runes: Uruz, Gebo, Hagalaz, Isa, Pethro, Ehwaz, Laguz, Dagaz

Animals: Dolphins, all fish, whales

I stand within my holy wood
and know that I am wild ...

Where's Your Wild?

As you finish the pages of this book and step back into the daily routine of your life, my hope for you is simple: that you are left inspired.

Inspired to slip out of your skin and let the milky glow of moonlight caress your curves as you dance to the music of the sea, for that is freedom. Inspired to run barefoot with moss in your hair through shadowy forests that carry the voices of ancient deities, for that is an awakening. Inspired to clamor up to the highest peak and yell your truth for all to hear, for that is power. Inspired to stand weary and parched but still able to look into the flames and know that transformation is never too late, for that is growth.

As you make your way back to the sacred, keep in mind we are not separate from the flesh of the earth but a part of her. Weave your magic well, wild soul, near babbling brook and under starry skies with your intuition as your guide. Remember, there is wisdom in every stone and root and flower, and it is the ones like me (and you), whose hearts beat with an unkept rhythm, who are responsible for sharing that knowledge so others won't forget.

Where is your wild? Making the realization is only the beginning... Now go outside and plant your bare feet firmly in the earth. Feel the stones under your arches and the soil between your toes and reclaim that fundamental connection that we as modern humans have lost.

Bibliography

Andrews, Ted. *Animal Speak: The Spiritual and Magical Powers of Creatures Great and Small*. Woodbury, MN: Llewellyn Publications, 2007.

Arrien, Angeles. *The Four-Fold Way: Walking the Paths of the Warrior, Teacher, Healer and Visionary*. San Francisco: HarperCollins, 1993.

Beth, Rae. *The Wiccan Way: Magical Spirituality for the Solitary Practitioner*. Blaine, WA: Phoenix Publishing, 2001.

Bratman, Gregory N., J. Paul Hamilton, Kevin S. Hahn, Gretchen C. Daily, and James J. Gross. "Nature Experience Reduces Rumination and Subgenual Prefrontal Cortex Activation." *Proceedings of the National Academy of Sciences* 112, no. 28 (July 2015): 8567–72. doi:10.1073/pnas.1510459112.

Bueke, Mary Beth. *The Ultimate Guide to Sea Glass: Finding, Collecting, Identifying and Using the World's Most Beautiful Stones*. Beach Comber's Edition. New York: Skyhorse Publishing, 2016.

Burne, Charlotte Sophia. *The Handbook of Folklore*. London, UK: Sidgwick & Jackson: 1914. https://archive.org/details/cu31924009657283/page/n8.

Cichoke, Anthony J. *Secrets of Native American Herbal Remedies*. New York: Penguin Putnam, 2001.

Conway, DJ. *Ancient & Shining Ones: World Myth, Magic and Religion*. St. Paul, MN: Llewellyn Publications, 1995.

———. *Maiden, Mother, Crone: The Myth and Reality of the Triple Goddess*. St. Paul, MN: Llewellyn Publications, 1999.

Cooper, JC. *An Illustrated Encyclopedia of Traditional Symbols.* London: Thames and Hudson, 1978.

Cotterell, Arthur, and Rachel Storm. *The Ultimate Encyclopedia of Mythology.* London: Hermes House, 2004.

Crosson, Monica. "Conjuring Up a Good Night's Sleep." In *Llewellyn's 2015 Magical Almanac,* 317–27. Woodbury, MN: Llewellyn Publications, 2014.

Cunningham, Scott. *Encyclopedia of Magical Herbs.* St. Paul, MN: Llewellyn Publications, 1985.

———. *The Complete Book of Incense, Oils and Brews.* St. Paul, MN: Llewellyn Publications, 1989.

———. *Earth, Air, Fire & Water: More Techniques of Natural Magic.* Woodbury, MN: Llewellyn Publications, 2010.

De Grandis, Francesca. *Goddess Initiation: A Practical Celtic Program for Soul Healing, Self-Fulfillment & Wild Wisdom.* New York: HarperCollins, 2001.

Deines, Tina. "Seashell Souvenirs Are Killing Protected Wildlife." *National Geographic.* July 16, 2018. https://www.nationalgeographic.com /animals/2018/07/wildlife-watch-seashells-illegal-trade-handicrafts/.

DeLys, Claudia. *A Treasury of Superstitions.* New York: Gramercy Books, 1997.

Douglass, Roy F. "Silvical Characteristics of Redwood (Sequoia sempervirens [D. Don] Endl.)." US Forest Service Research Paper PSW-RP-28. Berkeley, CA: Pacific Southwest Forest & Range Experiment Station Forest Service, 1966. https://www.fs.usda.gov/treesearch/pubs/28694.

Dugan, Ellen. *Natural Witchery: Intuitive, Personal & Practical Magic.* Woodbury, MN: Llewellyn Publications, 2007.

Dulsky, Danielle. *Woman Most Wild: Three Keys to Liberating the Witch Within.* Novato, CA: New World Library, 2017.

Frazier, James George. *The Golden Bough: A Study in Magic and Religion.* Oxford, UK: Oxford University Press, 2009.

Hardin, Jesse Wolf. *Gaia Eros: Reconnecting to the Magic and Spirit of Nature.* Franklin Lakes, NJ: New Page Books, 2004.

Ingerman, Sandra. *Walking in Light: The Everyday Empowerment of a Shamanic Life.* Boulder, CO: Sounds True, 2014.

———. *Soul Retrieval: Mending a Fragmented Self.* San Francisco, CA: HarperOne, 2011.

Kynes, Sandra. *Sea Magic: Connecting with the Ocean's Energy.* Woodbury, MN: Llewellyn Publications, 2008.

"Lawn Pesticide Facts and Figures." Beyond Pesticides. Accessed September 19, 2019. https://www.beyondpesticides.org/assets/media/documents/lawn/factsheets/LAWNFACTS&FIGURES_8_05.pdf.

Louv, Richard. *Last Child in the Woods: Saving Our Children from Nature-Deficit Disorder.* Chapel Hill, NC: Algonquin Books, 2005.

Matthews, Caitlin. *The Celtic Tradition.* Rockport, MA: Element, 1995.

Matthews, John. *The Quest for the Green Man.* Wheaton, IL: Godsfield Press, 2001.

———. *Robin Hood: Green Lord of the Wildwood.* Glastonbury, UK: Gothic Image, 1993.

McArthur, Margie. *Faery Healing: The Lore and the Legacy.* Aptos, CA: New Brighton Books, 2003.

Mehl-Madrona, Lewis. *Coyote Medicine: Lessons from Native American Healing.* New York: Touchstone, 1998.

Miyazaki, Yoshifumi. *Shinrin Yoku: The Japanese Art of Forest Bathing.* Portland, OR: Timber Press, 2018.

Monaghan, Patricia. *The Encyclopedia of Celtic Mythology and Folklore.* New York: Facts On File, 2004.

Montgomery, Pam. *Plant Healing: A Guide to Working with Plant Consciousness.* Rochester, VT: Bear and Company, 2008.

Morrison, Dorothy. *Everyday Sun Magic: Spells & Rituals for Radiant Living.* Woodbury, MN: Llewellyn Publications, 2005.

Müller-Ebeling, Claudia, Christian Rätsch, and Wolf-Dieter Storl. *Witchcraft Medicine: Healing Arts, Shamanic Practices and Forbidden Plants.* Translated by Annabel Lee. Rochester, VT: Inner Traditions, 2003.

Nahmad, Claire. *Earth Magic: A Wise Woman's Guide to Herbal, Astrological & Other Folk Wisdom.* Rochester, VT: Destiny Books, 1994.

Opsopaus, John. "The Ancient Greek Esoteric Doctrine of the Elements: Air." Biblioteca Arcana. Last modified 1999. http://opsopaus.com/OM/BA/AGEDE/Air.html.

Park, Bum Jin, Yuko Tsunetsugu, Tamami Kasetani, Takahide Kagawa, and Yoshifumi Miyazaki. "The Physiological Effects of *Shinrin-yoku* (Taking in the Forest Atmosphere or Forest Bathing): Evidence from Field Experiments in 24 Forests across Japan." *Enviromental Health and Preventative Medicine* 15, no. 1 (January 2010): 18–26. doi:10.1007/s12199-009-0086-9.

Paterson, Jacqueline Memory. *Tree Wisdom*. London: Thorsons, 1996.

Roads, Michael J. *Talking with Nature*. Tiburon, CA: H. J. Kramer, 1985.

Roberts, Llyn. *Shapeshifting into Higher Consciousness: Heal and Transform Yourself and Our World with Ancient and Modern Methods*. Alresford, Hants, UK: O-Books, 2011.

Rose, Carol. *Spirits, Fairies, Leprechauns, and Goblins: An Encyclopedia*. New York: Norton, 1996.

Rysdyk, Evelyn. *Spirit Walking: A Course in Shamanic Power*. San Francisco, CA: Weiser, 2013.

Sir Gawain and the Green Knight. Translated by Ernest J. B. Kirtlan. London: Charles H. Kelly, 1912. https://archive.org/details/sirgawaingreenkn00 kirtuoft.

Skelton, Robin, and Margaret Blackwood. *Earth, Air, Fire, Water*. London: Penguin Books, 1990.

Tate, Karen. *Sacred Places of Goddess: 108 Destinations*. San Francisco, CA: Consortium of Collective Consciousness, 2006.

Thoreau, Henry D. *Walden; or, Life in the Woods*. Boston, MA: Ticknor and Fields, 1854. https://archive.org/details/waldenorlifeinwo1854thor/page /n4.

Walker, Barbara J. *The Woman's Dictionary of Symbols and Sacred Objects*. Edison, NJ: Castle Books, 1988.

Wesselman, Hank, and Jill Kuykendall. *Spirit Medicine: Healing in the Sacred Realms*. Carlsbad, CA: Hay House, 2004.

Wohlleben, Peter. *The Hidden Life of Trees: What They Feel, How They Communicate*. Vancouver, BC: Greystone Books, 2016.

Index

To Write to the Author

If you wish to contact the author or would like more information about this book, please write to the author in care of Llewellyn Worldwide Ltd. and we will forward your request. Both the author and publisher appreciate hearing from you and learning of your enjoyment of this book and how it has helped you. Llewellyn Worldwide Ltd. cannot guarantee that every letter written to the author can be answered, but all will be forwarded. Please write to:

Monica Crosson
℅ Llewellyn Worldwide
2143 Wooddale Drive
Woodbury, MN 55125-2989
Please enclose a self-addressed stamped envelope for reply,
or $1.00 to cover costs. If outside the U.S.A., enclose
an international postal reply coupon.

Many of Llewellyn's authors have websites with additional information and resources. For more information, please visit our website at http://www.llewellyn.com.

GET MORE AT LLEWELLYN.COM

Visit us online to browse hundreds of our books and decks, plus sign up to receive our e-newsletters and exclusive online offers.

• Free tarot readings • Spell-a-Day • Moon phases

• Recipes, spells, and tips • Blogs • Encyclopedia

• Author interviews, articles, and upcoming events

GET SOCIAL WITH LLEWELLYN

Find us on
www.Facebook.com/LlewellynBooks

GET BOOKS AT LLEWELLYN

LLEWELLYN ORDERING INFORMATION

WITHDRAWN

2-18-2020

$17.99